Erin Millar is one of Canada's leading post-secondary education journalists and has written about education for publications such as *Maclean's, Chatelaine, Readers' Digest* and *The Globe and Mail*. She has also appeared as an expert on university life on radio and television across the country. Erin is perhaps best known for her work as a founding editor of *Maclean's* OnCampus, a section of Macleans.ca dedicated to university life.

Ben Coli contributes to a weekly advice column and blog at *Maclean's* OnCampus about university life. He was a property tax consultant before turning to writing full-time and brings his knowledge of financial planning and marketing to *The Canadian Campus Companion*.

Books of Merit

Library and Archives Canada Cataloguing in Publication

Millar, Erin, 1982–
The Canadian campus companion : everything a student needs to know
about going to university and college in Canada / Erin Millar, Ben Coli.

ISBN 978-0-88762-640-1

1. College student orientation—Canada—Handbooks, manuals, etc.
2. College students—Canada—Life skills guides.
3. Universities and colleges—Canada. I. Coli, Ben, 1976–
II. Title.

LB2343.34.C3M55 2011   378.1'980971   C2010-903804-5

Editor: Janice Zawerbny
Cover design: Sputnik Design Partners Inc.
Cover image: Corbis Images
Illustrations: Shutterstock

Published by Thomas Allen Publishers,
a division of Thomas Allen & Son Limited,
390 Steelcase Road East,
Markham, Ontario L3R 1G2 Canada

www.thomasallen.ca

ONTARIO ARTS COUNCIL
CONSEIL DES ARTS DE L'ONTARIO

Canada Council
for the Arts

The publisher gratefully acknowledges the support of
The Ontario Arts Council for its publishing program.

We acknowledge the support of the Canada Council for the Arts, which last
year invested $20.1 million in writing and publishing throughout Canada.

We acknowledge the Government of Ontario through the Ontario
Media Development Corporation's Ontario Book Initiative.

We acknowledge the financial support of the Government of Canada
through the Canada Book Fund for our publishing activities.

1 2 3 4 5   15 14 13 12 11

Printed and bound in Canada

The Canadian Campus Companion

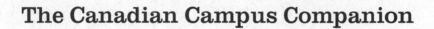

Contents

The Canadian Campus Companion

Both of us (the authors of this book) went on to post-secondary education immediately after high school because we were expected to. We had good grades, and college or university was where students with good grades went, simple as that. We each developed different reasons for going to school along the way, and we both ended up learning things from the experience that we never would have imagined beforehand.

There's a good chance that the best thing you're going to get out of university or college is something you haven't even thought of yet, so keep yourself open to the possibilities. It happened to us: Erin went to college to get a degree in jazz studies, became the editor of her school's student newspaper and is now a freelance magazine journalist. Ben went to university for a business degree, picked up a philosophy-reading habit and has ended up writing advice books for students. Neither of us could have guessed at age 18 that this would happen.

What you end up getting out of your education will depend a lot on what you decide to put into it. If you attack academics with zeal and enthusiasm, you're going to learn way more than if you do the bare minimum to pass your classes. If you attend events, join campus clubs, participate in student government, and get involved in the life of your school, you'll have a richer experience and meet more people than you will if you don't spend any more time on campus than you have to. All of these things take time, of course, so you'll have to evaluate your commitments and decide where your priorities lie.

We can't tell you what you should want from your education and how you should go about it. This is your life, and these are your choices to make. This book instead aims to provide you with information to help you make thoughtful, conscious decisions. We won't tell you what to do. Instead, we'll alert you to potential pitfalls and difficulties you may encounter. We'll pass on the advice and share the experiences of students who have already been through this. We'll relate the wise words of the dozens of professors, counsellors, university officials, and other experts we spoke to. We'll also give you a heads-up about choices you'll have to make in a few years, such as what kind of career you want and whether you want to go to graduate school, so you can have a good, long time to think about it and prepare for those decisions.

This book is divided into seven chapters.

- **Chapter 1: Before Classes Start.** It's time to get ready for school. You'll have to pick which school you're going to go to, figure out what you're going to study while you're there, and come up with a plan that will begin with registering for your first courses and end with you graduating.

- **Chapter 2: A Roof Over Your Head.** Whether it's your parents' house, a residence, or an apartment of your own, you're going to have to live somewhere while you're going to school. We'll talk about the benefits and drawbacks of these options and give you tips on surviving residence and making sure the apartment you rent isn't a total slum.

- **Chapter 3: Making the Grade.** This isn't high school anymore. At universities and colleges, students are much more responsible for their own learning than they were in high school, and classes move a lot faster. You're going to need to sharpen your academic skills and learn how to use your studying and reading time more effectively.

- **Chapter 4: Student Life.** You're going to be at a campus full of hundreds or even thousands of energetic, intelligent young people, and there's going to be so many awesome things to do. Read about how to make the most of your school's non-academic life.

- **Chapter 5: Finance.** Getting an education is expensive, but every year, more than half a million new university and college students figure out how to pay for it. We'll point you in the direction of the best sources of scholarships and loans, help you make a budget, and give tips on how to make the money last.

- **Chapter 6: Health and Safety.** Going to college isn't exactly a dangerous activity, but you'll probably run into issues you've never had to deal with on your own before. This is also a great time to establish healthy eating and exercise habits that will stay with you for the rest of your life.

- **Chapter 7: The Future Is Coming.** It might be the last thing on your mind when you're starting university, but some day you're going to graduate. There are things you can start doing now to prepare yourself for that next step, whether it's a career or graduate school.

If you're looking for some piece of information in particular and you can't figure out which of these chapters it would fall under, check the table of contents or the index. Otherwise, settle in and read the book. We tried to make it reasonably entertaining, and it's jam-packed with information, advice, and stories from students and professors about topics you're likely already wondering about and some you haven't even thought of.

Visit our website for links to more in-depth information, forums where you can chat with other students about your experiences, and downloadable guides for high school counsellors, parents, and university advisers.

As we'll remind you throughout this book, you'll never be alone when you're going to college or university. If you run into a problem that this book doesn't cover, one no amount of additional research can solve for you, you can always turn to your school's counselling services for help, so you can get back to learning about atoms and Julius Caesar and dialectics and whatever else you're studying.

The Canadian Campus Companion

Before Classes Start

YOU PROBABLY HAVEN'T made many decisions about your studies up to this point in your life. Sure, you chose a few options in high school and you might have decided whether to take the advanced math class or the not-so-advanced class, but for most high school students, that's pretty much it. Now that you're thinking about going on to post-secondary education, you've got all the choices in the world; you can choose from hundreds of different educational institutions in Canada where you'll be able to study literally thousands of different subjects.

Having so much to choose from might feel a little overwhelming, but trust us, choice is a good thing. If you take the time to research and think about your options, you will find a school, program, and course of study that will suit you perfectly.

In this chapter:

- Learn about the different kinds of institutions you can pick from when **Choosing Your School**.

- Do your research and try to keep your options open when you're **Choosing Your Major**.

- Design your education and strategically pick classes by **Planning Your Degree**.

- Get a preview of the differences between high school and college or university when we ask, **What's It Going to Be Like?**

1.1 Choosing Your School ✓

On one hand, picking which institution of higher learning you'll attend is a huge decision. Your choice will affect the kind of education you'll get, where you'll live, the lifestyle you'll lead for the next few years, and how your degree or diploma will be regarded by others.

On the other hand, you're lucky enough to live in a country with an exceptional post-secondary educational system, so it's difficult to make a truly terrible choice.

Your choice of schools will be partly determined by the kind of education you want. If you're looking for a practical, skills-based education that will get you out and into the job market in a couple of years, your choice will be narrowed down to colleges and trade schools. If you've got your heart set on a degree, on the other hand, you'll likely be looking at universities—although there are a lot of colleges that offer good degree programs, and there are plenty of reasons to seriously consider them, as you'll read later.

Once you come up with a short list of schools that can give you the education you want, you'll have to choose one of them. The education they offer and the certification or degree they'll give you might seem identical, but there are bound to be a lot of differences between schools, including where they're located, what it will cost to attend them, and the kind of campus life and educational atmosphere you'll experience when you get there.

You very well might end up choosing the school you always assumed you'd go to, but it's worth the effort to take a look at what other options are available so you can be sure you're choosing the right school for you.

In this section:

- Learn about the different **Types of Schools** you can choose from.

- Research your potential schools and ask, **So What's the Difference?**

- • Sooner or later, you'll have to stop researching and get down to **Making the Choice.**

Types of Schools

In Canada, there is a huge variety of different kinds of institutions to choose from, each of which provides a different education in terms of both form and content. You may have already decided that you want to go to a particular kind of institution, but you should be aware that different kinds of schools offer different versions of the education you want. For example, colleges offer skills-focused nursing certificate and diploma courses as an alternative to the more academic nursing degree programs offered by universities. Before you switch on the autopilot and go to the same university your father or your older sister went to, consider your options.

Universities

Universities come in all shapes and sizes, from the enormous, research-intensive and internationally recognized, like the University of Toronto, McGill University, and the University of British Columbia, to smaller schools that are more focused on providing undergraduate education, like St. Francis Xavier University and the University of Lethbridge. What these schools all have in common is that they grant bachelor's degrees and have faculty members who are engaged in research.

Most students who earn a bachelor's degree get it from a university, although they may attend a college first. Universities also offer a myriad of non-degree programs, from specialized diplomas to non-credit courses for students who wish to continue learning after they are finished their formal education.

Colleges

The word "college" can mean a lot of things; colleges can be private high schools like Upper Canada College in Ontario, and in the U.S., "college" often means a university. However, for the purposes of this book, colleges are post-secondary schools that offer diplomas and sometimes degrees. Colleges typically focus more on preparing students for the workforce than fostering intellectual exploration, and their faculty members are usually not required to engage in research.

Students who are eager to begin their career often attend college to enrol in vocational diploma programs that will get them through school and into their chosen industry quickly. Many colleges have strong ties to industry and boast high graduate employment rates.

Some colleges offer first- and second-year academic courses to students who plan to transfer to a university in their third year to complete a bachelor's degree. This can be an excellent choice for students who wish to stay closer to home for a couple of years before relocating to a university.

the college alternative

Many students never seriously consider attending a college instead of a university. A common (and unfounded, in our opinion) perception of colleges is that they don't offer the same quality of education as universities. A 2006 Queen's University study found that many parents believe "university is the only real path to success and college is the option you settle for if you can't get into university." However, the reality is that university isn't for everyone, and college might be exactly what you're looking for.

Many colleges boast very high graduate employment rates. More than half the students who graduated from NAIT in 2009, for example, had job offers before they finished final exams. In Ontario, the unemployment rate of college graduates between 25 and 29 years old is lower than that of university graduates.

College transfer programs can be a great way to begin a university career. These programs are common in Alberta and B.C. and increasingly popular in Ontario. They are agreements between colleges and universities that allow students to take the first year or two of their bachelor's degree at a local college, and then transfer to a university and receive full credit for the courses they've completed. This allows students to benefit from the advantages of a small college (such as lower tuition, smaller classes and a more intimate setting) for the first half of their degree and then have the advantages of a full-sized university (greater variety of courses, top-notch professors) for the second half, and get the prestigious name of the university on their degree.

Technical institutes

Technical institutes such as SAIT Polytechnic in Calgary and the British Columbia Institute of Technology focus on teaching students a specific trade or skill. Trade schools are often thought of as the training ground of electricians and carpenters, but many offer programs in a variety of different professions. Students can still land a trades apprenticeship in a subject like ironworking at a technical institute, but they can also get diplomas in journalism, accounting, engineering, health care, and many other fields.

Specialized schools

Every province has a number of schools that specialize in a particular subject or in providing a particular educational atmosphere. Students of fine art might benefit from the specialized education offered at a school like the Emily Carr University of Art and Design. Students wishing to pursue a university education in a faith-based environment may thrive at Trinity Western University. Want to be a trained engineer in the Canadian military? Consider the Royal Military College of Canada.

Private colleges and universities

While most of Canada's post-secondary system is publicly funded, there are a number of private colleges and universities. These institutions are usually focused on providing an education geared toward a specific industry. For instance, a large number of private schools focus on providing culinary training for future chefs.

Private colleges often offer smaller class sizes and more personal instruction, but because they're not government-funded, they tend to be much more expensive than public colleges. A word of warning: an unsettling number of private colleges have come under fire in recent years for poor-quality instruction and violating provincial education laws, so ask about the institution's accreditation and find out about its reputation in the related industry before enrolling.

CEGEP (collège d'enseignement général et professionnel)

In Quebec, students enrol in CEGEPs after high school if they want to prepare for university (similar to taking Grade 12 in other provinces and territories) or earn a diploma in a technical field. CEGEPs are similar to colleges in many ways, but because they are essentially part of pre-university education, this book will focus on students' educational experience after they graduate from CEGEPs.

So What's the Difference?

It can feel like you're splitting hairs when you're trying to tell the difference between several schools that promise to provide basically the same education. There is a difference between those schools, however; if it isn't in the classroom, it's in the campus atmosphere outside the class and in the city or town surrounding the campus.

Your goals and an institution's reputation

There are no really bad publicly funded post-secondary institutions in Canada, but some do certain things better than others. Some schools have a reputation for a really great business faculty, for example, and some are famous for producing engineers.

If you have a clear idea of what you want to gain from your post-secondary education, research which programs are the most respected in your field of interest, find out where the leading researchers work, and enquire about the employment rates of graduates. Don't just assume the university in your province with the biggest name has the best reputation in your field of interest; just because a school has a high profile doesn't mean it offers the highest-quality education in every faculty.

If you're unsure about where your education will take you, choose a school that offers a wide variety of courses so you can explore your interests in a lot of different subjects. And don't let a school's reputation be the only factor in your decision; the most prestigious school won't necessarily be the best match for your learning style and desired lifestyle.

Big schools versus small schools

Schools vary greatly in size, from universities like York University or the University of Alberta, which educate tens of thousands of students every year, to small community colleges, where fewer than 1,000 students study. The size of your school will have a huge impact not only on the education you receive, but also on what your life there will be like.

Large universities tend to gather faculties composed of world-class researchers, so undergraduate students have a huge number of experts to

Post-Secondary Jargon Dictionary

- Certificate: An accreditation received after completing a one-year program made up of courses that prepare students for a specific occupation. Certificate programs are generally offered by colleges and technical institutes.

- Diploma: An accreditation received after completing a program usually lasting two years, which prepares students for employment in a specific field. Diplomas are usually offered by colleges and technical institutes.

- Bachelor's degree: An accreditation received after completing a program offered by universities and some public and private colleges, and technical institutes, which usually takes four years. A bachelor's degree, also known as an undergraduate degree, is the first level of degree a student can receive.

- Undergraduate degree: See bachelor's degree.

- Undergraduate student (or undergrad): A student working toward a bachelor's degree.

- Graduate program: Education following a bachelor's degree, generally leading to a master's or doctoral degree.

- Graduate student: A student enrolled in a graduate program.

- Master's degree: A second degree earned after an undergraduate degree. A master's usually takes about two years to complete.

- Doctorate: A third level of degree earned after a master's degree through a program of study and research. Also called a Ph.D.

- Major: The main subject or specialization of study for a student pursuing a degree.

- Minor: A second area of specialization for a student pursuing a degree.

- Double major: Two different fields studied simultaneously. Double major programs typically allow students to earn two degrees in a shorter amount of time than if they were to pursue each degree separately.

- Co-op: A co-operative arrangement between a student, their school and an employer that allows students to gain work experience in a chosen field by alternating semesters of study with semesters of employment.

- Honours program: An extended research project, supervised by a faculty member, that typically culminates in a thesis. An honours bachelor's degree is good preparation for graduate school.

Small Can Be Beautiful

"I enjoy how small and personal my program is at McMaster. In my first year, I did not feel so much like a small fish in a big pool. I also love the mixed neighbourhood that allowed me to make connections in the wider Hamilton community, which helped me get out of the university bubble."

— Adira Winegust, psychology, McMaster University

learn from. This is of particular interest to students who are considering going on to graduate school and possibly becoming academics themselves. Almost every topic under the sun is taught at these schools, giving students a huge variety of subjects to explore, either as potential majors or as options.

On the other hand, the emphasis on research and graduate-level studies at large universities sometimes comes at the expense of undergraduate education. It's not uncommon for first-year students to find themselves in classes of 300 or more students. Not surprisingly, the large classes limit the amount of interaction students have with their professors. So while you might be taught chemistry by one of the country's foremost researchers, you might not have much opportunity to talk to him or her.

Smaller schools tend to have much smaller class sizes, and consequently, in the National Survey of Student Engagement, students typically rate them higher than the big schools in categories like "student-faculty interaction" and "enriching educational experience."

Size greatly affects campus life, as well. Ask yourself whether you prefer the intimate setting of a small campus or the diversity and excitement offered by a larger school.

City campus, suburban campus, small-town campus

The atmosphere of a campus will depend a lot on where it is located. Urban campuses such as the University of Toronto and McGill University feature the excitement of being connected to the city and to the rest of society. These campuses are often surrounded by neighbourhoods full of rental housing, restaurants, shopping, and bars that cater to students, and have good access to public transit that can take you to the rest of the city.

Suburban campuses, such as the University of Calgary and the University of Manitoba, are usually distinct areas that are separated from the rest of the city. They often have large open spaces and a lot of greenery, and because they're removed from the rest of the city, they can feel like a tranquil oasis specially made for students.

Some schools are located in towns so small that students almost outnumber the non-student population. The town may feel like an extension of the university campus. For example, St. Francis Xavier University (student body 4,900) is located in Antigonish, Nova Scotia (population 5,000).

contrasting school settings

The University of Toronto is built right into the fabric of central Toronto. It is surrounded by neighbourhoods full of cheap restaurants, student nightspots, and rental housing.

Simon Fraser University is located on top of a small mountain (elevation 370 metres) covered in trees and mountain-biking trails. On a clear day, you can see across the Strait of Georgia to Vancouver Island.

Close to home or far away

Most students choose a school close to home. At the University of Toronto and the University of British Columbia, 80% of students are from the province. At the University of Northern British Columbia and at Guelph University, that number jumps to 95%. There are a lot of advantages to going to school close to home, many of them economic. If you choose a school that is close enough that you can live at home with your parents, you'll save a pile of money on rent and other expenses, such as the cost of plane or bus tickets for visits home. Also, the transition of going from high school to university is a lot to take on; not everyone wants to have to get used to a new city at the same time.

However, taking the road less travelled by moving to a different part of the country can have its advantages as well. If you're willing to relocate, you'll have a much broader selection of schools to choose from, and there might be a school that is better suited to your academic goals in another city or province. Perhaps more important, you'll learn a lot and grow as a person if you leave home and experience another part of the country.

Your Choice Is About More Than Adademics

"I think that clubs and extracurricular activities like student newspapers aren't advertised very much. . . . I'm happy I found out about the student-run newspapers and the employment and writing opportunities they offer, but this isn't something I was even remotely aware of when applying to university."

– Evan LePage, journalism, Concordia University

"When I was reading guides on Canadian universities, the biggest complaint about Ryerson was that there was no sense of community. Looking back now, I wish I had realized how much that would actually affect the quality of the university experience I was getting. I transferred from Memorial and that's a school with an amazing community, and an excellent student life. Ryerson is primarily a commuter school and no bonds between fellow students. It's really frustrating to not have support from your fellow students."

– Alex Fox, design and fashion, Ryerson University

Costs

A major issue to take into consideration when choosing your school is what it will cost. Tuition and the cost of living vary greatly between institutions and locations. You might be able to save a significant amount of cash by choosing to start your education at a college or at a school close to home. Read more about costs in **Chapter 5.1: Costs and Budgeting.**

Making the Choice

So how are you supposed to choose between all these schools? A good place to start is to think about your goals, both career and personal, your interests, and your preferences about the type of campus where you'd like to spend the next few years. Ask yourself questions like: Is it important for me to be able to visit home on weekends? How is my choice of school going to affect my career goals? Am I prepared to deal with a large campus or a big city? Discuss your options with family members, friends, and your high school counsellor.

From there, create a list of schools you're interested in and start investigating. Find the answers to questions like: Which schools offer the best programs in the subject I want to study? Does this campus offer activities related to my interests? Does this school have an educational environment that suits me?

You can enquire about universities in a number of ways. To get an idea of how various schools compare, check out either *Maclean's* University Rankings or the *Globe and Mail*'s Canadian University Report. Go to university fairs and find out what the schools have to say about themselves. *Maclean's* and the *Globe and Mail* both run annual virtual university fairs, where you can learn about a huge number of schools without leaving the comfort of your bedroom.

Once you have narrowed your options and created a short list, you can start investigating those schools more intensely. Check out the "prospective students" section of the schools' websites and see what they have to offer. They may have virtual tours and other online tools, along with loads of information to help you make your decision. Talk to people who are employed in your field of interest to get a feel for which schools are most highly regarded. Seek out students at the schools you're considering and ask for their opinions.

If you're able to, visit the campus to see what it's like. Some schools offer programs that allow prospective students to follow a current student for a day, so you can talk to professors and see what classes are like. It's even possible that a school will pay for your transportation for a campus visit.

Ultimately, the choice is yours, and you should follow your instincts.

1.2 Choosing Your Major ✓

You may have decided to be an electrical engineer when you were a precocious eight-year-old, or you may still have no idea what field interests you. Depending on your program, you probably don't have to decide just yet; most courses of study don't require students to choose their major or specialization until their second or even third year of school. However, you should start thinking about this decision from the very beginning of your education. You'll have to complete certain classes in order to take other ones down the road, so you should start preparing yourself now for your future area of study. Having one or more potential majors in mind will help you plan which courses to take during your first few semesters.

In this section:

- Find out how to narrow down the options by **Exploring Possible Majors**.

- Read **A Tale of Two Students** who stumbled upon their majors in very different ways.

- Find out why it's okay if you are experiencing **Indecision**.

Exploring Possible Majors

Even if you think you know what you want to study, it's not a bad idea to explore what else is out there before you make your decision. Have a thorough look through your school's calendar of courses; there might be subjects in there you never realized existed and never considered as an option. Consider which subjects you enjoyed or excelled at in high school, think about your interests and hobbies, and ask an academic adviser what courses are related to them.

There are often several different ways to approach a subject. In some cases, you have a choice between getting a practical, hands-on trade-school certification, an arts degree, a science degree, or an honours degree—all in the same subject. You can also combine more than one subject, either by taking a minor along with your major or by taking a double major. Sometimes it's possible to enrol in an integrated degree program, where you design your own degree by combining classes from more than one field of study. You don't necessarily have to choose one of these possibilities right now, but it's good to be aware of them and consider which approach suits how you learn.

Research your major before you commit yourself to it. This may sound like an obvious piece of advice, but many students don't do it. You may have a preconceived notion of what a field of study involves, but your notion probably includes only a small part of what falls under the subject—and it's possible your understanding of a subject is completely wrong.

The very best sources of information are people who are involved in your field of interest. Talk to students, professors, and practitioners and ask them detailed questions about the subject. Your school's advising department can also be a huge help in providing information about different subject areas, types of related jobs, and how to choose a major.

Even if you do have a very good grasp on the material you'll be studying, it's also a good idea to find out what kinds of careers your major could lead

Don't Get Stuck on One Subject

"To me, university is where most of us decide what we want to do. There are so many classes you don't get exposed to in high school."

– Alexia Paquette, academic adviser, University of Saskatchewan

to when you graduate. You may enjoy studying a subject but hate the jobs in that field. If you can, talk to people who have graduated with the degree or diploma you're thinking about pursuing and ask them about the employment opportunities in the field. Don't just ask about the job market or the pay; find out what a typical workday is like.

A Tale of Two Students

For many students, choosing a major is a complicated process—and a glorious voyage of exploration. It can take time for some students to find out what they really want to study, and that can add semesters to the time it takes to get a degree—but it doesn't have to.

Jill MacPhee (not her real name), who graduated in 2010 with an education degree from the University of British Columbia, entered university as an English major, then switched to political science, then to sociology, then back to English before finally settling on education. She spent five years earning her bachelor's degree, but when she left high school, Jill didn't know what interested her or what she excelled at. "It wasn't until I went to college," she says, "that I discovered so many different ideas and beautiful writers. It was mind-blowing."

accountants: men of mystery

Rows of pallid workers in green visors poring over ledgers and pulling the handles of mechanical adding machines? That's an entertaining stereotype, but it has little to do with the actual profession. What do they really do? You better ask an accountant before you decide you want (or don't want) to be one.

Even if you switch programs, it is possible to graduate in four years. For 2009 St. Francis Xavier graduate Danielle Webb, it wasn't until the end of second year that she decided on a history degree; that's a year later than most universities recommend declaring a major. But because she consulted with advisers from the beginning, she'd chosen courses that left doors open.

Like many students, Danielle had to finance her own education. Financial realities often lead students to reduce course loads in order to work, which means staying in school longer. Danielle stayed on the four-year schedule by working less and taking out larger student loans, a decision she doesn't regret. She also found flexible, on-campus jobs, such as working for the athletics department and university newspaper. She took summer classes so she could work while she was enrolled part-time in her final year. (We'll cover more strategies for graduating on time in the next section.)

Indecision

Some students know exactly what they want to study and exactly what career they want to pursue when they graduate—but most don't.

The choice of what to study when you begin your post-secondary education might seem like the most momentous decision of your entire life. This one decision will determine your future career, your income, how attractive your spouse will be, the happiness of your future children, the obedience of your future pets, and what will be written on your tombstone, won't it?

If this thought panics you, you'll be happy to know that you're allowed to change your mind. More than half of Canadian students change their major, their program, or their school before they graduate.

There are loads of reasons for changing your major. You might learn more about the subject that seemed so attractive to you back in high school and decide that it's not for you. You might find out that you're actually really bad at your major, or that you're really good at another one. Or maybe you'll be exposed to a subject you never realized existed before, and discover that you love it.

Post-secondary education is at its core an opportunity to explore. There are literally hundreds of different specializations you can get an education in, many of which a typical high school student has never even heard of. If everyone had to choose their future career at the age of 18, there would be no neurolinguists or biophysicists or ethnobotanists.

There are often drawbacks to changing your major, particularly if you do it late in the game, like during the third year of a university degree. You probably won't be able to use some of the courses you've already finished to satisfy the requirements of your new program, which means you'll have to take more classes and possibly spend more time in school. If you really hate what you're studying, or you've learned that you really love some other subject, it's probably worth the time and money it takes to switch to a new program.

1.3   Planning Your Degree

I magine this: you're in the last semester of your undergraduate degree. You've studied hard, worked your butt off, and passed every class during the past four years, and you're going to graduate on time. You've got a job lined up after graduation and you can't wait to begin the next stage of your life. But when you apply for your degree, you learn—surprise!—that you're one course short and you'll have to come back next year.

What a nightmare!

It's a more common mistake than you might think. Even someone as organized and admirable and plain awesome as Ben Coli, a co-author of this book, can space out and make a mistake while planning fourth-year registration by taking the wrong course. Ben was lucky: he was able to take the course he needed in the summer session, and his boss let him take an afternoon off

be open-minded

K irk was studying veterinary ophthalmology when he developed allergies to both animals and eyes. He switched majors to dance, earned an honours BFA, and now works as a choreographer for the National Ballet. (Warning: not a true story.)

every week so he could attend lectures. Under different circumstances, a small mistake in planning could cost you a year of inconvenience.

It's becoming increasingly common for students to take more than four years to complete a four-year degree, and not always because of a failed class or a registration screw-up. Many students choose to take longer to complete their education so they can work while going to school, take semesters off to work or travel, or simply to avoid being driven crazy by the pressure of a full course load.

However long you intend to stay in school, it's important to plan carefully. Effective planning will keep you on track to graduate when you want to and it will allow you to enjoy other exciting opportunities such as international exchanges and co-op work semesters.

In this section:

- Ask yourself **What's Your Plan?** so you can design a strategy.

- Learn why **Academic Advising** is essential to staying on track.

- Get tips on **Choosing Courses**.

- Find out what to expect when **Registering and Scheduling**.

What's Your Plan?

Registering for college or university courses will be a whole new experience if you're coming straight from high school. Picking classes isn't just a matter of choosing between two options (sewing or cooking class?); depending on your school and your program, you might have to choose every single class you take. If you want to graduate at the end of this, you're going to have to figure out your program's requirements, plan which courses you'll take, and in what order you'll take them.

Don't worry, though; you'll make it. Plenty of people who are less organized than you have graduated from university before (we don't know who you are, but we know that this statement is true). Plus, you'll have plenty of help figuring things out.

Most programs of study offer a road map of classes (it might be called a "program planner" or a "degree navigator" or something else) available in your school's calendar that will get you through to graduation in the minimum amount of time. The road map will tell you which courses you need to take in each year of study, and it will tell you how many electives you should take. The nice thing about following your road map exactly is that it will ensure you take the classes in the right order, so you complete the prerequisites you need before you register for the next class.

Things get a little more complicated if you fail classes or switch majors, because you probably won't fit exactly into the four-year timeline anymore, but it will always be helpful to refer to your road map and get an idea of where you are in your program. (For example: "I'm in third year, minus those two second-year courses I'm missing.")

Acceptance into a program doesn't guarantee that you'll be able to get into the courses listed on that road map, however. Sometimes courses are full, and sometimes you'll run into scheduling conflicts, where two courses you need are offered only in the same time slot.

Prepare to be flexible with your plan. You might have to take courses earlier or later in your program than your degree's road map says you should. And be careful about prerequisites. If you put off taking Chem 101 until a later semester, you might not be able to register for other chem classes you planned to take because they require you to have taken Chem 101 first.

For various reasons, many students plan to take a break during their studies. Some students take off semesters for co-op programs, or they take a year off to travel or to participate in an exchange program. (To read about co-ops, see **Section 7.2: Co-ops and Jobs**.) You don't have to decide in your first year that you're going to take a semester off in your third year, but having flexibility in your academic plan will keep your options open.

Academic Advising

Whatever your plan is, you should take full advantage of your school's academic advising services. Your institution has an office full of experts whose job is to help students sort out their scheduling dilemmas and make good decisions for their future.

Most advising offices offer special orientations for first-year students that will teach you how to plan your schedule and register for classes. Whether you attend an orientation or not, schedule an appointment with an adviser at the very beginning of your first year to talk about your alternatives and make sure you're off to a good start. It's best to see an adviser every year and make sure you're on the right track, even if you feel like you know exactly what you're doing. It might seem like a waste of half an hour, but that beats screwing up and wasting a whole semester.

Most schools also offer online resources, such as degree navigation tools, scheduling tools, and graduation checklists you can use to make sure you're not missing anything that might prevent you from graduating on time.

Choosing Courses

The amount of choice you have will depend on what you're studying. Specialized programs, like engineering, will often lay out exactly which courses you need to take in your first year, while other programs, like an arts degree in English, will give you almost unlimited flexibility.

The freedom to choose your classes can feel like a curse if you don't know what to take or if you want to take more classes than you could possibly fit into your schedule. The most important things to keep in mind are fulfilling the requirements of your program and completing the prerequisites for classes you'll need to take in future years. Figure this part of your schedule out first and then fit the optional courses around this core of requirements.

Read through the calendar to find optional courses you might want to take in later years, and find out what prerequisites are required for them. Philosophy 100: Introduction to Philosophy might sound like a real snorefest, but if you don't take it this year, next year you won't be able to take

there's no reason to rush

McGill engineering student Veronica Pinchin decided to add a semester to her program to avoid the pressure of having to take six classes per semester for four semesters in a row. She says the decision was good for her sanity—and her marks. "Since I started school at 17, if I'd completed my degree in four years I would have graduated at 21. As it is, I'll have just turned 22. That doesn't seem too old to be starting the rest of my life."

Philosophy 240: Knowledge and Reality, which, if you're anything like us, sounds fascinating.

consult advisers from the beginning

Ann Tierney, vice-provost for students at the University of Calgary, has seen too many students in their final year discover they've erred in planning their degree. According to Tierney, general arts and science students are most affected by the problem because they have so much freedom to choose their classes. The university system can be difficult to navigate, and anyone, no matter how conscientious they are, can make a small mistake that can add a semester. "For some students, the first time they see an adviser is in a reactive way, when they're going into their last year. Sometimes students feel they do not need any help and then realize late in their program that they should have sought the advice of an adviser earlier."

Apart from those considerations, take the classes you enjoy. You'll be more likely to attend classes and do well in a course if you look forward to going. That being said, try to take a variety of classes instead of taking all your options in the subject you love the most. You'll have a much more well-rounded educational experience if you occasionally take yourself out of your comfort zone. And who knows, maybe one of those oddball classes will turn out to be your true calling in life.

Students are often tempted to take classes that have a reputation for being easy, to improve their averages without taking on a lot of extra work. It's true that grades are important, but make sure you don't take an "easy" course that you find so boring you can't muster enough attention and effort to get a better grade than a C.

A boring professor can make you hate a subject you would otherwise enjoy. Before you register, ask other students about the reputations of various professors. Interesting professors can make a boring subject come to life, just like boring professors can put you to sleep even if they're lecturing about a rock-and-roll sex orgy on the moon.

Strategies for Graduating on Time

- Consult an academic adviser at the beginning of the year, every year.

- Learn about your university's system. Do you know your program requirements? Are you sure you'll have completed all the necessary prerequisites in time?

- Research your major and talk to professors before you commit yourself.

- Apply for all scholarships and bursaries, work during the summer, and take out student loans to limit how much you have to work during the academic year.

- Make school your top priority. If you must work, look for jobs that are flexible.

- Take summer courses to lessen the course load during the academic year.

Registering and Scheduling

At a post-secondary school, there is no alarm bell in the morning that tells everyone to start class and no scheduled time when everyone has lunch. Each student assembles his or her own schedule out of lectures, seminars, and labs listed in the calendar, so it may be that on some days you won't start until noon, while on other days you'll start at 8:00 A.M. This system can allow you great flexibility in building a schedule that suits your preferences and your other activities, but putting a schedule together can be frustrating.

Imagine this: You've been poring over the calendar, reading class descriptions and blocking off courses in your hypothetical schedule for the next year. You've got everything scheduled just so. It's perfect: you get to sleep in two days a week, you've got lunch hours, and you get to go home at two o'clock three days a week.

Then, when you try to register for your Monday morning physics class, it's full. The only other time that class is offered is Tuesday and Thursday at 1:30, at the exact same time as your Portuguese class. Portuguese is also available Tuesday and Thursday at 10:30, but that's when you were going to take Prehistoric Archaeology.

Everything's falling apart!

Don't stress out. People rarely get their ideal schedule.

It's wise to select backup courses and create alternate schedules before

research
potential
classes

Rey Buenaventura, director of academic advising at Simon Fraser University, says it's important to know what you're getting into when you sign up for a class. Find out what the class is about and how many mid-terms, finals, and essays will be required. "Then do some self-evaluation. You have to be honest with yourself and have an idea of your strengths and weaknesses. If you prefer to write essays, taking a math course might not be a good idea."

registration day rolls around so you don't have to choose a course at the last minute. In the end, you may be forced to take classes at awkward times, like 5:00 o'clock at night or 8:00 o'clock in the morning, but such is the life of a student. Inasmuch as you can control the timing of your classes, try to create a schedule that is conducive to learning.

Avoid scheduling classes for those times of the day when you're not going to be awake enough to pay attention to a lecture. You know yourself— maybe you're not a morning person, or maybe you burn out in the after- noon and can't understand anything anyone says after about 3:00 o'clock. Figure out what time of day works best for each activity you have to do, and schedule accordingly; for example, if you read best early in the morning, don't schedule any classes before 10:00, and plan a two-hour reading period starting at 8:00 A.M.

Avoid scheduling more than three consecutive hours of lectures. Your brain needs time to recover between classes. As attractive as the prospect of getting all your classes out of the way in three days might seem, it's probably a bad idea. Those three days are going to be exhausting, and your marks could suffer for it.

Schedule lunch. Hungry students think about sandwiches, not about Shakespeare or semiconductors. And besides, taking a break in the middle of the day helps you rest and reset your brain and get ready for the next subject.

Don't forget to check if any of your classes have labs or seminars. It's easy to forget to leave room in your schedule for those little guys, and you'd hate to finish registering for everything and then have to go back and change your whole schedule to fit in your labs.

move over, social studies

Forget the boring subjects of high school and embrace the wild, wonderful and just plain weird classes that some post-secondary institutions offer. For example:

DRAM 236.3: You can spend an entire semester learning how to achieve the illusion of physical violence onstage in this University of Saskatchewan stage-combat course.

ENV 2401: The University of Winnipeg offers an intensive two-week course on forestry skills that includes safe use of chainsaws and basic bush-survival skills.

MUSC 2022: Students must bring an approved hand drum to this class at Dalhousie University, where they study the art and science of drumming.

CNST 451: The University of Calgary offers an entire course on the culture and history of a famous local festival: the Calgary Stampede.

TG PEAC 245: Improve your swing and learn golf etiquette in this Medicine Hat College physical education and activity class.

MIT 3371 F/G: At the University of Western Ontario you can learn about video-game addiction and the history of gaming in this course on the culture and technology of video and computer games.

Take a variety of courses each semester, instead of cramming all four of your English Lit. courses into the first semester and all four of your biology courses into the second semester. Those four Lit. courses are going to have you reading a ton of novels, and those Bio. courses are going to have you spending half your life in a lab. Too much of any one kind of course can burn you out.

At many schools, students with the best marks and those who have declared their major get first crack at registering for certain courses—but this helps you only if you get around to doing it. Make sure you register on the very first day you're able to, and register for the courses that are most important to you first.

Other students will be changing their schedules right up until the first day of class (and sometimes even after that), so keep checking to see if any space has opened up in classes that were full when you tried to register for them.

You Might Need Some Discipline

"Some days, only having class at seven in the evening meant I wouldn't get out of bed until noon, which didn't necessarily do wonders in terms of productivity."

– Jesse Willms, political science, University of Ottawa

If you can't get into a course you absolutely need, get on the waiting list and show up for the first class even if you aren't enrolled. Often it's up to the professor to choose who on the waiting list gets into the class, and he or she might sign you up that day if you're there. If all of that fails, it might be time to start begging your professor, your registrar, your department head, or whoever else is in charge of making special exceptions for hard-luck cases.

1.4 What's It Going to Be Like?

If you're feeling nervous about making the transition to college or university, you're not alone; almost everyone feels at least a little anxious about what it's going to be like, mostly because they don't know what to expect.

We've got bad news for you: we don't know what your university or college experience is going to be like, either. Everyone's experience is different,

think outside the box

Throw aside your course calendar and try using social media to find exciting and fulfilling courses. Use Facebook to ask friends about courses they loved, question the masses on Twitter, or log onto www.Ratemyprofessor.com and review candid peer comments. You're bound to stumble across an interesting university course you may otherwise have overlooked.

Work Hard and You'll Be Fine

"The big fears turned out to be no big deal. University courses aren't impossibly difficult. If you do the readings and take good notes, you'll do fine."

    – Scott Dobson-Mitchell, medical
    sciences, University of Waterloo

and besides, what are we, fortune tellers? Psychics advertising on late-night TV? No, we're just advice-book writers.

Oh . . . We guess we should offer some advice. Disregard that last paragraph. We're experts on everything, including your future!

We talked to a lot of students who, a year or two ago, were where you are now. We asked them about their first year of post-secondary education and what it was like to make the leap from high school to college or university.

Now, here's the good news: it sounds like post-secondary education is going to be an improvement over high school in most ways. Basically, it sounds like you're in for some hard work, but you're going to meet a bunch of new people, escape from the cliques and torments of high school, learn a lot about yourself and about the world, and have a whole pile of fun (if you let yourself).

You're the Boss

"There's no one constantly on you to do what you're supposed to do—this is both a relief and a curse, because it means that the only person around to make sure you do your assignments is you."

    – Samantha Thompson, global
    stewardship, Capilano University

Academically, college or university is probably going to be a lot tougher than high school was, although some programs are more challenging than others. Typically, you'll spend much less time in the classroom than you did in high school, but you'll have much more work demanded of you outside of class time. In some classes, you'll read more than you ever imagined possible back in high school, and you'll have to stay caught up on your reading if you want to follow what's going on in class.

In class, you'll cover material more quickly than you did in high school, even though you've got less class time to cover it in. Grading standards are

Don't Worry, Be Happy

"University is nothing to be afraid of: My last month of summer vacation was spent worrying. Worrying that university courses would be impossibly difficult, worrying that I wouldn't be able to keep up with the readings, worrying that I'd fail miserably and have to drop out. What I didn't know is that in university, you're given every opportunity to succeed."

– Scott Dobson-Mitchell, medical sciences, University of Waterloo

Expect Grading Standards to Change

"I found that despite the assignments . . . not becoming any more difficult or challenging, to achieve the same mark did prove more challenging."

– Jesse Willms, political science, University of Ottawa

going to be higher than they were in high school. Professors are going to demand higher-quality work to earn an A than your teachers did.

On the bright side, you'll be studying things you chose to study, and the faster pace will help keep things from getting boring. Some students take to it like a fish to water, having finally been freed of all the courses they hated in high school. (Would you prefer never to take a math class again? That can be arranged.) For many students, there is a period of adjustment while they get used to the change, and some students' first-semester grades are worse than they were used to getting in high school. But you will get used to it, and you'll learn the tricks and techniques of the game before long.

Something else you'll get used to (if you're going to college right after high school, anyway) is being treated like an adult. In some ways, it's great—you'll be able to have a conversation with your professors as one human being to another. You'll have the freedom to make your own choices, to set your own bedtime, and to eat nothing but chocolate chips right out of the bag, if you want. Depending on your school, you probably won't even have to go to class if you don't want to—most professors don't bother taking attendance, and if it's a big class, they might not even notice if you don't show up.

There's a downside to all of this, of course. If you eat all those chocolate

Be Open to Making New Friends

"Don't come into post-secondary so worried about losing your friends from high school that you forget to make new friends."

– Samantha Thompson, global stewardship, Capilano University

chips, you'll get a stomach ache, and if you don't go to class, you're going to flunk out. Nobody's going to hold your hand anymore and tell you what to do and when to do it. You're the one who's responsible for making sure you complete your assigned reading and finish your school work, and that means you'll have to learn some time management skills.

Your fellow students will also likely treat you more like an adult than your classmates in high school did. The cliques and bullying you might have seen in high school rarely transfer over to college or university. People tend to treat one another much more civilly, and nobody has to worry about being called a nerd for being good at school because at an institution of higher learning, being good at school is the whole point.

If you're moving to a different town to go to school, you'll probably miss your friends from home. But your school will be packed with other people your age, many of whom will have similar interests and like all the same cartoons as you. And if you don't like cartoons, you'll probably find other people who don't like cartoons for the same reasons you don't like them, and maybe you can talk about that. The point is, there are loads of people around you can get along with. You'll make new friends, as long as you keep yourself open to people.

Although you'll come across many challenges during your first year of studies, there are people all around you who can help. You only have to ask. Your school employs counsellors who can help you with any problem you might run into, academic or personal. If you leave home for the first time and move in to residence, there are people there called residence advisers (RAs) who can help you with that transition. You're going to be treated like an adult, but you're not going to be left all on your own, so you don't have to be too stressed about it.

Every college and university also offers orientation sessions, or other workshops in which you can learn about how your university works and what to expect. During the summer, look online or call an academic adviser to find out when these sessions are offered and what you should be doing to prepare for the coming academic year, like picking up your identification card, paying tuition, or registering for courses.

And if you're still worried about how you're going to cope with this frightening adventure you're undertaking and you're wondering what other challenges you'll run into, we have one final tip: read the rest of this book.

2

A Roof Over Your Head

NOW THAT YOU'VE CHOSEN your school, picked your classes, and assembled the perfect schedule, the next question is, where are you going to live? Where you choose to hang your hat will affect your marks, your budget, and your social life.

If you're going to a school that isn't close to home, you've got the choice between living in a university residence or finding your own place somewhere off-campus. Both have their benefits and drawbacks, and before you default to one or the other, take a second to consider your options. Are you going to be able to be a successful student in a crowded, social place like a residence? On the other hand, are you ready for the work and responsibility of cooking, cleaning, and paying rent in your own apartment?

If you're going to school close to home, you may have a third option, which is to continue living with your parents. You already know how to live at home, so we're not going to include a section about it, but this is an option you should give serious consideration because it can have major benefits. Depending on your situation, you might be able to score free rent and food while avoiding the difficulties of transitioning to a new living arrangement and a new school at the same time. As for the disadvantages—well, they're your parents, so you've got a better idea than we do.

In this chapter:

- Find what's so great about **Residence Life** and how to actually get something done when you're sharing a bathroom with 40 other people.

- Figure out whether **Renting Off-Campus** is right for you, how to score a great apartment, and how to stay out of disputes with your landlord and roommates.

2.1 Residence Life

I f it's time to move out of your parents' house but you feel like you're not quite ready to live completely independently, residence can be a great option.

Residence isn't like living with your parents, but it's also not quite the same thing as living independently. Nobody will set a curfew or tell you to clean your room (unless it's dirty enough to be a health hazard), but you won't have to worry about paying the electricity bills or cleaning the toilets, and if you've got a meal plan, someone else will cook for you. Plus, you'll be living with hundreds of other students, which can be really fun or a huge pain in the butt—or both, depending on what you're trying to do that day.

In this section:

- We'll talk you through the question: **Is Residence Right for You?**

- Get tips on **Applying for Residence**.

- Get an idea of what to expect while you're **Surviving the First Month**.

- It's a small room for two people, so learn about **Living With a Roommate**.

- Living there is one thing, but you're going to need **Residence Study Tips** to get decent grades.

- Turn res into a chance to thrive by **Participating in Your Residence**.

- Finicky eater? Read about **Surviving the Meal Plan**.

Is Residence Right for You?

Jesse Whitehead was 17 when he moved from a small town to a residence at the University of Alberta.

In the first month of the semester, the guy who lived in the room next door spent his scholarship money on a booming stereo and played terrible music at top volume all the time.

Another guy on the floor spilled his fish tank on his bed, put his mattress in the showers to dry and, being too lazy to put his room back together, spent the rest of the semester sleeping on the couch in the lounge.

In the women's wing of the floor, a student entered her room with her mother to find her roommate in bed with a guy.

And Jesse had the time of his life living in residence that year.

Communal living definitely has its challenges. Residences, especially first-year dorms, can be pretty crowded places. You're going to have to share a small space with a bunch of people who will at first be strangers, and deal with their weirdness and their bad habits. Plus, you're actually going to have to get stuff done while you live there; you'll have to read a mountain of books, study for exams, and write coherent papers, which can be a serious challenge if you happen to live in a particularly rowdy residence. But if you can adapt to living in residence, you will have a great time and meet lifelong friends.

In spite of the challenges, every single former residence-dweller we spoke to recommended living in residence for at least your first year—even the people who hated it.

What's so great about living in residence? We came up with three things:

The social scene

Residence is a great place to meet people. If you're from a different town, you'll need to build a whole new support network of friends, but it can be hard to make social contacts in a lecture theatre with 300 students in it. In residence, you're going to meet a lot of people, and you're going to get to know them very well, very quickly.

Imagine having an instant social scene of 20 or 40 people. Everywhere you go on campus, you'll run into people you know, even in the first month

Automatic Community

"One of the most advantageous things about living in res when you start university is that there's this immediate community."

– Lizzie Blundon,
physics and psychology,
University of British Columbia

of class. And if some night you feel like going bowling with a dozen people, there's your crew, right there on your floor.

Residence will also help connect you to a much more diverse group of students than you'll meet in class. You tend to meet only artsy people in art history class and engineers in an engineering class, but in residence you'll meet all kinds of people and get in touch with what's going on all over campus.

Residence is convenient and easy

In your first year, you'll be learning to cope with the workload and responsibility of university, and for most people, that's enough to deal with. You might find it too much to also learn to feed yourself and run your own household.

Worry-Free Accommodation

"It's really hard to get yourself settled off-campus if you don't know the town or the city that you're going to, so res provides one less thing for a new student to worry about."

– Danielle Webb, history, St. Francis
Xavier University

Living in residence means you won't have to look for an apartment in a strange city, deal with a landlord, or buy furniture. If you sign on to a meal plan (in most residences they're mandatory for the first year), you won't have to plan meals, shop for groceries, or cook, which will save you time you could otherwise spend studying or socializing.

Living on campus also means you won't have to commute to and from school, which can save a ton of time and make it easier to get involved in campus life. It's also a lot less time-consuming to be a good student when you live within walking distance of all the academic resources on your campus, such as libraries, computer labs, and your professors' and TAs' office hours.

You'll learn a lot

It's true: you'll learn a lot about yourself and other people living in residence. Breaking out of your comfort zone by leaving your family and high school friends and getting that up-close exposure to people from different backgrounds will teach you about how to deal with people.

Learn About Yourself

"You get to figure out who you are in the context of other people."

— Jesse Whitehead, psychology, University of Alberta

Residence is like having roommates, but with training wheels on. You'll be living in close quarters with people you may not have a lot in common with, but if you have any serious conflicts, there are residence advisers (RAs) to help you sort it out.

After you've survived residence, you'll be an expert at dealing with roommates, which will make things easier when you live independently for the first time. After all, one or two roommates are a cinch after you've gotten used to living with 39.

Applying for Residence

Research your residence

Residences come in all shapes and sizes, and all the big universities have several to choose from. Which residence you end up living in will make a huge difference to the experience you have. Some residences are more social, some have nicer rooms, and some allow (or force) you to live more independently than others. It's important to think about the kind of living situation you want and to find the residence that suits you best.

Not All Residences Are Equal

"The Lansdowne rooms seem like they're the smallest out of all the rooms on campus. I've been to other ones and ours seem about 3/4 of the size. Plus, our walls are highlighter yellow with these awful orangish-brown colours that look like pumpkin and oatmeal puke."

— Stephen Finnis, environmental sciences, University of Victoria

residence advisers: your guides to first year

Residence advisers (RAs) are just ordinary students who live in res, except that they are endowed with superpowers they use to solve other students' problems. RAs run orientations and other residence activities, and generally make themselves available to help students with problems. RAs are connected folk, so if your RA can't get you out of a bind, they know someone who can.

This is the place you'll be living for a whole academic year, so at least take the time to read the descriptions of the different residences on your university's website. If you're able to, take a tour of the residence buildings before you choose, and if you know anybody who is going or has gone to your future university, talk to him or her about what kind of reputations the various residences have.

Don't lie on your application

Your residence application form will probably include a few questions about your habits, to help residence administrators match you to a roommate and floormates with compatible lifestyles. Are you messy? Noisy? Are you an early bird or a night owl?

Everyone is terrified of getting a total slob for a roommate, but resist the temptation to lie about your own habits. If you're messy and you lie on your application to get a roomie who is neat, it could cause conflict. If you're a social person, don't claim to be quiet—you'll probably have more fun with someone who is a chatterbox like you.

Surviving the First Month

The move-in date for most residences is about a week before classes start. During this week, there are usually orientation activities. It's a good idea to move in early and to go to the orientation, even if you know the city well and think you have a pretty good handle on the campus. That first week is a great opportunity to get to know everybody on your floor and to get settled before

Practise Sleeping

"You become good at sleeping through anything as a matter of necessity. You get to know people really quickly and you become comfortable with sharing a bathroom."

– Jesse Whitehead, psychology, University of Alberta

the pressures of classes start.

You can expect lots of partying in the first week or two you're there. If it feels a little crazy, don't worry; soon everyone will start getting assignments, and they'll have to get to work. Each residence and school has its own culture, but by and large, weekdays are relatively tranquil times during the semester.

There is going to be a lot of stuff to get used to. You may not be comfortable sharing a bathroom at first, and having all those people around all the time might be a bit overwhelming. If you've got a roommate, you might miss having a space of your own where you can hide from the world. You will get used to it, though, and by the time the year is over and you go home for the summer, you might even miss it.

Living With a Roommate

You and your roommate are going to learn more than you ever wanted to know about each other in a very short period of time. The room you share will probably be very small, so you'll be studying, reading, and sleeping within arm's reach of each other, and it's extremely easy to get on each other's nerves in those circumstances. It helps to get to know each other's schedules and arrange to have the room to yourself sometimes. You'll both be there at the same time often, though, so you're going to have to figure out how to get along.

The key to having a good relationship with your roommate is communication. If she does something that annoys you, tell her. It can be really awkward to have to tell someone that you can't stand how messy they are, but it's much better to be open about it and to give your roomie a chance to fix things than to let the resentment build up for months until it explodes in a big fight. By the same token, if your roomie tells you about something that annoys him, try to understand where he's coming from instead of getting defensive.

Come up with a set of ground rules at the very beginning to avoid misunderstandings before they start. Some universities have roommate contracts to get roommates to discuss issues at the beginning of a semester, but if yours doesn't, you can come up with your own understanding with your roommate.

Things you'll want to discuss with your roommate include:

- How clean do you expect to keep the room? How will you divide the responsibility?
- What is the policy for having an overnight guest in the room? How much notice should you give each other? Can you arrange a signal so you don't walk in on each other at an awkward time?
- Do you need permission to borrow each other's things?
- Is it acceptable to have alcohol in the room?
- What are your sleeping schedules like?
- At what times of the day is it acceptable to make noise during the week? And on the weekend?
- At what time do the lights have to be out?

It might feel a bit nerdy to break out this list at the beginning of your roommate relationship, but if you don't talk about this stuff right away, later on you'll wish you had. And remember, they're your rules; if you both agree, you can change them anytime you want. The important thing is getting in the habit of talking to each other and getting things out in the open.

Try to settle your differences together, but if you can't, talk to your RA. RAs are trained in conflict resolution, and they've dealt with disagreements like yours before.

Residence Study Tips

Residence is an extremely social and sometimes very loud place, especially on weekends. It can be hard to get any work done in your room if you're surrounded by the distractions of your floor's social life.

It's generally a good idea to leave your room when you're trying to work. Your room is probably full of distractions—it's where your roommate is playing video games and where people who want to hang out with you come to find you.

Scout out quiet places to study on campus. The library is a good bet, but there are probably lots of other good places as well. Some people swear they can study in their residence's lounge, but that usually consists of hanging out and chatting with people with an open book on your lap. Unless you've found a way to absorb a book's knowledge through your skin, it doesn't count as studying if you're not actually reading.

A laptop computer can be a lifesaver in residence because it gives you the ability to write papers and do other computer-based assignments anywhere on campus. If you've got a desktop computer, you're anchored to your room, and you'll have to negotiate with your roommate for some quiet time and somehow shut out all the distractions coming in from outside your room. If you find that's not working for you, head to a computer lab.

Participating in Your Residence

Residence, of course, isn't just something that needs to be endured; it can be tons of fun, you can make lifelong friends, and you can grow as a person. Residence veterans told us over and over again: "You get out of it what you put into it," meaning, if you stay in your room and keep to yourself, you're not going to love the experience. But if you participate in activities and socialize with your floormates, you're going to have a blast.

Residence offers opportunities to volunteer, to play on res intramural sports teams, to participate in residence government (which can be a gateway to student politics), and even to opportunities for employment, such as being a residence adviser. RAs get paid or receive free accommodation or both; they get connected to the university community in a big way, and they get a great experience to put on their resumé.

Surviving the Meal Plan

The bad news is that residence meal halls have a terrible reputation. The food is said to be bland, repetitive, unhealthy, and, perhaps worst of all, expensive. We too have heard the rumours that the catering company that provides meal plans on campus also caters to prisons, and the prisoners get higher quality food because they would riot if they were served the stuff students get.

The good news is that this reputation isn't always deserved, and many cafeterias are making a real effort to get better. Meal-plan providers have started working with campus health offices to offer more nutritious food, and some residences and student unions have set up committees to communicate concerns and ideas to meal-plan providers.

Despite what you might think after having a particularly bad meal, your meal-plan providers aren't monsters. They want to give you decent food, and if you have special dietary requirements, they will accommodate you. But they can't fix problems they don't know exist, so if you can't stand the food, tell them. If your residence doesn't have a student committee that communicates with your meal-plan provider, form one. Even if you plan to leave residence next year, you'll learn from the experience, and next year's residents will thank you for it.

It is true that a meal plan is more expensive than cooking for yourself, but you have to expect that—you're paying someone to cook for you. If you're a gourmet chef or just a super-picky eater and you really want to cook for yourself, then find a residence that doesn't have a mandatory meal plan.

If you can't escape the meal plan, buy a mini-fridge for your dorm room, where you can keep fresh vegetables and other healthy snacks to help round out your meal-plan diet. For more tips on eating well, see **Section 6.6: Eating Well and Being Active**.

2.2 Renting Off-Campus ✓

Living off-campus entails a bit more work and responsibility than living in residence, but it also gives you a lot more control over your living circumstances. You can choose what neighbourhood you live in and which roommates you live with, instead of being assigned a room in a dorm with 40 random strangers on your floor.

You'll get to choose a space of your own and decorate it how you like, and you and your roommates will get to set the rules you live by, instead of living by the rules your dorm gives you. On the other hand, you'll have to do your own cooking and cleaning, remember to pay all the bills, find your own social scene, and, perhaps toughest of all, find a place you can afford.

In this section:

- Think about **Your Housing Requirements** before beginning your search.

- **Finding Roommates** can make renting much more affordable.

- Learn how to go about your **Accommodation Search**.

- **Understanding Your Lease** is important before you sign on the dotted line.

- Protect your security deposit by filling out and documenting your **Condition Report**.

- Find out about **Your Rights as a Tenant**.

- And finally, prevent the whole thing from falling apart by learning about **Living with Roommates**.

Your Housing Requirements

Before you start looking for a place, take some time to think about what's important to you in a house or apartment. You can narrow down your search a lot if you decide in advance how much rent you can afford and which neighbourhoods you would like living in.

If you're from out of town, it's best to make the trip to your future alma mater a couple of months before classes start and check out the neighbourhoods near the school. If you can't make the trip, talk to someone who lives in town and make sure your target neighbourhood isn't a dangerous hellhole or a two-hour commute away. Research the transportation options from your future neighbourhood to your school. Pay attention to the frequency of the bus service and the hours the system operates.

Ideally, you'll find somewhere within walking distance of school. A half-hour bus ride may not sound too bad, but those half-hour trips add up to a lot of time—particularly if an awkward school schedule demands two trips to school every day.

Make yourself aware of the kind of housing options you have in your target neighbourhoods. Apartment towers, walk-up apartments, townhouses, houses, and basement suites all have unique advantages and disadvantages. Think about which housing styles appeal most to you.

Once you figure out how much you can afford to spend (see **Section 5.1: Costs and Budgeting**), a quick look through the local classified ads or Craigslist should tell you whether it's realistic for you to rent a place on your own in the neighbourhoods you want to live in. If it is too expensive, you may have to look in a cheaper part of town (which often means somewhere farther from school) or team up with one or more roommates to share a house or apartment.

Finding Roommates

You might know people who go to your school who are also looking for a place to live, but even if they're your best friends, you have to ask yourself if you could really live with them. You want to keep them as your friends, and if you have incompatible lifestyles it could be a total disaster.

Before you get too enthusiastic about all the fun you're going to have living with your buddies, talk to them about their habits. Are they tidy? Do they like to have a lot of people over and throw parties every weekend? Do they wake up super-early in the morning and blast Beethoven symphonies to get psyched up for their 8:00 A.M. physics lab? Do they smoke? What do they smoke? Do they mind if you smoke? Do they play the drums? Do they have pets? Do they mind if you teach their pets to smoke?

There are no right answers to these questions, only answers that are right for you. Maybe you want a drummer roommate who throws outrageous parties every weekend—but take a minute to think about what that will do to your marks before you sign up for it.

If you don't know anyone to share a space with, but you need to find a roommate, check Craigslist, the classified ads in the local paper, or your school's housing registry, where you'll find tons of listings for shared accommodation.

Be sure to meet your new roommates to get an idea about who they are and whether you could live with them before you make any commitments. If the listing is for a room in a space your prospective roommates already live in, have a good look around the house or apartment for evidence of how they actually live.

Strangers can sometimes make the best roommates, especially if you want a less social atmosphere; people tend to show more consideration and give more space to strangers than they do to their best friends. It can be difficult to study and work in a space you share with people you socialize with. You may find it easier to live with other students. You'll all be on the same schedule, studying most evenings and cramming at exam times, and you'll understand each other's needs.

Searching for Accommodation

Many schools have housing registries, run either by the school or the student union; this is the best place to start, as the listings tend to be posted by student-friendly landlords at prices students can afford in locations near the school. Other places to look include Craigslist and the classified ads in the local paper.

Don't spend hours looking for the ideal listing; instead, complete several listings that might work for you and your roommates, and look at all of them before you make a commitment to one of them. It's hard to tell if a place is a good deal or not until you've looked at several places.

It's extremely difficult to find housing if you're out of town, particularly if you're not familiar with the city you're moving to. It's best to go in person to see what the neighbourhood is like and whether the apartments are decent places to live. Don't take a landlord's word about the condition or quality of an apartment, and don't rent it sight unseen over the phone; you may be setting yourself up for an unpleasant surprise. If you absolutely can't go and look at the place yourself, ask someone you trust to look at it, or get the landlord to take photos and ask him or her a lot of questions. Be sure you know who the landlord is and where he or she lives before you send a deposit cheque to a stranger in a distant city.

When the time comes to look at a place, dress decently and behave politely. Refrain from cracking jokes within your landlord's hearing about how you or your roommate are going to pass out drunk in the hallways. Your landlord is looking for someone who isn't going to destroy the place or scare off the other tenants. Bring a list of questions you want to ask your landlord so you don't forget anything important.

If you're not familiar with the area the apartment is in, show up early and take time to look around the neighbourhood. Ask yourself whether you'll feel safe there. Then go back to the neighbourhood late in the evening and see how safe it feels after 9:00 P.M. Check out transportation options to school; a quick search on the local transit authority's website will give you an idea of how long your commute will be. Find out where the nearest grocery store is.

Take note of the building's security when you enter; do you have to get buzzed in the front door, or can just anyone walk in? The lobby and the hallways will tell you a lot about your landlord's standards of maintenance. Pay even closer attention to the inside of the apartment. Don't just check to see that there's enough space for all of your stuff; also look for:

- Is the place clean? Check the toilet, fridge, and drawers.
- Is there adequate lighting? Enough windows?
- Does the plumbing work?
- Are the windows properly sealed? Does the glass look thick enough to keep out the cold?
- Do the windows and patio doors have decent locks on them?
- Is there a deadbolt on the front door?
- Does the place have all the appliances you'll need?
- What's the landlord like? Does he or she seem reasonable? Do you think you can count on the landlord to fix problems promptly?
- Do you see any bugs? See any mouse poop?
- Is the place adequately heated? Do you have control over the heat?
- Is the cost of utilities included in the rent? Or will you have to pay for heat and electricity separately? If so, what do utilities cost for an average month?
- Are there closets in the bedrooms? Is there other storage space?
- Are there laundry facilities in the unit, or in the building? If not, where's the nearest laundromat?
- Are the building and location noisy? Can you hear the upstairs neighbours' footsteps? Is there loud traffic on a nearby major road? Is there a dance club downstairs?
- Are there water stains on the ceiling or walls from a leaky roof? Or are those bloodstains? Or something worse?

The most important question you can ask yourself: Can you imagine being happy here? Some places are just too depressing and dreary for human habitation. You'll thank yourself for getting a place with more windows when January rolls around and it seems like the sun sets about an hour after it rises.

Understanding Your Lease

Before you submit an application for an apartment, be sure you understand the deal that's being offered to you. You'll be told a monthly rent, but you need to know what that includes. Does the rent include heat, electricity, gas, water, use of laundry facilities, or parking? If it doesn't, you'll have to make room for all those expenses in your housing budget, on top of the rent. If you're renting a house, ask who is responsible for shovelling the walks and mowing the lawn.

You'll also want to know how long a lease your landlord will expect you to sign. In many provinces and territories, one-year leases are the norm, which doesn't work well for students who intend to stay for eight months and then go home for the summer. Avoid signing a lease for longer than you intend to stay; you'll be left having to find a replacement tenant to take over your lease, or you'll forfeit your security deposit, as well as any chance of getting a decent reference from your landlord when you want to rent your next apartment.

Your landlord will probably ask for references from past landlords. If you're reading this, it's probably your first apartment, so you won't have any. Don't make up fake references; explain to your landlord that this is your first apartment, and offer other references instead, like former employers who can tell your landlord what a responsible and upstanding young person you are.

Your landlord may also want to perform a credit check on you (if you don't understand what this is, see **Section 5.3: Borrowing Money**). If you don't have much of a credit history (most students don't), your landlord might ask you for a guarantor to co-sign the lease for you. That means that someone with decent credit (typically a parent) has to sign the lease, guaranteeing that they'll pay the rent if you don't.

In most cases you'll be asked to pay a security deposit, which is an amount of money your landlord holds on to until you move out. If you skip out on your last month's rent or if you wreck the place, the landlord is allowed to deduct any of his or her losses or repair bills from the security deposit. The maximum legal amount of a security deposit varies by province or territory.

Your landlord will present you with a lease agreement and ask for your signature. Make sure you read and understand everything in the lease. "Standard agreement" doesn't mean it's not up for negotiation, especially if there's a high vacancy rate in the local rental market. If there's anything you don't like in the agreement, discuss it with the landlord: see if you can get the agreement changed. Before you sign, make sure to write down, on the rental agreement, any changes your landlord agrees to make. You can cross out passages that don't apply and write in your amendments. If there's anything in the suite or apartment that needs to be repaired, get your landlord to agree, in writing, and specify a deadline for the repair. Be sure you get a copy of your amended lease with your landlord's signature on it.

Condition Report

Before you move in to your apartment, take the time to inspect it with your landlord and fill out a condition report. Condition reports are mandatory in most provinces and territories and are optional in others, but they are always a good idea. (Visit our website at campuscompanion.ca for links to information on renting in specific provinces.) A condition report is a document you and your landlord fill out together, making note of the condition your apartment is in and recording details of any existing damage to the apartment.

renters' rights
resources

The Canadian Mortgage and Housing Corporation offers a series of fact sheets, giving a rundown of tenants' rights in each province and territory. Many provinces and territories have tenants' rights organizations that produce more comprehensive handbooks for tenants, often named something like "Tenant Survival Guide." If you can't find one, as a last resort you can always take a crack at reading the tenancy act. These are readily available online. Reading the legalese is good practice for any of you pre-law students.

Visit campuscompanion.ca for links to resources for tenants in each province and territory.

When it comes time to move out, you and your landlord will inspect your apartment again to see if you've done any damage to the place that goes beyond normal wear and tear. If you and your landlord disagree about whether something was broken before you moved in, you can check to see if the damage is noted on the condition report. Even better, bring a camera to your move-in inspection, so you'll have photos to back you up when you move out.

Your Rights as a Tenant

The rights discussed in this section apply to landlord-tenant contracts only, not to roommate arrangements. Tenants' rights vary by province and territory, so we'll discuss the rights that tenants generally have. Before you go to your landlord and complain that he's violating your rights, familiarize yourself with your province's or territory's laws on the subject, so you know what your rights actually are. Google "tenancy act" and your province or territory, or visit our website at campuscompanion.ca for information about specific provinces and territories.

When you apply to rent an apartment, it is illegal for a landlord to deny it to you on the basis of your race, sex, sexual orientation, religion, and (important for students) your age. Unfortunately, it's usually easy for a landlord to find another reason not to rent a place to you, and it's hard to prove that he or

Can You Trust Your Landlord?

"A lot of landlords will try to get away with charging you for things they aren't really allowed to, so know what you have the right to demand and leverage. You are entitled to a lot more than you think. Make sure that you trust your landlord before signing the lease, because even if you ask for something specific—we asked for our counter to be finished by a certain date—to be written in the lease, it doesn't mean it will end up happening (unless you're willing to bring the landlord to court, but usually it isn't worth it). Our counter was never finished at all."

– Stephanie M., arts and sciences, McMaster University

"Speak to the previous tenants and ask about the suite and the landlords, so that you avoid unpleasant surprises in the first place. Be a responsible tenant. Know and follow the responsibilities you have, and expect your landlord to do the same. Know your rights as a tenant in and out. If you have any doubts, phone your local tenancy office and ask."

– Christine McLaren, German, University of British Columbia

she didn't rent it to you because you're a 74-year-old Buddhist or an Albanian lesbian or whatever—but it's a nice law, anyway.

All things pertaining to money are pretty tightly regulated in most parts of Canada. There will be a maximum size of the security deposit your landlord can ask of you, and your landlord may be required to pay interest on the deposit when your lease is up. Every province and territory demands that a landlord give ample notice before he or she is allowed to increase your rent—generally three months—and a landlord can typically increase rent only once per year. Many provinces and territories have a maximum rent increase as well—in Manitoba, for example, it was only 1% in 2010.

If anything breaks in your apartment for reasons other than outright abuse, it's your landlord's responsibility to fix it—and that includes appliances. Landlords can sometimes drag their feet about fixing things, but they are obligated to make repairs in a timely fashion. If your landlord is being uncooperative, make your requests for repairs in writing and keep a copy of your request. If the repairs are still not completed, you can complain to your province's or territory's tenancy regulatory body—often called a Residential Tenancy Board.

You have the right to privacy in your apartment. Your landlord owns your apartment but can only enter it only under specific circumstances.

Generally, a landlord can't come in without first giving you 24 hours' notice, unless there's an emergency.

A landlord can evict you from your apartment, but only under very specific circumstances, which vary by province or territory. In most places, you can get kicked out only if the landlord wants to renovate or demolish your apartment, or if you give cause. "Cause" for eviction could be:

- You regularly disturb your neighbours.
- You repeatedly don't pay your rent on time.
- You are doing something dangerous or you damaged the building.
- Too many people are living in your suite.
- You broke a rule in your tenancy agreement.

Whatever the reason for your eviction, your landlord has to give you notice. The length of the notice varies by province or territory. Landlords may have to give three months' warning if they're renovating, for example. If they think you're doing something dangerous in your apartment, like manufacturing homemade fireworks, they might have the right to kick you out within a few days.

If you think your rights are being violated or that you've been evicted illegally, contact your province's or territory's tenancy regulatory body immediately. Often the tenancy board stops your landlord until a hearing can be scheduled, but if you wait too long to file a complaint, you lose the right to complain.

Living With Roommates

Living with roommates in private accommodation is a little different from living with a roomie in residence. On one hand, you probably won't have to share a tiny dorm room with anyone, but on the other hand, you will have to make arrangements to determine who is going to clean the toilet. Nevertheless, the key to a good roommate relationship in either situation is the same: communication.

If your roommate is doing something that drives you crazy, tell her so. Don't roll yourself up into a resentful, passive-aggressive ball and find little ways to annoy her until finally one of you snaps and blood is spilled. After all, if you kill your roommate, you'll be stuck paying all the rent by yourself.

Being Passive-Aggressive Doesn't Work

"Dealing with problems up front the first time it happens as politely as possible usually solves the situation. After a few reminders, if it keeps happening, someone is either an idiot or willfully neglectful, in which case you can't do anything to change them. As tempting as they are, passive-aggressive notes usually don't do anything except piss your opposite party off and let them feel justified in ignoring you. And really, in the end, you might just have to live with ignoring someone until you or they can leave."

– Ruth C., arts and sciences,
  McMaster University

Start off on the right foot with a roommate agreement. Suggesting the idea might sound nerdy, but it doesn't have to be like contract law. You can sit down over a beer and come up with some general principles about how you'll live with one another. Big areas to discuss include:

- Sharing. Are you going to share food? What's okay to share and what's not?
- Borrowing. What type of stuff can you use and under what circumstances?
- Quiet times. When is it all right to be noisy?
- Guests. How often is it reasonable to have guests over? How are you going to deal with those special naked sleepover guests?
- Cleaning. How will you decide who's turn it is, and when it's time to clean?
- Rent and other bills. Who is responsible for paying for what, and how will you arrange to transfer money back and forth?
- Smoking, drinking, messy home crafts, amateur taxidermy, and other potentially obnoxious habits. Find out who does these things and define where and when (if ever) it is acceptable to do them in the apartment.

The discussion doesn't have to stop there. There are a ton of other things worth talking about. Is it okay to leave dishes in the sink, or does everything have to be washed immediately after it's used? If someone has to move out before the end of the lease, who is responsible for finding a replacement roommate? What happens if you want to watch TV shows on different channels?

Get Your Frustrations Out in the Open

"A roommate would not clean up suffi-ciently and freaked out at me any time I asked her to do so. I admit that at times I lost my patience being so frustrated over the mess and wasn't particularly tactful, and she also later admitted she'd been going through some serious health issues. Unfortunately I ended up treading on eggshells around her for most of the summer. The cleaning was still an issue but at least I knew she was trying and there was a reason she wasn't fully keep-ing up her end of the bargain all the time. We just needed to get it out in the open like adults and talk about it. I wish I had been mature enough to realize that this was how I should have handled it but it's hard to get away from being passive-agressive."

– Catherine Wells, psychology, Simon Fraser University

And so forth.

When it comes to living with one another, there are no rules but the ones you agree to. Here's a good code to keep in mind, though: treat each other with respect, forgive each other for occasionally being wrong, and give each other space.

Making
the Grade

YOUR ACADEMIC EXPERIENCE at college or university is going to be very different from high school. Your instructors will likely move much more quickly through material, and you will be graded on standards that are different from what you are used to.

In college or university, you are responsible for your own learning to a much greater degree than ever before. In most programs of study, you will be in much larger classes, so your professors aren't going to have as much time to give you individual attention as your high school teachers did. Much of your learning will occur outside of the classroom, when you're studying and reading under nobody's supervision but your own. If you fall behind, it's up to you to find out how to catch up.

This change can be a shock for many people. Students who were able to get through high school on pure brainpower, without doing much work, may find that they are woefully underequipped with the academic skills needed to excel in college or university. Even those who were diligent students in high school find they need to sharpen their academic tools and adapt themselves to new strategies for succeeding at university.

Your first semester might be a little rocky as you get the hang of it, but a combination of hard work and the strategic building of skills will get you into the swing of things.

Don't skip **Section 3.1: Assessing Your Learning Style**. It might not look super-interesting, but it's the most important section in this chapter. As Sun Tzu would have said if he had followed up *The Art of War* with a book called *The Art of Going to College or University in Canada*: "Know yourself and know your course material and you need not fear the result of a hundred exams."

In this chapter:

- Become aware of how you learn and what methods of teaching work best for you by **Assessing Your Learning Style**.

- Effective listening and note-taking skills will help you with **Getting the Most Out of Class**.

- Deal with the largest volume of words you've ever read in your life by learning about **Effective Reading**.

- Organize and clearly express all your brilliant thoughts while **Writing Papers and Essays**.

- Learn to coordinate with others and deal with different personality types when you are assigned **Group Projects**.

- **Studying and Exam Preparation** will help you get ready for that nerve-racking moment of truth.

- Calm down, pace yourself, and accurately read the questions when you get down to **Exam Writing**.

- You may never again have access to such brilliant minds, so now's the time to think about **Getting the Most Out of Your Professors**.

- Even great students sometimes make mistakes and run into a **Grade Crisis**.

3.1 Assessing Your Learning Style

Before you start working on your academic skills, take a minute to think about yourself as a learner. By figuring out how you learn best, you can develop techniques to learn things more quickly and thoroughly, with less pain and effort than before, leading to better grades and an easier, more pleasant time at school.

You've probably noticed that most people learn better in some ways than in others. For example, think about the way people communicate and understand directions on how to get somewhere. One person might say, "Take a left at the blue house," without knowing the name of the street, while someone else would say, "Take a left at Willow Street," and not remember that there's a blue house on that corner. Some people have difficulty understanding verbal directions, but they can take one look at a map and find their way. Other people might have to walk the route a few times before they really remember how to get there.

If you know how you learn best, you can focus your attention on the style of explanation that works best for you, which will save time and help you learn material more effectively. If you know you're hopeless at reading maps, you can save time by skipping the map and getting out there to walk the route; if you know you have trouble remembering street names, you can pay extra-close attention to the blue house on the corner.

In this section:

- Read about common **Learning Styles**.

- Find out how you learn by **Identifying Your Learning Style**.

- Tailor your studying habits to suit your style by developing personalized **Strategies for Learning**.

- Work on your weaknesses by **Developing New Learning Strategies**.

Learning Styles

Education researchers talk about people's learning preferences by assigning them broadly defined "learning styles." These styles work as a framework for thinking about the subject; they're not strict, mutually exclusive categories. Your learning style is probably some combination of the styles listed below, or it may not closely resemble any of them.

Your learning preferences are formed by experiences, past choices, and subjects of interest. Although you may have developed a preference for a certain learning style at a very young age, there is no reason you can't develop new learning skills. Since some subjects require the use of certain methods of learning (for instance, literature courses depend heavily on reading, while engineering courses may depend on an ability to visualize concepts), the best students are flexible enough to adapt to different ways of learning.

Researchers define learning styles in various ways, but there are three common groupings:

Auditory learners internalize information best through hearing. They benefit from lectures and class discussions and prefer to study with other students so they can talk through concepts. They are usually good at remembering details, but they may struggle to understand the big picture and how concepts are related.

Visual learners take in knowledge through seeing. They benefit from drawing diagrams and charts, viewing videos, and reading text accompanied by pictures. They may remember ideas by visualizing them in their mind's eye. They tend to be good at grasping the big picture and seeing how concepts relate, but sometimes struggle to remember details.

Kinesthetic learners learn best by doing. They like "hands-on" activities, such as working in a lab. They benefit from field trips, demonstrations, and working in small groups. They sometimes struggle to stay engaged during lectures or extended reading sessions.

Identifying Your Learning Style

You may have immediately identified yourself with one of the three learning styles. Perhaps you find yourself reading aloud from your textbook to remember certain passages. Or maybe your notebook is full of elaborate flow charts that map the events that led to the Second World War or show you how to solve a complicated math problem. However, 60% of people have multiple learning-style preferences, so there's a better chance that you learn well in a combination of ways.

Begin exploring your learning type by thinking about how you remember phone numbers. If you have an image in your mind's eye of the numbers or how they look on the phone pad, you may be a visual learner. If you "hear" the numbers or recite them silently to yourself, you may be an auditory learner. If you can only recall phone numbers when your fingers are dialing them, you may be a kinesthetic learner.

Another way to determine your learning style is to think about the teachers you've enjoyed learning from, and those you struggled with. Make a list of the things your favourite teachers did in class to explain concepts, then make a list of the reasons you hated that terrible Grade 11 math teacher (other than her terrible body odour).

Ask yourself questions about how you prefer to learn:

- Do I need hands-on experience with something to remember it?
- Do I prefer listening to podcasts or watching TV?
- Do I learn more from reading books than from going to lectures?
- Do I study best alone or during discussions with a study group?
- Is my time best spent in a lab or a library?

There are a number of surveys and tools online that will help you identify your learning style. Take some of these quizzes and explore the workings of your brain. They're pretty fun. Visit campuscompanion.ca for links to resources.

Strategies for Learning

You don't have to define your learning style in exactly the above terms, but it's important that you think about how you learn, because the more you understand the way you learn, the more successful you will be as a student. As an academic adviser we spoke to says, "It's not about studying harder, it's about studying smarter."

As you read the following sections and think about how you study, how you take notes, and so forth, consider how you can develop strategies that work with your learning style.

Using the three-style framework we discussed earlier, we came up with some examples of ways you can tailor your academic habits to fit your learning style.

Auditory learners

Since you find it easy to remember what is explained to you verbally, make the most of your lectures. Sit close to the front of the room and away from windows and doors so you can focus on your professor without being distracted. Participate in class discussions. Avoid missing lectures. Seek other opportunities to have course material explained to you, including making use of your professors' office hours, attending seminars, or speaking to your TAs.

To supplement your notes, readings, and lectures, organize study groups with fellow auditory learners so you can practise explaining concepts to one another. Ask a librarian to help you gather audiobooks or videos that relate to your subject of study.

When studying for exams, read important sections of the textbook aloud to yourself. Describe key diagrams and graphs to yourself in words. Create rhymes or songs to aid memorization. Talk yourself through a difficult problem by describing each step you need to take to solve it. When you answer questions in exams, imagine how you would explain the answer to someone else.

Visual learners

Since visual aids help you learn, seek out professors who make heavy use of overhead projectors or blackboards in their lectures. Draw your own diagrams and flow charts when you take lecture notes, and use highlighters to make your notes visually interesting.

Supplement your notes and reading by seeking handouts and other visual aids your professor may have posted on the class website. Create concept maps to show visually how the ideas in your notes tie together and to show steps for solving problems.

Make Your Notes More Visual

"The best strategy for me was rewriting my notes and making bright flash cards or posters that helped me to visually remember."

– Julia Bolzon, arts and sciences, McMaster University

When you study, find a quiet place where you can focus in silence. Create flash cards, and take mental pictures of them. When you're reading or reviewing notes, pause frequently to visualize the material in your mind's eye.

Kinesthetic learners

Since you learn best when you're actively participating, lectures and extended reading sessions can be sleep-inducing. Make the most of class time by participating in class discussions when you can, by sitting close to the front where you are more likely to be engaged by your professor, and by actively taking notes throughout the lecture. Always attend seminars, labs, and field trips.

Supplement your lecture notes and readings by seeking hands-on experiences that relate to your subject of study, such as work experience or clubs. Find ways to make the course material concrete with case studies and examples.

When you study for exams, take frequent breaks to aid concentration. Listen to relaxing music to stay engaged. Move around or stand up while you're reading or reviewing notes. Use highlighters and pictures to create visually interesting study guides.

Get Active With Studying

"I always study best and enjoy myself most doing practice questions, especially in math and science courses. When there is no choice but to memorize, flash cards with terms on one side and their meaning on the other are very helpful."

– David Campbell, arts and sciences, McMaster University

Developing New Learning Strategies

As we mentioned earlier, your learning style isn't something you're stuck with. Most people use a combination of more than one style, and sometimes you're forced to learn in a way that isn't your favourite. For some people, the whole university lecture-and-textbook thing is far from their favourite way to learn, but that doesn't mean they're doomed to failure.

With practice, you can adapt to new ways of learning. None of us could read when we were born, but most of us get pretty good at absorbing information that way after 18 or more years of practice. And listening to lectures might not be the method of absorbing new information that comes most naturally to you, but if you focus and make an effort, you'll find that it becomes easier with time, and eventually you'll become a more rounded and flexible student.

3.2 Getting the Most Out of Class ✓

In university and college, classes are often separated into different components, including:

- *Lectures*, which mostly consist of listening to the professor speak, but may have some degree of class participation.
- *Seminars or tutorials*, where a smaller number of students discuss the course material with a professor or TA.
- *Labs*, where you get hands-on experience doing the thing you're being taught.

Classes are also increasingly incorporating an online component, where students can access supplementary materials, participate in forums, and engage in discussions on message boards.

Depending on the subject you're studying, you'll probably find that there is much less class participation in lectures than there was in your high school classes. A lecture will often consist of listening to an intelligent old guy talking about the same subject for 75 minutes straight, stopping occasionally to answer questions. Even if you find the subject matter really interesting, you might find yourself struggling to stay focused and take good notes for that long.

It does get easier the more you do it, however. Listening and note taking are just two more skills you'll pick up on your way to your degree or diploma.

In this section:

- Learn about the skill of **Effective Listening**.

- Improve your **Note-Taking** skills.

- Increase your retention of what you learned in class by **Following Up**.

Effective Listening

You may not be used to thinking of listening as a skill, but it is. Listening to a friend tell a funny story is easy; listening to and understanding a philosophy professor explaining Hegelian dialectics requires real effort.

Effective listening involves more than casually taking in the words you hear. Instead, it requires listening actively, keeping your brain one step ahead of your professor, thinking about whether you understand what he or she is saying, and asking yourself how all the information ties together.

Prepare to listen effectively

Effective listening doesn't just happen. You've got to be ready for it. You've got to get psyched for it. You've got to get yourself into top physical form so you're 100% psyched and ready to do some listening!

Okay, maybe you don't need to be *100%* psyched, but it definitely helps if you do four things:

- **Come to class prepared.** It will be way easier to understand the material in a lecture and connect it to other things you've learned if you've kept up with your reading. Before you go to a lecture, review your notes from the last class and check the current topic in the course outline so you know what your prof is talking about and how it relates to previous classes.
- **Avoid distractions.** Find a seat where you can focus on what the professor is saying. This is most important in the classes you find the most boring. If friends or other classmates distract you during lectures, don't sit next to them. If you find your mind wandering and your eyes straying to nearby windows, sit at the front of the room away from the windows. And if you can't take notes on your laptop without checking Facebook continuously, it's time to ditch the laptop and get back to pen and paper.

- **Show up fed and rested.** There's nothing more distracting than a growling stomach or eyes that won't stay open.
- **Keep your attitude positive.** It's only going to make it harder to pay attention if you tell yourself in advance that you hate the class and that the prof is the worst lecturer in the world. Make an effort to listen for interesting topics within a boring lecture. Focus on the material instead of how the lecturer is delivering it. And try to be open-minded about topics you find uninteresting or viewpoints you find disagreeable; try to understand your lecturers' viewpoint before you start arguing with them.

Focus your efforts effectively

Paying attention to the stream of words coming out of your prof is a good start. Next, you'll have to figure out which words are the most important, so you can effectively take notes and piece all the bits of information together into a coherent whole.

Familiarize yourself with the format of the course. Make sure you go to the first lecture of the semester, so you can hear what the professor says about how he or she will approach the course. This will provide a framework for thinking about the course material and the relative importance of each part of the material.

Think about the purpose of the lecture. Lectures don't all have the same purpose, and you need to respond to each lecture appropriately. For instance, a professor might use a lecture for explaining readings, instead of introducing new material. If that's the case, it may be best to take a minimal amount of notes and spend most of your time focusing on whether you understand the readings. Other lectures will be very fact-intensive and might even be the main source of the material you need to know for an exam, in which case you'll want to be very detailed in your note taking. Check the course outline to see if the learning outcomes are listed for each class.

Listen for your professor's thesis. Figuring out the main idea your professor is trying to convey will make it a lot easier to understand how everything he or she says is related.

Find out what to expect on the exam. If you know how you'll be tested, it will be easier to focus your efforts in class and take more effective notes. Multiple-choice exams may require more detail- and fact-heavy notes; essay questions will require a broader understanding of the big ideas.

7 Bad Listening Habits

1. **Getting bored:** Even if you feel that you know all about the topic, listen for tidbits of new information and new perspectives.

2. **Criticizing your prof:** Pay attention to what your prof is saying, not how he or she is saying it or the horrendous shirt the prof is wearing.

3. **Getting bogged down:** If you don't understand something your prof has said, make a note and move on. Don't miss the next point because you're still struggling with the last one.

4. **Listening only for facts:** Don't miss the big picture by getting lost in details.

5. **Writing down too much:** Don't get so caught up in taking notes that you miss what's being said.

6. **Getting distracted:** Avoid distracting classmates, and don't create distractions for others.

7. **Letting your opposition get in the way:** Many university topics are controversial. Don't allow your disagreement to prevent you from hearing your prof out.

Some professors will make a point of formally outlining the content and structure of a lecture at the beginning, but this is seldom the case. You'll have to listen for clues that hint at the structure and ideas behind the lecture and which facts are important. For instance, listen for addition words, like "furthermore," and for phrases used to contrast ideas or examples, such as "on one hand." Pay special attention to ideas your professor emphasizes through repetition or tone of voice.

PowerPoint slides and any other visual aids your professor employs might serve as an indication of which facts are most important and can make it easier for you to understand the way the professor has structured the lecture. Sometimes professors summarize the material at the end of a lecture; this won't help you understand the lecture while you're listening but it might help you make sense of your notes afterward.

If you're confused about what the professor is talking about, raise your hand and ask. There's a good chance you're not the only one who is lost, and other students in the room will silently thank you for asking. If you don't understand the explanation the second time around, however, let the class move on. After class, schedule an appointment with your professor to talk about it one-on-one.

Don't waste time taking detailed notes about things you already know, and don't spend all your time writing down facts and figures you can easily look up later. Instead of writing obsessively, put more of your energy into listening and understanding what the professor is saying, and strategically take the notes you need to take.

Note Taking

There is no way you're going to remember everything you hear in every lecture you attend in a semester. By the time your final exam rolls around, one of the most important results of all of the good listening you did will be the notes you took.

Most high school students are never taught how to take notes. Some students start off trying frantically to write down everything the prof says, and others don't write down much of anything at all, and it's not until mid-term exams that they realize how useless their notes are. You'll have to invent a style of note taking that works for you—some amount of trial and error is unavoidable—but it helps to think about note taking as a skill before leaping into it. Here are a few general tips:

- Invent a system of symbols and abbreviations to help you write faster.
- Highlight, or put a star next to, the most important points and items you know will be on the test.
- Clearly title, date, and organize your notes. If you can't find your notes, they won't do you much good when it comes time to study.
- Leave lots of white space so you can add to your notes later on.
- Use lots of headings and subheadings to help you identify the subject of each part of your notes without having to read the notes themselves.
- Find a note-taking medium (e.g., a notebook, binder, laptop, clipboard) in which you can take legible notes and keep them organized. Many students recommend using a three-ring binder and loose-leaf paper so you can reorder notes and add pages as necessary.

Most students come up with their own system of note taking that works well for them, but which may not be comprehensible to other people. To give you some ideas you can adapt to suit your style, here are some common systems that are taught at universities around the world:

Cornell note-taking system

One of the most popular systems of note taking was developed by Dr. Walter Pauk at Cornell University. *Use columns* Start by drawing a vertical line to create a 2 1/2-inch (that's 63.5 mm—if you're off by half a millimetre it will ruin everything!) margin on the left side of the page. Write your notes in the larger right-hand column. When your prof moves on to a new topic, skip a few lines to leave space so you can fill in more information later.

After class, add all the extra information you didn't have time to record and flesh out your notes while *Add cues* the lecture is fresh in your mind. Then review your notes and write "cues" in the left-hand column to summarize the major points.

When it comes time to study, cover up the right column. Read the cues in the left column and try to *Cover to study* remember as much information as you can about each of the cues. Then uncover the right column and read the information you might have forgotten.

Outlining method

- In classes where your professor provides an outline at the beginning of the lecture, use the outline to organize your notes.
- Write the most general topics as headlines on the left side of the page.
    1. As your professor gets more specific and provides examples, write notes in point form, indenting under your heading to keep the page organized.
        a. For example, you might indent the first example of a series like this.
        b. And a second example of the same kind could be done like this.
    2. Use underlining, bullets, or numbers to identify how concepts are linked and <u>what is important</u>.

Mapping method

Visual learners might benefit from spatially mapping their notes, to help visualize the connections between different ideas. Write major themes and topics as headings and use lines to connect ideas that are attached. You can also use highlighters and colours to help keep your notes organized and visually interesting:

NOTE-TAKING STRATEGIES:

(three types)

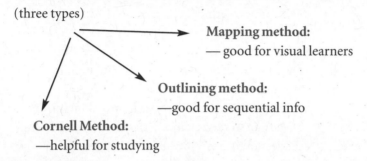

Mapping method:
— good for visual learners

Outlining method:
—good for sequential info

Cornell Method:
—helpful for studying

Taking Notes on Your Laptop

Pros:

- Wireless Internet can connect you with online course material.
- You can avoid having to decipher your messy handwriting.
- You won't lose paper versions of your notes.
- You can easily organize notes by cutting and pasting.

Cons:

- Laptops can be distracting, especially if you have wireless Internet access, because you'll be tempted to check Facebook or check the latest news headlines.
- It's difficult to draw diagrams and charts.
- Your battery may run down.
- It can be a pain to carry a laptop around all day.

Following Up

You've just walked out of your lecture, having listened carefully to your prof and taken excellent notes in a style that works for you, but you still have one more job to do: you've got to review your notes and think about what the lecture meant.

Research shows that students who don't review and think about material learned in a lecture forget 50 to 80% of the knowledge within 24 hours. One week after the lecture, the amount of knowledge retained drops to a fraction of what you originally understood. Thirty days later—about the time your mid-term is scheduled—you will only remember 2 to 3%. If you don't want to relearn your entire course every time you have to study for an exam, it's important to follow up after your lecture.

You Might Learn Better From Handwritten Notes

"I prefer taking notes by hand rather than on a laptop. This is because I think I retain the information better, and I have to be more selective about what I write down."

– David Campbell, arts and sciences, McMaster University

Scheduling 10 to 15 minutes after each lecture to read over your notes and write down any questions will save hours of studying later. Edit your notes and fill in any gaps you left within 24 hours of the class. Review all your lecture notes at the end of each week. Creating a one-page summary sheet for each set of notes will help you retain knowledge and stay organized. Finally, take five minutes before each class to remind yourself of the material your prof covered last time.

If you keep up these short study sessions all semester you'll be amazed at how much you remember when it's time to study for your exam.

3.3   Effective Reading

The transition to post-secondary-level reading can be quite a shock. Some (but thankfully not most) classes require students to read 100 or more pages a week. The task becomes even more formidable if you fall behind early in the semester so you have even less time to get through it all. And if you don't keep up with your readings, it will be more difficult to understand lectures, participate in seminars, and grasp the context of hands-on practice in labs.

In desperation, some students fall back on skimming their readings and highlighting things seemingly at random, and then find that for some reason they don't remember the material come exam time. Others read every line, but get bogged down in the detail and don't come away with a good understanding of the material. This section will help you avoid these pitfalls by learning strategies for improving how you read, which will help you retain the knowledge contained in the pages of your textbook.

In this section:

- Avoid being overwhelmed by the amount of reading by **Getting Organized**.

- Battle distractions by improving your **Concentration**.

- Make the best of your time by developing **Methods of Reading**.

- Keep that precious information in your brain by **Following Up**.

Getting Organized

You make a nice cup of tea, put on your comfiest clothes, and snuggle into a nice, comfortable chair—and then you look at the huge stack of textbooks you need to read and you feel like vomiting with dread. Can't you just wait for the movie version of "Molecular Biology of the Cell" to come out? (It could star Robert Pattinson as mitochondria!) Alas, even if they start making that movie now, it's not going to come out before exam time. You're going to have to read the book.

Although reading the entire text is a daunting task, by organizing yourself you can break it up into manageable, digestible chunks and work your way through it over time.

For most classes, your readings will be listed on the course outline or class website. At the beginning of the semester, figure out how much you'll be required to read every week for each class, and then schedule an appropriate amount of time to take on the task. Instead of making all of Saturday your reading day, schedule smaller chunks of time throughout the week. Long reading sessions often lead to burnout and make it less likely that you'll retain the information. When it's absolutely necessary to schedule a long reading session (when you're behind or have to read a lot before exams), plan

Make Readings Manageable

"To get through large amounts of readings, I tend to break it down into smaller pieces. Instead of trying to suffer through a whole chapter in one night, it is easier to split it up into equal sections throughout the week. I always take notes on my readings so I won't have to do them again! This helps me to remember what I've read, but condenses it down into an easy-to-read format. Textbooks are often more long-winded than they have to be, and putting the main ideas into your own words helps you to read and understand it later."

– Amy Kluftinger, medicine, University of British Columbia

to take 10-minute breaks to go for a walk or clear your mind in other ways. It can help to switch subjects during a long reading session: for example, try to use your history reading as a break from your biology reading. (Read Chapter 4.1: Time Management for more on organizing your academic tasks.)

Concentration

Find your happy place: a spot where you can focus on a book without interruptions from others and without temptations to slack off.

Maybe you need the silence of the library or the solitude of a closed room to read. But maybe your happy place is a crowded café, where you can anonymously sit and read while the voices and clamour of activity in the background wash together into a pleasant, unintelligible, distraction-cancelling drone.

You'll have to experiment and figure out what works for you. You might try reading in your room and find that the constant temptation of your computer is too much to resist; go somewhere else without your computer and see how that works.

Most people don't find reading textbooks in bed useful. It's hard to take notes, and it's easy to start confusing the two functions of your bed and either fall asleep while reading or lay awake thinking about school work while you're trying to sleep. And don't fool yourself into believing that you can effectively read while watching TV. Even if you do get something out of your book, it'll take you four times longer than it will if you just read the thing.

Your body will have a lot to say about how well you read. It's hard to concentrate when you're tired or burned out. Figure out when your down times are during the day, and don't schedule your reading for that time. You might be fresh and calm early in the morning and find that an hour's reading before

Read During Your Up Times

"Try not to do your readings at night. It's when you are most tired, you'll have to reread lines, and you'll never retain any information. If I had time in the morning, I would always go to the library and do my reading there, after I'd eaten breakfast and I felt more awake and studious."

— Julia Bolzon, arts and sciences,
McMaster University

class works great for you, or you might be a total mess at that time and not be able to uncross your eyes long enough to get through a paragraph.

Your ability to concentrate can also be affected by your health, so take care of yourself. Eat decently, exercise, and get enough sleep; cutting out any of these things to spend more time reading and studying could hurt your academic performance more than it helps.

If you find yourself distracted by worries, stop reading and write down the problem and steps you can take to solve it. This will help free your mind from worry so you can focus on the book in front of you.

If you're having a hard time motivating yourself, set rewards for yourself. If there's something you'd really rather do, like watch a TV show or hang out with friends, then tell yourself you're allowed to do it only if you finish this chapter first.

Methods of Reading

To retain the information you're reading, it's important to engage yourself in the material as you read it. Avoid reading passively, with your eyes bouncing over the words, your hands turning the pages, and your mind wandering off to more interesting topics. Come up with strategies that force your brain to interact with the text, and you'll understand and retain much more of the material. Try reciting important passages out loud, discussing the readings with classmates, or drawing concept maps as you go along.

Develop an effective strategy for taking notes from your readings. Creating summaries of the key concepts in a reading will provide you with something to study from later on, without having to reread the entire section before an exam. Taking notes is also a great way to force yourself to engage with readings, because you'll have to understand what you've read in order to summarize it and write it down. (For more on developing your own style of note taking, see Section 3.2: Getting the Most Out of Class.)

Don't rush through your reading. It's better to read half as much material and understand it than to put yourself through the ocular exercise of looking at twice as many words without taking the time to let any of them sink in. Even if you're able to comprehend readings at high speed, chances are good that you won't remember much of them if you don't take the time to think about them. Many people find that speed reading costs them more time in rereading than it would have taken to read carefully in the first place.

SQ4R strategy

Each student learns in his or her own way, so you'll have to figure out what reading techniques work best for you. Take a look at this summary of the SQ4R method, which has helped thousands of students since the 1960s. You might find that it will work for you, or you might be able to adapt it to better suit your style of learning. The method may seem time-consuming, but it will likely save you time in the long run, particularly when it comes time to study for exams.

- *Survey:* Before diving into the reading, take a quick scan of the cover, table of contents, chapter outline, headings, diagrams, and conclusion. This will give you an idea of the big picture behind what you will read, and it will put the details into context, which will help you remember the material.
- *Question:* From the general ideas you read when you survey the section of reading, write down questions that ask what you hope to learn from your reading. For instance, if you are reading a section titled "SQ4R Strategy," ask yourself, "What the hell is the SQ4R Strategy and how do I use it?"
- *Read:* Then read through the text slowly, looking for the answers to the questions you wrote down. Don't skim the text looking for the answers; pay attention to all the information the section contains.
- *Recite:* After you've read the section, recite the main points you've just read, either out loud or on paper. Try to answer all the questions you wrote down. Return to the text for any points or answers you can't remember.

- *Record:* When you're done reciting the main points and answering all your questions, take notes to record the information for later. Make sure to put everything in your own words. You can also highlight the important points in your text at this point.
- *Review:* Schedule a time to quickly review all your reading notes once a week. This will help you retain the information so you don't have to relearn it by cramming right before the exam.

This method won't work for every kind of reading assignment; it will be pretty much useless for reading a poetry anthology for English class, for example. You may have to adapt it to fit the content of the reading and your learning style, but it's a good starting point for thinking about your reading strategy.

Following Up

As with your notes from lectures, you'll retain much more of what you read if you return to it, think about it, and try to use it in some way. You should review your notes once within 24 hours of taking them, and then regularly throughout the course, including immediately before reading new chapters or attending lectures that are related to the topic. Not only will this help you remember, but it will also help you understand the lectures and labs.

You will find that while it may take a significant amount of time to review your notes the first time you do it, every subsequent time it will take less and less time. By the end of your term you should be able to glance at a topic for only a few minutes and feel confident you know the material.

Depending on your learning style, you may benefit from forming a small group of students to discuss and review

It Takes More Than Just Reading

"Before I start reading, I skim through the chapter and look at the headings and subtitles to get a general idea of what the text is about. Then I read through each section, and usually take notes on terms in bold, or ideas relating to concepts we covered in class. I try to relate what I read to what we have learned in class so that there is context to the material."

– Leanna Katz, arts and sciences, McMaster University

readings. Explaining concepts and listening to how others explain them can be an excellent way to remember and understand.

3.4 Writing Papers and Essays ✓

Although the amount of writing demanded of you will depend on your classes, it's almost impossible to get through a diploma or degree without writing at least a few essays. In many classes, virtually the entire term's mark will be based on papers, and marking standards tend to get higher in third- and fourth-year classes, so it's important to start working on your writing skills early on. Besides, effective writing is a career skill that will help you later in life.

Many first-year students are surprised when they discover that college and university professors have very different standards than those of high school teachers when it comes to grading papers. In high school, you were often asked to write reports, which consisted mainly of compiling information from various sources and presenting it without analysis. In post-secondary education, you are expected to display critical thinking and contribute some of your own original thought to virtually everything you write.

It may take some time for you to get used to these new expectations. You may have been used to getting As on written assignments in high school and find that you're a B-grade essay writer when you start college. If you apply yourself and learn from your mistakes, you can get yourself back into A country again.

In this section:

- You'll find it much easier to write if you **Know What Your Paper Is About**.

- Learn how to marshal your sources while **Researching**.

- Keep your paper on the academic up and up by learning about **Citation and Plagiarism**.

- Make your paper clear and logical by **Organizing and Outlining.**

- Finally, you're ready to start **Writing.**

- The best way to improve your writing is to get in the habit of **Reviewing Your Graded Paper.**

Know What Your Paper Is About

The very first thing you need to do when you write a paper is to make sure that the paper has a clearly defined topic. The second thing you need to do is to make sure that you know what that topic is.

Read your assignment carefully and if you find the wording confusing or ambiguous, ask your professor for clarification. You can write the most beautifully worded and logically coherent paper in the world, but if you don't answer the question asked or follow the terms of the assignment, you're going to get a bad grade.

Even if you don't plan to start writing the paper right away, read the assignment as soon as you get it. Thinking about the subject in advance will help you recognize information you can use. For example, your prof might lecture about your essay subject; if you don't realize you need that information, you're going to kick yourself later for not paying better attention.

There are many different kinds of papers, and every department in a school may have its own guidelines and expectations for writing. Make sure you understand what type of paper you're being asked for and what the department's expectations are. Most papers assigned are argumentative essays that involve some amount of research, so this section focuses on that style of paper, but pay close attention to the wording of your assignment; if you've been assigned a personal essay or a book review, make sure you write one, instead of launching into your standard essay format. If you don't know how to write the style of paper you've been asked to write, visit your school's writing centre and get help.

Your assignment may ask you a very specific question, it may give you the choice of a few questions, or you may have the freedom to choose your own topic. Freedom sounds great, but it can actually be quite difficult to come up with a suitable essay topic. You need to select a subject that is focused enough that you can cover it in depth in the scope of the paper you're writing, but not so focused that you run out of interesting things to say.

If you're having trouble coming up with ideas or if you're unsure about the appropriateness of your subject, talk to your prof or TA about it. Don't go into the meeting completely unprepared and ask them to come up with an idea for you, though; put some thought into it first. Be prepared to take their advice: they know when a subject is too small or too big for an essay, and they can save you a lot of time by alerting you to the fact.

Relatively early in your process, start thinking about your thesis statement, which is a statement that summarizes what you're going to argue to be true. You won't necessarily have your thesis statement finalized before you start doing your research, but the sooner you have an idea what it will be, the easier it will be to focus your efforts. You don't have to be artful in the presentation of your thesis statement; it can be something as straightforward as, "This essay will argue that thesis statements should be straightforward."

If you have no idea how arguments are expected to be presented, or even what a good paper looks like, find an academic journal on the subject you're writing about and read a few papers written by professional academics.

Common Essay-Writing Mistakes

- Failure to offer a clear thesis and argue for it systematically.
- Failure to delineate an essay so as to have space to make one's case.
- Failure to anticipate likely objections and address these.
- Failure to frame the essay in terms of core themes and questions of a given course.

– Dr. David Kahane, political science professor, University of Alberta

---

Researching

The amount of research you need to do depends entirely on your assignment. If you've been asked to analyze an article, your research might consist of nothing more than rereading the article. If, however, you're writing about the cultural impact of Russia's defeat in the Russo-Japanese war of 1904–05, you'd better head to the library.

If it's not clear in your assignment how much research is expected of you, ask your professor, who can tell you how many sources you should use.

Be Original

"Imagine that your paper is the very last one a professor is going to correct at the end of a very long evening. Try to write something original, or at the very least, clear and logical."

– Dr. Sorel Friedman, English studies professor, Université de Montréal

If you use too few, your paper might come out superficial and one-sided. If you use too many, you might not have enough room left for your analysis— and besides, tracking down all those sources will take up time you could have spent writing a better paper.

It's also important that you know the kind of sources you're expected to use. It might be completely acceptable in a first-year history class to rely on secondary sources (like history textbooks), but a third-year history professor might expect you to use primary sources (like eyewitness accounts).

As you get more experienced at this, you will learn to judge which sources are considered academically credible and which are not. You'll learn to draw the line between what you can call an academic source and what books are popular non-fiction. Your high school teacher may have been okay with you using Wikipedia, but at the post-secondary level, Wikipedia should never be used as a source unless your paper is *about* Wikipedia. That being said, Wikipedia and other encyclopedias can provide a good initial overview of a subject, and their bibliographies can point you in the direction of better sources.

Often, your professors will be explicit about the kind of sources they expect you to use, and they might even suggest specific books. If not, ask your profs before you go through the effort of tracking down information from sources that aren't considered reputable. Librarians are also excellent judges of sources, so when in doubt, ask a librarian.

Academic journals are a great source of the most up-to-date information in a field, and they're searchable through academic databases. If you're new to this researching business, you probably don't know how to operate these databases, but your friendly librarian definitely does, so ask for help.

As you gather your information, make sure you keep track of where you got it from in your notes. Make a record of the bibliographic information of every source you use. Put any quotes you write down word for word in quotation marks and note their source, so you don't mistake them for your own words.

Why? So you can avoid committing plagiarism, of course.

Citation and Plagiarism

Citation

Every piece of academic writing is expected to be original. That doesn't mean that it has to contain some stunning new advance of knowledge that nobody has ever thought of before—just that the piece of writing has to have been created by the author and not copied from someone else.

Of course, every academic work is based on the ideas and knowledge of other people; we're all standing on the shoulders of giants, after all. When we use the ideas, words, or knowledge of someone else in an academic work, we have to credit, or "cite," the source so a reader can tell the difference between what in the work is the original thought of the writer, and what has been taken from other sources.

Generally speaking, there are four situations that require citation:

1. Using direct quotes or paraphrases
2. Making reference to the work of another
3. Using specific facts from another source
4. Using a distinct idea you got from someone else

You do not have to cite any fact that can be considered common knowledge in the field. For example, the statement "China has a population of over one billion people" does not require a citation because the information is common knowledge. However, if you write, "China had a population of 1,324,655,000 in 2008," you'd better properly cite the World Bank's website. If you write, "Marx was a Marxist," you don't have to cite it, because what else would he be? But if you want to write, "From each according to his ability; to each according to his need," you'd better strap some quotation marks on that pearl o' wisdom and tell us that it was Karl Marx who said it, and where he said it.

If you're not sure whether you should cite something, cite it. Unnecessary citation will take a little extra work and clutter up your paper a little, but it's better than inadvertently committing plagiarism.

Citation standards vary from school to school, subject to subject, and professor to professor. The most common styles are called MLA (Modern Language Association), APA (American Psychological Association), and

Chicago (*Chicago Manual of Style*), and all three are easily looked up on the Internet. Some professors don't care which style you use as long as you use it consistently, but most do care, so find out which style your prof wants and learn how to use it. You can learn about citation and style at your school's library and writing centre.

Plagiarism

Failure to properly cite sources is known as plagiarism. Whether plagiarism is done accidentally or deliberately, it can have serious repercussions.

Deliberate plagiarism—such as buying essays off the Internet or copying whole paragraphs from sourcebooks and passing them off as your writing—is easy to avoid: just don't do it.

But it is easy to accidentally commit plagiarism if you don't know what you're doing or you're not careful. You might mix up your notes and forget where you got a piece of information, or you might write down a quote and later mistake the words for your own—hence the importance of keeping your research notes organized, with all your sources noted.

Students also often run into trouble with paraphrasing, which is putting someone else's ideas into your own words. When you paraphrase, it's not enough to change a couple of words in a sentence and include it without quotation marks, even if you cite the source. If you include a passage that uses the same wording as the original document, the passage should be put into quotation marks and cited. If you intend to paraphrase, the passage should be substantially rewritten without changing the original meaning, and then attributed to the original source.

Students are often surprised to learn that it is possible to plagiarize yourself. This isn't copyright law we're talking about—it doesn't matter who owns the rights. Each academic work is expected to be original, so if you turn in the same paper to two different professors and try to get credit for it twice, you are committing plagiarism.

In this age of fancy electronic gizmos like computers, it is extremely easy for professors to catch plagiarizers. Professors use a website called turnitin .com to compare students' papers to a database of thousands of books, magazines, and journals, millions of other student papers, and billions of web pages to detect improper citation and give papers an originality score. It's not only cut-and-paste plagiarism that gets detected; the website can also detect improper paraphrasing.

Pick Relevant Information

"Don't try to say everything you know about the subject, whether it's relevant or not, in hope that you will impress the reader with your knowledge."

– Dr. Malgorzata Dubiel, mathematics professor, Simon Fraser University

Plagiarism is a serious offence, and getting busted is no fun at all. Depending on the school and the severity of the plagiarism, a first offence can get you a verbal warning, a zero on the assignment, or a zero on the course. Repeat offenders can be suspended or expelled from school.

If you get in trouble for plagiarism, contact your students' union or your school's ombudsperson for help.

Organizing and Outlining

A well-defined thesis will make it much easier to organize your paper. You are arguing a point, so your paper should have a logical flow that takes the reader from the thesis statement through a series of coherent, well-ordered arguments toward your destination, which is the conclusion that the thesis statement is true. This is the nuts and bolts of what an argumentative essay is, and you'll save yourself a lot of time and trouble if you keep this in mind throughout the process.

Draft an outline of your essay that details the arguments you need to make to reach your conclusion, with the supporting arguments and facts you'll use along the way. Think of the steps you'd need to take to convince an intelligent person who is not your professor of the truth of your thesis. Avoid the temptation to include every piece of information you have about a subject. Stick to the argument.

A good outline will act as a guide while you're writing, preventing you from straying off onto irrelevant tangents and keeping you focused on your objective. If you've been given a specific length your paper is supposed to be, you can also use your outline to give you an idea of how long each section should be. This will stop you from spending the first 1,000 words of your 1,500-word paper making the first point of your six-point argument.

Writing

Your Thesis Should be Crystal Clear

"Before I start writing my paper, I make sure that I have a crystal-clear thesis statement. If someone asks, 'What are you writing about?' you should be able to clearly state what your main point is in two sentences or less. Make sure you can do this clearly, concisely, and completely before you start writing. The thesis statement should be the beginning of your essay, the end, and it's the compass that guides you through the paper. It's what gives the reader a sense of continuity when they read your work."

– Sandra Duffey, social work, McMaster University

We'd all love to be poets. We'd love to write an eloquent, even lyrical paper that will entertain and elevate readers while it enlightens them. But hey, it's a paper about fluid dynamics, so let's just settle for making it understandable.

Clarity is much more important than style in academic writing. The most important thing is that you are understood. Short, simple, to-the-point sentences and clear language will be more appreciated by your professor than verbose, run-on sentences that are confusing.

Be very careful about how you use your thesaurus. A thesaurus can suggest words with similar meanings, but it doesn't tell you how the words are used, the context in which they're used, or the subtle connotations a word might carry. It's usually wisest to put your thesaurus in the drawer and use the first word that pops into your head, since you probably understand the nuances of its usage and meaning.

For example, if you're looking for a way to spruce up the sentence, "I am going to pay my landlord," a thesaurus will tell you that the word "liquidate" can be used as a fancy way to say "pay." Your thesaurus may not tell you that you liquidate a debt, not the person you owe the debt to, and it may fail to mention that "liquidate" is also used as a euphemism for "murder," so you'll have no idea that you and your thesaurus just changed your innocent sentence into a death threat. As a rule of thumb, your thesaurus should only be used to remind yourself of words and word usages you're already completely familiar with, never for learning new ones.

Get to the point very early in your paper. Your reader shouldn't spend the first page wondering what the paper is about. Get that thesis statement down on paper early in the game, then start making your argument. Refer to your outline continually and make sure you're staying on track.

Leave Time to Revise

"I make sure that I leave at least 2 or 3 days in between the first full written version of a paper and the due date so I can reread and reorganize it a few times, because I know that once I've read it so many times it's just going to cease making sense to me. I always employ the help of my roommates, friends or mom, who, luckily, is a university professor herself. Now not everyone has a university prof as a mother but my roommates are a great help for merely seeing if the paper flows and makes sense—many profs and TAs will tell you to write a paper so that it could be understood by someone outside of the field, so the use of friends is great, especially when they're in a different field than you."they're in a different field than you)."

– Catherine Wells, psychology, Simon Fraser University

The best way to find out if someone else will understand your writing is to get someone else to read what you've written, preferably a fellow student. It's easy for you to understand your writing because you already know what you are trying to say. Another person will have a much easier time spotting problems in your language and your logic than you will.

As embarrassing as it may be, the best way to catch awkward language is to read your paper aloud to another student or even just to yourself. Grammatical problems and clunky sentences that look fine on the page will become obvious when you hear them out loud.

Be prepared to write several drafts of your paper. This means starting it well in advance of your deadline. This is a foreign concept to many students, but the difference it makes in your mark will be worth the discipline it requires. Often, the best thing you can do with a piece of writing is to put it away for a day and then come back to it; mistakes and awkward phrasings you couldn't see the day before suddenly become apparent after a night's sleep.

Reviewing Your Graded Paper

You researched, you outlined, you cited, you wrote, and you stayed up all night revising so you could hand your paper in on time. But you're not done with it yet. Not quite.

When you get your paper handed back to you, don't just flip to the back page, check the grade, either smile or groan, and then go on with your life,

Make Your Writing Seem Unfamiliar to Edit

"Writing is a process. Unless you're a genius, sentences don't come out clean; they are revised many, many times. Once you have a draft, change the font, arrange the words into columns, print it out, and then read it again in a different place than where you wrote it. Make the writing seem unfamiliar, like it was written by someone else. This is a good way to edit. But to do all this you can't procrastinate. The whole process takes time. Reading aloud helps, too."

– Paul H., master's of journalism, New York University

forgetting you ever wrote the thing. Your graded paper is full of remarks from the professor or TA who graded it. They might look like meaningless hieroglyphics, but they are actually hints from a very intelligent person about how you can write a better paper next time.

If you have any serious objections to the way you were graded, or if you want a more detailed explanation than you found in the grader's notes, talk to your professor or TA. You'll probably get some personalized advice about your shortcomings as an essayist, and tips on how you can improve your writing.

And if you still need more help, your school has tons of resources for helping you improve as a writer. The librarians will help you research, and the writing centre will help you with everything else, from citation to punctuation—but you've got to ask for help to receive it.

3.5   Group Projects

When Jean-Paul Sartre said, "Hell is other people," he was clearly referring to a university group project. Working with a group of other students can be a nightmare of conflicts that ends with a terrible grade—or it can be a super-fun and rewarding experience. Either way, you'll learn a lot about how groups work or don't work together.

A group's dynamics depend a lot on the personalities of the individuals it contains, but it's not all in the luck of the draw. With some good communication, organization, and well-timed intervention into personal conflicts, a good group member can turn a potential disaster into a well-oiled, project-completing, grade-getting machine—or at least a tolerable situation.

In this section:

- Get off on the right foot when you're **Forming the Group**.

- Learn how different people can play different roles, depending on their **Personality Types**.

- Equitably distribute the responsibility by **Sharing the Work**.

- Help defuse those potential personality clashes by **Dealing with Conflict and Problem Group Members**.

Forming the Group

Whether you chose your fellow group members or your professor put you together, you can't know in advance how a group of people will work together, even if you know each of them individually. Every combination of people is different, with different personalities that will create unique group dynamics. Each member brings his or her past experience (or lack of experience) of working in groups and associated ideas about how things should be done.

The only way to avoid conflicts caused by these differing expectations is to communicate with one another from the beginning; it's worth the time it takes to get to know one another and discuss your expectations before you get to work.

If you're in a group of strangers, start out by introducing yourselves and exchanging contact information. Find out everybody's major, what year they're in, and talk a little about your strengths and weaknesses, and the skills you bring to the project.

Your classmates may have different expectations about the project you're about to undertake. To avoid misunderstanding, discuss the amount of time each member is able to dedicate to the project and what he or she hopes to get out of it. Not everyone will be committed to getting an A, for example;

Groups Can Be Awesome— Or Mediocre

"Every single group work scenario I experienced was mediocre. If you throw together a group of different people with different working styles, levels of comprehension, and levels of motivation, no one will be satisfied with either the experience or the grade."

– Bronwyn Guiton, library studies, University of British Columbia

"We were all friends in the same program, and the group dynamic was great because we had an online Google doc and all committed to researching. When we got together to study, it was effective and efficient, but also fun. We joked around at times, but only because we knew we were getting the work done."

– A.C. Gage, arts and sciences, McMaster University

you may find that some of your fellow group members are busy with other classes that are more important to them and would be content to get a B on this project. If that's the case, it's better to have it out in the open from the start. If you are the only student in the group with the goal of earning an A, you may have to take a lead role in the project.

Discuss the project and make sure everyone has the same understanding of what is required. Talk in general terms about what you each think is the best way to go about completing the project, and discuss the roles each of you can fill on the team.

Leadership can be an awkward issue; in the professional world, there is usually a leader everyone is forced to accept (i.e., the boss). As students, however, you're working together as equals, and people may react negatively if some stranger unilaterally declares himself or herself the leader of the group. It isn't necessary for one student to be in charge, anyway. Leadership in a student group project usually takes the form of consensus-building rather than dictatorship.

You don't have to formally assign roles to people, but you can if you want. One group member can be designated the facilitator or chairperson, in charge of running meetings; another can be the designated note taker who keeps minutes at the meeting; a third can be in charge of tracking progress and making sure group members are staying on schedule.

Finally, discuss when everybody is available to meet. Students can be very busy people, especially those who have outside commitments such as work, so everyone is going to have to be flexible. It's possible that the only time everyone can get together will be on a Saturday morning and to make this group work, you might have to give up on sleeping in on Saturdays.

Personality Types

Everyone responds to working in a group differently, and it's a good thing they do. The best group dynamics are often found in groups composed of a mix of different kinds of personalities. If every person in a group had a strong, take-charge personality, it could lead to a lot of conflicts, but if everyone in a group is conciliatory, understanding, and compromising, the group may never find any direction or come to any decisions.

A good place to start thinking about different personality types is to take the group behaviour style test you can find at campuscompanion.ca.

This test measures your tendency toward the roles of director, supporter, analyzer, and creator when you're working in groups. This isn't to suggest that there are only four personality types, or that you'll play the same role in every group. Often, you will find that the role you fill will depend on the other personalities in the group and the skills and knowledge each group member has. It's good to take some time to think about how you participate in groups, though, particularly if you're in a program that has a lot of group projects.

Sharing the Work

Once you've talked through the project and decided what the group is going to do, you have to figure out how you're going to do it. Working collaboratively on every part of the project is a nice idea, and it could result in a better product if everybody has some input into every part, but it's incredibly difficult to do efficiently and in a way that will fit everyone's schedule.

Depending on the size of your group and the nature of your project, it might make sense to divide things up into subcommittees of two or more people, or it might be simpler to distribute the work to individuals. It's important for everyone to have input into the process of dividing up the work and to be as fair as possible.

It isn't in anyone's interest to overload a particular group member with work, or to assign someone a bunch of work they're not very good at; the unfairness will show in the work that person puts out, and that will have a negative impact on everyone's grade. By the same token, if you're a perfectionist and you don't trust anyone else to do things right, it's not in your interest to try to take on more work than you can handle; you'll land up either burning out or doing a lousy job if you overload yourself. The ability to delegate is a skill every perfectionist should learn before they become stressed-out micromanagers who are working on their second heart attack before they turn 40.

Look for Committed Group Members

"Try to pick students who seem committed to their classes and projects. Clearly define your tasks, and then have one person committed to collecting all the data and ensuring the research is submitted by each member. Have set deadlines, and make everything very clear and concise."

– A.C. Gage, arts and sciences, McMaster University

Make sure the group's expectations of each individual are explicit. Agree to expectations as a group, and have your note taker write them down. This will help avoid finger-pointing later on.

These expectations shouldn't be set in stone, however. Sometimes a job that appeared to be simple on the surface turns out to be difficult or time-consuming. Be prepared to reallocate the workload if one member runs into trouble and ends up needing help.

Create a schedule, including your professor's due dates, and other intermediate deadlines your group creates for itself. Check each member's progress on a regular basis; you'd hate to discover a few days before the project is due that one of your group members hasn't been doing any work at all.

Make sure the whole group knows that if a member is having a hard time with the work or just doesn't know how to do it, he or she should go to the others for help. You're all in this project together and you're all going to get the same grade. If you're particularly strong at this subject, you should expect to help your fellow group members along the way. On the other hand, if you know you're one of the weaker students at this particular subject, don't be afraid to ask for help, but don't expect the rest of the group to do your work for you; compensate for your lack of knowledge with a strong work ethic and a cheerful willingness to do whatever work you're able to do.

When your group gets together, it's important that you run your meetings efficiently. Some members might be happy to socialize and waste half an hour before getting started, but other members might have much busier schedules, so put off the socializing until the end of the meeting, when the busy people can leave if they want to. Have clear objectives for each meeting before you begin, start the meeting on time, and stay on topic. If your group has a hard time with this, appoint someone to be the meeting chairperson, whose job it will be to keep the meeting on track.

Dealing with Conflict and Problem Group Members

Real Stories of Group Projects

"The difficulty with group projects is that there is always somebody who takes control and ends up doing more work than the others. I was in a group with a grad student and another girl much more experienced in the field than me. The grad student took control and I definitely did less work than the rest, not because I am a slacker but because they knew more about the subject than I did.

"In the worst group I've ever been in, one of the students wouldn't return our calls or emails and wouldn't show up for meetings. We ended up ratting on the student who did literally nothing, and he got zero. The teacher gave the two of us that did the majority of the work some extra marks."

– Caitlin Millar, integrated science, University of British Columbia

Conflict of some sort is inevitable and can even be desirable. Groups that have absolutely no conflict can fall into a sort of groupthink, where everyone automatically agrees with the first suggestion put forward, even if the idea is really stupid. Constructive conflict can help a group achieve better results by putting ideas into competition with one another and (hopefully) allowing the better idea to win.

Too much conflict can be poisonous to a group, particularly if disagreements start getting personal. It's easy for two people with strong opinions to butt heads. Each group member should keep an eye out for nasty conflict like this developing in the group, and be prepared to intervene and help the parties talk it out before things get really ugly.

When people start arguing, it's important that they address the cause of the conflict. It's best if one person speaks at a time (preferably in a calm voice) while the other listens respectfully and waits his or her turn. Keep the conversation focused on the problem rather than on personal attacks and maintain focus on the interests of the group, instead of abstract discussions of right and wrong.

You won't necessarily be able to resolve the conflict; there's nothing you can do to force two people with intractable positions to come to a compromise. The important thing is to find a way to keep the group moving toward its objective in spite of the conflict. The conflicting parties don't have to like each other afterward, either—what matters is that they are able to work with each other without disrupting the rest of the group.

Sometimes the problem in a group isn't overt conflict but a group member who is uncooperative, unproductive, or just plain unreasonable. Often, it's best to deal with problem group members one-on-one, so they don't feel like they're being ganged up on by the rest of the group. They may not even realize that there is a problem, so give them the benefit of the doubt and explain the situation to them without making any accusations.

If members aren't contributing to the group, ask them why. It could be that they're just lazy, but there might be another reason. They could be shy, and they might feel overwhelmed by the more assertive (and louder) members of the group. Perhaps they feel in over their heads and don't know what they're doing but are embarrassed to admit it. Or maybe they're really busy with other classes and they don't care that much about this project. In any case, it will be much easier to deal with an individual's underproductivity if you know the cause of it.

If people are really acting unreasonably, you may have to report the situation to your professor—after all, your project mark is at stake. Your professor may or may not bail you out of your problem, though; the entire point of group projects is to teach students how to work together, and dealing with conflict is a part of that.

3.6 Studying and Exam Preparation

Exam time: this is where the rubber hits the road. A whole semester of learning, reading, and note taking come together and transform themselves into a grade.

You're going to need all of your academic skills to get ready for your exams, so if you haven't yet, read the sections on understanding your learning style (page 60), getting the most out of class (page 64), and effective reading (page 71) before you jump into this section—unless you're in a panic because the test is in two days; in that case, skip straight to the cramming tips (page 96).

Preparation for an exam should begin long before you start officially studying for it. Ideally, you'll have been getting ready for it all semester long by keeping up with your readings, taking good notes in class, reviewing your notes, and keeping the whole semester's material fresh in your mind.

But in those last couple of weeks before the big test there is a lot more you can do to get ready. Make sure you're physically ready by eating decently, getting enough sleep, and leaving yourself some time for exercise; a rested, healthy body is a good home for an intelligent, active mind. Then make sure you're mentally ready, by strategically studying for the exam.

In this section:

- You can tailor your studying to the test if you **Know Your Exam**.
- Make the most of your limited study time by learning to **Pace Yourself**.
- Actively engage with the material while **Reviewing Notes**.
- Round out your studying experience with **Other Study Strategies**.

Know Your Exam

To study efficiently, you need to know what you're studying for. This means knowing not just the course material the exam will cover, but also the format

Study Strategically

"Before I seriously start studying I sit down and think what type of questions will be asked and plan my studying accordingly. If the exam is multiple choice I will spend a lot of time rereading my textbooks and notes. If it's short answer or essay-based I always brainstorm for all possible questions that might be on the exam and make notes based on that."

— Laura Carlson, communications,
Wilfrid Laurier University

of the exam and as much information about the style of the questions and the weighting of the various parts of the course material as possible.

Every professor provides some information about the exam, but the depth of that information varies. You might have to rely on a brief description in the course outline, or the professor may give an in-depth description of what you should expect in the last class before the exam. If you think that attending that last class is a waste of an hour, think about how much time you might save if you know exactly what (and what not) to study for the coming exam.

The format of the exam (e.g., multiple choice, essay, short answer) will have an impact on how you study. Multiple-choice questions tend to be based on a wide variety of simple facts, so you'll have to do a lot of memorization. Essay questions, on the other hand, tend to require deeper knowledge of narrower subject matter and require students to have a strong conceptual understanding of the course. We'll go into much more detail about exam formats in **Section 3.7: Exam Writing**.

The material the exam covers will dictate what you study. For example, some final exams will only test you on material covered since the mid-term exam, and knowing that will save you a lot of time you might have spent studying stuff you won't be tested on. Your professor may come right out and tell you exactly what material will be covered and what percentage of the exam will concern each part of the course, but some professors are coy and drop little hints for attentive students to pick up on, so pay attention in class.

Find out if any study help is available. Professors and TAs sometimes offer special pre-exam study seminars; some post practice problems on the course website. As well as being good practice, these official study aids can provide insight about the content of the exam. It is sometimes possible to find copies of exams from previous years; although the tests won't be identical, last year's is usually a good indication of what kinds of questions to expect, particularly if the course was taught by the same professor.

Finally, find out what you're allowed to bring into the exam room. Exams are sometimes open-book, and you're allowed to use anything you want, or sometimes professors will allow students to use a set number of pages of notes or other materials, like calculators, dictionaries, and other reference materials. An open-book exam can be extremely hard to write if you've left your book at home, and you're going to want to kick your own ass if you flunk just because you missed this little nugget of information.

Pace Yourself

You learn best when you have time to process information and let it sink in. You'll be better off starting to study a couple of weeks in advance, instead of cramming the same number of hours of studying into the last few days before an exam.

Rather than spending all your time studying for your first exam and switching to the second exam only after you've written the first, divide your study time between all the subjects you have to study for. It's important to give yourself the time to absorb the material for your later exams, and the amount of study time you dedicate to each test should be set through rational planning rather than determined by the happenstance of scheduling.

Form a study plan by making a list of all of your exams and creating a schedule that dedicates an appropriate amount of study time to each of them. Treat your scheduled study time like it's a job and prioritize it above everything else.

Be realistic in setting your schedule; don't plan to study 16 hours a day, because you'll exhaust yourself and you won't remember anything you read. Plan to switch between topics in a study session instead of dedicating marathon study sessions to a single subject—studying a variety of subjects will make it easier to stay focused. Leave some time open at the end of your study plan so you can dedicate extra time to subjects you have unexpected difficulty with.

Don't plan to spend the same amount of time studying for each exam. The subjects you find most difficult will probably warrant more study time than the ones you find easiest, but that should be balanced against other strategic considerations, such as the percentage of the course's mark the final

cramming
tips

Maybe a personal emergency popped up and consumed most of your study time, or maybe you've just spent the last two weeks partying; either way, you've only got a couple of days left before the exam and you haven't studied. It's time to cram!

Don't panic, and don't just pick up the nearest book and start frantically reading as fast as you can. You might have been irresponsible, but at least you can be irresponsible strategically.

Start by making a plan. You may be in this situation because you haven't effectively managed your time—now you'll have to get really good at time management really fast. Make a list of topics you have to study, write up a list of learning goals, and then create a schedule—and stick to it.

First, do a quick inventory of the material you need to cover and the amount of time you have to cover it. You might not be able to cover everything, so you're going to have to do some studying triage. If you don't understand what "triage" means, don't worry—you don't have time to learn right now.

Read your course outline and try to figure out what material is most likely to be on the test and what is likely going to be worth the most marks. It's probably too late to hope to get an A on this one. Instead, you're going to focus on getting the most marks given the time you have left.

If there's some small part of the material you don't understand that will take you a long time to learn, you might have to make the decision to forget about it and lose those marks. Similarly, if there's something you know you understand really well, plan to give that material a quick review and be done with it. Focus your time on the part of the material where you stand to gain the most marks in the least amount of time, which is the part that you don't know, but you can learn quickly.

Create study aids that help you study quickly. Flash cards and mind maps are good ways to drill information into your brain in a hurry. If you haven't been reviewing your notes throughout the term, you'll have to recreate that process in a short time. The key is repetition; recite key terms over and over and create an abbreviated version of your notes you can reread repeatedly.

And most important, keep calm. What's done is done, and it's too late to get back that time you wasted. It doesn't help anything to beat yourself up. Calm down, get to work, and get some sleep the night before the test.

exam makes up. In some classes, your final will be worth 50% or more of the final grade, while in others it may not be worth much at all, and you'll want to prioritize accordingly.

Reviewing Notes

Rereading your notes and reciting the facts to yourself is extremely boring. It also happens not to work very well. After hours of reading and reciting, the words start to run off your brain without sinking in, like water off a duck's back.

You're much more likely to retain knowledge that you're actively engaged with and are using or manipulating in some way. Here are a few tips for playing with your notes to help you engage with them.

- Reorganize your notes following a logic other than the chronological order you took them in. Organize them in a way that demonstrates how ideas are related to one another.
- Think about the material in your notes actively, not as something that needs to be memorized. Try contrasting ideas or thinking through the steps of how you would argue to prove a point of fact or to support an idea. Conjure up visual images of the material. Recite tricky facts in your mind.
- Rewrite concepts from your notes using different wording.
- Come up with your own examples to illustrate concepts. It's often easier to remember a story than it is to remember an abstract concept, so try to make an idea concrete.
- Practise explaining concepts from your notes to friends or family, or if you're wearing out their patience and their interest in macroeconomics, explain it to your cat.

Other Study Strategies

There is more to studying than endlessly reviewing your notes. Your goal is to prepare yourself for a test, so try testing yourself.

At the end of each study session, quiz yourself to find out which topics you're still a little weak on. Go back over your notes, looking at the subject headings only and see what you can remember about each topic. If your textbook has practice questions about each chapter, adapt these into quizzes.

If you can track down practice exams, write them and take them seriously when you do. Try to recreate the atmosphere of an exam hall by going to the library, putting away your textbook and your notes, and timing

Write New Notes for Studying

"I highly recommend making study notes. The purpose isn't exactly to study from them; rather, the exercise of going through your notes and textbooks and distilling the important information into tidy point-form notes over only a few pages helps organize your thoughts, see the shape of the material, and better understand how things fit together. It's just an added bonus that the notes become a useful study tool."

— Jennifer R., religious studies, McMaster University

yourself. Not only will practising help make you less anxious on the day of the test, but it will also expose gaps in your knowledge of the course material so you can focus your studying on problem areas.

Reviewing the results of other exams you've taken can improve your awareness of your strengths and weaknesses in exam situations. Did you study enough? Did you study the right things? Did you get nervous and suffer from exam anxiety? Did you rush and make careless mistakes? Did you not read the questions well enough? Knowing why you got the mark you did on previous tests (good or bad) will help you get better marks in the future.

Studying with peers in groups can be a big help. You can help motivate each other, explain concepts to one another, and share notes and study aids. It's also a lot easier to make up practice questions for someone else than it is to do it for yourself. Make sure your study group is helping you, though, and not wasting your time. If you spend most of your time chatting and distracting each other, you're probably better off alone.

You might find that you are way ahead of your study buddies and that you spend most of your time explaining basic concepts to them instead of studying the things you need to learn. Explaining a concept to someone else can help secure the knowledge in your own mind, but there are limits to how much time you want to dedicate to this. Helping friends is great, but you've got to think about your own test performance. If time is tight, you might have to bid your study group adieu and go it alone.

3.7   Exam Writing

The grade you get on your exam isn't just an evaluation of how well you know the course material; it's also a reflection of your exam-writing skills.

Exam writing *is* a skill; there are loads of perfectly intelligent students who know the course material backwards and forwards but get lousy marks on exams anyway. They may get performance anxiety and forget everything they ever learned. (Question 1: What's my name? . . . Damn it! I knew this one just a few minutes ago! Argh!) And sometimes it's because they're not very good at reading questions, budgeting their time, or employing the right strategy to fit the test.

In this section:

- Develop your own **Exam-Writing Techniques**.

- Learn strategies tailored to each specific **Exam Format.**

- Conquer your **Exam Anxiety**.

Exam-Writing Techniques

You need to develop a strategy for each test you write. When you get into the exam hall, start by reading the entire exam to get an idea of what's on it. If there are a hundred multiple-choice questions, you might not want to read every single one, but skim them and figure out what they're generally about. Note any particularly easy or difficult questions. This will give you time to think about the difficult ones, and it will help you decide how much time you'll need for each question.

Next, plan your attack. Budget your time, taking into consideration not only how difficult questions are, but how many marks they're worth. Don't kill yourself solving a challenging two-mark question and then rush through a ten-mark question because you're running out of time. Leave yourself time to review your exam and to transfer your multiple-choice answers from the question sheet to the computer form, if necessary.

You may want to start somewhere other than at the beginning, but if you skip questions, don't forget to come back to them. Start with the easiest questions first, to warm up your brain and get them out of the way so you know exactly how much time you have for the harder questions. The easy questions sometimes contain information that will help you tackle the more difficult ones. Multiple-choice questions are often a particularly good source of information for your answers to short-answer and essay questions on a mixed-format test.

Read and reread every question before you start answering it. Writing a brilliant, analytic answer to a question that was never asked isn't going to garner many marks, even from the most generous of markers. Pay close attention to how questions are phrased, and watch for key words such as *define, describe, analyze, contrast, argue, explain, demonstrate,* and *summarize*; each of these words is asking you for something different, so be sure you understand what you're being asked for.

Keep an eye on the clock. That's not to say you should obsess over the ticking of the minute hand, but make sure you at least have an idea of how much time is left. If you find yourself running out of time, you may have to prioritize what's left. Focus your attention on the questions that are worth a lot of marks compared to the time they take to answer.

Unless your professor is one of that rare breed of academic sadists who deduct marks for incorrect answers, it's better to have some kind of answer than no answer at all. If you run out of time, try to have at least an educated guess for every question. For essay and short-answer questions, get down as much as you can in point form to save yourself the time of having to put together full, grammatical sentences. You're not going to get full marks, but you may at least get some marks for your ideas.

Exam Format

Different exam formats demand different strategies and preparation. A hundred-question slog through the multiple-choice Scantron will require a very different approach than an intimidating single essay question that will determine 50% of your course grade. In most cases your test will incorporate more than one of these categories; for example, you may have an open-book exam that is 50% multiple choice and 50% short answer.

Multiple choice

Multiple-choice directions consist of a stem, which asks a question, and one correct answer among a number of incorrect distractor answers. Multiple-choice tests are among the most complained about in post-secondary education because they are often overwhelmingly long. Many students tend to over-think their answers.

Always read the directions carefully. Pay close attention to double negatives and key words like "always" and "necessary" in the stem phrase.

Cover up the possible answers when you read the stem phrase and try to come up with the answer independently before you look at the possibilities. Reveal the possible answers one at a time, and read each of them. If you see the answer you guessed, tentatively select it, but read all the other answers to make sure there isn't another possible correct answer, such as "all of the above."

If you can't find the answer you think is correct, narrow down the options by crossing out the ones you know are incorrect. If you still can't figure out which answer is right, don't waste too much time. Make an informed guess and flag the question so you can return to it if you have time after you've completed the remaining questions.

Don't over-think your answer. If the answer seems simple, it probably is simple. Trust your first instinct, and don't change your answers when you review unless you have a good reason, such as new information you have just remembered or the realization that you read the question wrong the first time.

Essay and short answer

Professors use essay and short-answer questions to test whether you understand how concepts are related and whether you can critique ideas. Anyone who's ever experienced writer's block knows how easy it is to freeze up when you are forced to write under pressure.

Start by reading the question a few times to make sure you understand exactly what you're being asked to do. If you find the wording of the question confusing, ask for clarification.

Acing Long-Answer Questions

"The hardest part is conceptualization and structure. When you get your exam, pick the essays you're going to write (if you get a choice) and do all the thinking at the beginning of the exam when your brain isn't fried. Decide your thesis statement, your points and your proofs for all your essays before you do any writing. What's nice about this is that, even when you're writing the meat of your first essay, you've thought about all the questions and something might come to mind that would be useful in one of your other essays."

– Sandra Duffey, social work, McMaster University

Spend a couple of minutes writing down everything you can think of about the subject. Be sure to write down examples and pertinent facts so you don't forget them.

Spend 5 to 10% of your time creating a brief outline and planning the amount of time you will spend on each section. Make sure your planned thesis statement answers the question you've been asked.

Now write! Don't try for anything fancy; nobody's expecting you to produce literature during a two-hour exam. Use short, clear sentences, follow a straightforward, understandable structure, and try to write as neatly as possible so you don't have to rewrite sections later to make them legible. Don't waste time crafting a clever beginning or ending to the essay. Style matters less here than it does in a normal essay.

Provide examples, and be as specific as possible. The marker will have points in mind he or she is looking for you to touch on, so don't breeze by the details. Keep your writing objective; don't personalize the essay unless you've been asked to. Wrap up the essay with a conclusion. A two-sentence summary will do.

Under exam conditions, it's easy to write so quickly you skip a word that completely changes the meaning of a sentence, so make sure you leave yourself a few minutes to look for mistakes and to revise.

Quantitative

Quantitative questions ask you to solve mathematical problems, which you'll run into not only in math classes, but also in many science, economics, and business courses. Students often find these questions frustrating, because if you make a small mistake in one step, you'll come up with the wrong answer, even if you followed the right steps.

Before you start writing the exam, write down the concepts, formulas, and constants you have memorized on a piece of scrap paper so you don't forget them later. As always, carefully read directions and identify key terms, to ensure you're doing what you've been asked to do.

You may choose to work through your problems on a separate piece of paper, which helps keep your exam booklet from getting cluttered with notes and false starts. When you're finished the problem, however, be sure to neatly copy your work into the exam booklet, including all the steps, without skipping the mathematical signs. Even if you get the answer wrong, markers often give partial marks if they can see how you puzzled through the problem. Make it obvious which of the numbers in the jumble of your work is your answer, by underlining or circling it.

If you're struggling with a difficult question, try to break the problem down into smaller, more manageable chunks. Write down all the steps you need to take to solve it and avoid shortcuts, and see if that helps you think it through.

Leave yourself time to check over your answers. Pay close attention to the details such as decimal places and negative signs.

Open-book and take-home

Students often make the mistake of thinking they don't have to study for an open-book exam. However, because you're not being tested on your memory, you have to understand the content in more depth. Your prof has eliminated all the simple questions you can just look up in the book, so all that's left to test you on is in-depth analysis that shows a deep conceptual understanding of the course material. Take-home exams are a more extreme version of the open-book exam; the professor has opened the exam to all the research materials in the world and given you much more time to complete the exam, so you're going to be expected to produce a higher standard of work than you would in a two-hour exam.

First of all, make sure you know what material you're allowed to bring into the test. "Open-book" can mean anything from being allowed to bring just the textbook, without any notes written in the margins, to a free-for-all where you're allowed to bring in anything you want. If you're allowed to bring in notes as well as the textbook, consider making notes on how the information is organized in the text, so it will be easier to look things up quickly.

Be careful about what you choose to bring. It's better to have a few well-chosen sources and a manageable amount of neat, well-organized notes than a huge stack of books and reams of paper containing every note you've ever taken on the subject.

Be careful about copying long quotes from your textbook in the exam. The idea is to demonstrate your ability to think critically, not your ability to copy quickly. The same rules of plagiarism apply in open-book exams as in essays, so note sources and paraphrase correctly. (See **Section 3.4: Writing Papers and Essays** for more on plagiarism and citation.)

Exam Anxiety

A little bit of stress over writing exams is normal and can even help you focus by sharpening your senses and stimulating your mind. Getting too stressed out can hurt your exam performance, though, especially if you lose sleep or get so nervous that you freeze up in an exam.

A healthy lifestyle is key to managing stress. If you make sure your body is rested and in good condition, your brain will have a fighting chance. In the days leading up to your exam, eat properly, get some exercise, and avoid drinking too much coffee or booze. You'll benefit way more from a decent night's sleep before the test than from staying up all night studying and blasting your brain with caffeine and energy drinks.

You can also avoid anxiety by properly preparing for the exam. If you feel like you've studied well and you know the course material, you'll have less to worry about. Taking practice exams in an environment that mimics a real exam hall can help set your mind at ease.

Avoid cramming at the last minute. Give yourself some time to chill out so you can go into the exam feeling calm instead of frantic.

If you feel completely overwhelmed during the exam, take a 30-second break and calm down. Close your eyes and breathe deeply. Look around the room: there's no physical danger here—just a bunch of polite hominids making marks on crushed-up wood pulp with graphite sticks. Surely you can do that too. Now get back to work.

3.8 Getting the Most From Your Professors

Your professor is the person who is best equipped to help you understand a subject and excel in class, but professors often seem like intimidating, unapproachable people. Many professors are renowned scholars and widely published in their field; surely they're too busy being utterly brilliant to waste time addressing the banal questions of a lowly undergraduate like you, right?

There is a two-part answer to that question:

1. It's part of professors' freakin' job to talk to you, so like it or not, they have to.
2. They probably actually do want to talk to you.

Professors have office hours for a reason: so students can come and speak to them. Discussions with your profs are an important part of your education, and it's part of what you're paying your tuition for.

Perhaps more important, most professors like to talk to students, but many of them end up spending a substantial part of their office hours sitting in their office alone, because students are too intimidated or don't get around to taking full advantage of them.

In this section:

- Talk to one of the smartest people you've ever met, by **Meeting Your Prof**.

- Learn strategies for coping with **The Bad Professor**.

Meeting Your Prof

Can you imagine what it would be like to spend your days lecturing to students who never asked questions or came to office hours? It would be like lecturing to a brick wall. Discussions with students provide professors with feedback, so they know which parts of their lectures are getting through and which parts need clarification.

Your Profs Actually Want to Talk to You

"I love it when students come to me and ask questions. It shows they are interested in the material and I'll always spend time with them."

– Dr. Carolyn Eyles, geography professor, McMaster University

But we're not suggesting that you should go and visit your lonely professor as a favour. Your professor can do a lot for you.

You have never before and you may never again have access to so many intelligent people as you'll have at your post-secondary institution. Professors' whole business is being intelligent and writing and speaking intelligently, and they can be some of the most interesting and inspiring people you'll ever talk to.

On a more practical level, your professors can help you a lot with your studies. If you don't understand a concept from class or from your textbook, ask your prof to clarify it for you. There are many angles an idea can be approached from, and your prof can find another way to describe a concept to you so you understand it.

Professors also use office hours to clarify assignments and help you if you're struggling to choose a topic for an essay. Sometimes they'll be willing to go over your essay outline with you, or read a draft of your paper before you hand it in. Some will even give a preview of the material that will be covered on an upcoming exam for students who take the time and effort to ask about it.

Plus, getting to know a few of your professors can be helpful later in life. Professors are connected people and may tell you about opportunities around campus and in their field of expertise. For example, some professors are willing to help students find volunteer positions or summer jobs, often as lab assistants and the like.

> Dear That Guy, from my philosophy class at UBC,
>
> When we went out for a beer with our prof after the last day of class, the prof kept looking wistfully down the table at the rest of us laughing, but you wouldn't stop chewing his ear off about ethics. The poor guy just wanted to talk and joke with the rest of us, That Guy, not listen to you telling him how smart you are.
>
> Signed,
> Ben, co-author of this book

References from professors are vital for anyone who plans to continue their education beyond the bachelor level—and they're great to have even if you're not. However, professors who don't know you will likely be reluctant to write a reference letter on the basis of nothing but the coursework they've seen. (For more on reference letters, see **Section 7.4: Reference Letters**.)

When you go and see your professors, be sure you make good use of their time. Most of them are busy people, and while they probably are happy to talk to you, they'd like it to be about something worthwhile. Come in to your discussion prepared. Don't ask questions that you could have easily answered for yourself if you had only taken the time to read the textbook or the course website.

That being said, if you are genuinely struggling, don't worry about asking a question you're afraid will make you look stupid. It's much better to get your question out of the way and look stupid now, rather than look stupid later when you don't know the answer on your final exam. And don't wait until the last week of class to tell your prof that you didn't understand a single thing she said the entire semester; visit early on if you're falling behind, and give yourself the chance to catch up.

Don't arrange meetings with your professors just to show off how smart you are or try to wow them with your understanding of the course material. The best way to demonstrate your intelligence is by asking an intelligent question you genuinely want to have answered, not by setting yourself up for a monologue on your favourite topic and boring the hell out of your professor by trying to show off.

And if at the end of the semester your professor invites the class out for a beer, you should go, because it will be fun and it's a great way to get to know a prof personally, but don't be that guy who monopolizes the professor and won't stop talking about the class. Your prof is human, too, and he just wants to have a beer and talk about normal human things.

The Bad Professor

Until now, this chapter has focused mainly on things you can do to improve your grades. But let's face it: there are factors that will affect you that are outside of your control. A problem most students come across at least once during their education is the bad professor.

The bad teacher

Often, bad professors are just bad teachers, whether it's because they don't have the skills or because they don't have the inclination. Maybe your physics prof is one semester away from retirement and doesn't care about lecturing anymore. Or maybe your mathematics teacher is a brilliant researcher—but barely speaks English. Or maybe you encounter a professor who just doesn't suit your learning style. You can complain all you want to your classmates over pints at the campus pub (which can be therapeutic), but at some point you have to figure out how to learn from this person.

The first thing you should do when you're having difficulty learning from professors is approach them about it during their office hours. Don't tell them that you think they are lousy at teaching, but explain that you're having difficulty following their lectures or participating in discussions. A professor may be able to suggest extra reading or give you some context that makes the subject make more sense.

If you still can't wrap your head around the way they are teaching the material, you may have to look to others to help you learn. Often your TAs will be an invaluable source of knowledge; they are usually graduate students who just a couple of years ago were where you are now, and they may be able to explain the subject from a perspective that works better for you. They may even have struggled taking the same course from the same teacher, and know first-hand what you're going through.

Other students will also be able to help you. If you're really struggling, chances are that others are too, so form a group of students who can meet after class to go over the material and try to decipher your bad professor's terrible teaching. Split up the subjects of the lectures between the members of your group, and have each member prepare his or her own mini lecture on the week's topic.

You may have to supplement your course material with other sources of information. Ask a librarian to help you find material on your subject of

the bad
TA

While your professor is the main guy in charge of your class, in many cases TAs (teaching assistants) do a lot of the important work, including marking exams and papers. Most TAs are very helpful and intelligent, but there are of course exceptions. Misha Warbanski, who studied journalism at Concordia University, encountered one of these bad TAs.

"It was a first year Political Science class. The professor was young and energetic and with the exception of the textbook it was a good class. The teaching assistant was pretty mean right from the get-go and acted like he had something to prove. I'm pretty opinionated and took issue with many of the points of view expressed in the textbook. The answers on my mid-term reflected this differing view. When I got the test back with a dismal failing mark, I felt it had more to do with this guy's attitude and political leanings and less to do with the substance of my answers.

"I first met with the TA (who marked the papers) and got nowhere. Just attitude. So I booked a time with the prof. He was really clear from the get-go that if he was going to take the time to regrade a paper the marks could go up or down. I thought that was fair and agreed. In the end, I got a near-perfect grade and then he bought me a beer for my troubles."

study, including other books, videos, audiotapes and so on. If the course is offered by a number of professors, look at the course descriptions of other classes to find alternative material related to your subject. You may also be able to sit in on lectures delivered by another professor if it works with your schedule.

If you feel that the professor's poor performance affected your mark unfairly, or you disagree with the mark you received, you may have to be more direct with your professor. The first step, again, is to approach him or her during office hours, but if you can't get anywhere you may have to discuss your situation with someone else.

Every university has a process for appealing grades and resolving other disputes. An academic counsellor can explain how these processes work and can help you think through how to move forward. Also, many student unions offer confidential help to students in these situations. Your school will also have a student advocacy office or an ombudsperson whose job it is to mediate in cases of disagreement.

The really bad professor

Your problem may go beyond your prof's bad teaching. This is the enlight-ened world of academia, but it's certainly not unknown for students to encounter discrimination or sexual harassment from their professors. It can also happen that professors are so uninterested in teaching that they fail to live up to the most basic requirements of the job, like keeping office hours or consistently making it to lectures.

If your conflict with your professor is serious, you may have to bypass the step where you speak to the professor in person and go straight to the administration or ombudsperson. Don't just suffer through a clear-cut case of harassment; think about the poor students who are going to have to put up with this jerk next semester. Report your prof. (See **Section 4.4: Diversity on Campus** for more information on discrimination.)

3.9   Grade Crisis ✔

So, you just got back a mid-term exam or a major paper and you got a terrible grade. It's not just a disappointing grade; it's a hideous, dis-figured little mutant of a mark, and the sight of it stings like a slap in the face.

Before you burst into tears, drop out of school and join the circus, take a minute to ask yourself why you got this lousy mark. The answer to this ques-tion will determine how you should react to it.

You didn't work hard enough

Did you fail because you didn't study enough or put enough time into the as-signment? If that's the case, ask yourself why you didn't put in the necessary time. If it's because you were way too busy doing other things, then your problem might be time management. (See **Section 4.1: Time Management**.) You may need to give up other activities to make more time for school work, or you might just have to learn how to make better use of your time.

It's also possible that you didn't work hard enough because you had a hard time being interested in or caring about the assignment. Maybe you don't like the subject you're studying. If the course is totally optional to your degree, then the solution is obvious: don't take another course in the subject. If it's a one-off prerequisite to your degree, like that one calculus course you need to take to get accepted into the management faculty, then you'll just have to force yourself to redouble your efforts and suffer through the class.

But if this class you're not interested in is the main subject matter of your degree, then it's time to do some soul-searching and ask yourself whether you're taking the wrong degree. Make an appointment with an academic adviser to talk through your options.

You worked your ass off, but still got a lousy mark

Maybe you put your blood, sweat and tears into this test or assignment, but you still got a terrible mark. There's a chance that you made some simple mistake that explains your mark. Maybe you wrote a great essay, but it had nothing to do with what you were assigned to write about. Maybe you mis-read an important question on the exam, or maybe you studied hard, but you studied all the wrong material and came into the test unprepared. If that's the case, then the solution is that you'll just have to be more diligent in the future.

Talk to your professor about your performance and find out how you could have done better. The explanation might be simple, or it might be that you really need to brush up on some of your core academic skills, like writing (section 3.4), studying (section 3.6) or exam writing (section 3.7). Your professor or TA might be able to help you and explain concepts you missed, and you can also check out your school's academic support programs, such as the writing centre and tutoring programs.

Or maybe you're having a really hard time understanding the material you're being taught. Maybe you took the class too early in your degree and you're in over your head, maybe you're having a hard time learning from your professor (see section 3.8), or maybe you're just really bad at this subject.

Don't conclude that you're terrible at a subject after you screw up the very first pop quiz. Sometimes it takes awhile to get the hang of a subject, and maybe some help from your prof or TA will help. However, if the evidence starts to pile up and your efforts to improve get you nowhere, you might have to admit to yourself that this subject isn't your strong point.

Your reaction will depend on how this course relates to your major: if it's not central to your major, you can either drop it or suffer through it and then avoid similar courses in the future. If this is a core subject, however, it might be time to consider whether you're getting the right degree. Unless you decide to drop the class, however, you should still go to your prof, your TA, and your school's academic support programs for help.

To drop or not to drop

It is said that quitters never win, but it's often said by people who've had the crap beaten out of them because they refused to quit when they should have.

Sometimes it is the right decision to drop a class. Persevering through a difficult class can cost so much time and energy that it will hurt your marks in your other classes. You might be better off focusing your time on getting better grades in your other classes and adjusting your schedule to make up for the lost class.

That being said, dropping a class isn't a decision to be taken lightly. It's important that you consider everything that dropping will impact. First of all, how will the class show up on your transcripts and how will it affect your GPA (grade point average)?

Policies vary from school to school, but generally, if you drop a class very early in the semester, it won't show up on your transcripts at all. If you drop it a little later, the class will register as a "W" for "withdrawal" on your transcripts, but won't affect your average. And after a certain date, you won't be able to drop a class anymore—you'll just get an F, or you'll get the percentage mark for whatever work you've done so far in the semester. Make sure you understand your school's policies before you make any rash decisions.

Schools have similar policies regarding tuition refunds—if you drop a class very early in the semester, you'll usually get a full refund, but if you drop it later on, you may have to kiss your tuition money goodbye. You might have spent $500 or more to register for that class, and you have to ask yourself whether you want to spend another $500 to register for another course to replace it.

And finally, you have to think about your schedule. How hard is it going to be for you to make up this class? Are you going to have to take a summer class, or is it going to delay your graduation? Don't just speculate—take a look at your school's calendar and figure out when you can retake the class or take a suitable replacement for it.

Make sure you think about how it's going to affect the rest of your schedule. Dropping a class that is a prerequisite could mess up your whole sched-

a story about academic probation

Brian Li hasn't had the smoothest path through his post-secondary education: he's switched majors six times and he's been put on academic probation three times. With the help of academic advisers, however, he's now on the path to successfully completing a double degree in music and anthropology.

Academic probation is a warning to a student that gives the student the opportunity to rectify failing grades or misconducts before suffering consequences like being asked to leave school. Regulations vary from school to school; for example, the first time Brian was put on academic probation, it was because he failed a course and dropped below the required GPA. To continue studying his chosen major, he was required to withdraw from school for 12 months and then reapply. At a second school, Brian was again put on academic probation for his grades because his GPA dropped below 2.0 out of 4. That time around, he received a letter of academic warning and a guide on how to use the academic advising and tutoring resources at his school.

Brian, a singer, attributes his low GPA and subsequent academic probation to the stress of studying for exams while preparing for vocal competitions and concerts. After taking a "much needed year-long break" and enrolling in a different school, he found himself on academic probation for a third time, and he knew that his next semester was the "make-it-or-break-it semester." He began seeing his academic adviser every other week and eventually pulled himself out of his GPA rut. Brian credits his academic advisers with helping him find a major he enjoys and with helping him transfer credits and get on the path to graduation.

ule next semester. In that case, you might have to figure out how to somehow pass this course, come hell or high water.

Before you go dropping courses willy-nilly, see an academic adviser and make sure you understand exactly how it is going to affect your path to graduation.

Student Life

YOUR LIFE at school is going to involve a lot more than just attending class and studying. With campus pubs and parties, lectures, events, and everything else this exciting atmosphere has to offer, there is no end to your possibilities on any night of the week. You will have the opportunity to try many, many new things, from athletics to politics to knitting.

At the same time, your social life will be transformed as you explore this weird and varied place, and your relationships with your parents and the people you knew in high school will be changing. You are going to encounter hundreds of new people. Some may become your new best friends, others may introduce you to a whole new way of thinking. Some might confound and confuse you, while others may offend you.

You'll have to learn to balance the time you spend on all of these activities with your school work, to make sure you're still achieving academically while making the most of the opportunities for growth and fun that your campus offers.

In this chapter:

- Make time for exciting new activities by learning about **Time Management**.

- Take advantage of everything your university has to offer by exploring **Life Outside the Classroom**.

- Cope with leaving your old friends and embrace **Your Changing Social Life**.

- Get the support you need and broaden your horizons by experiencing **Diversity on Campus**.

- Supplement your educational experiences by **Going Abroad**.

4.1 Time Management ✓

Get ready for what could be the busiest years of your entire life. Suddenly, you're enrolled in more challenging classes with an insane amount of required reading and you're living at a campus with an amazing social scene. You could probably handle that, but you also joined the school's Clowning Club and discovered a love for juggling, your intramural lacrosse team plays every Wednesday, and you've got two shifts every weekend at your part-time job. Now you have a choice: are you going to spend the evening doing laundry, or are you going to go to that Engineering Society beer garden and spend the next week recycling underwear by wearing it inside out?

University isn't only about understanding Aristotelian philosophy or quantum mechanics; it's also about figuring out how to live a full life as an adult. Effective time management is essential not only to your marks, but also to your quality of life because it enables you to make time for what is really important to you.

In this section:

- Find out where all your time goes by **Assessing Your Time**.

- Dedicate time to what's really important by **Making a Schedule**.

- Avoid wasting time by learning strategies to avoid **Procrastination**— or watch TV now and read about procrastination later.

Assessing Your Time

Where does all the time go?

No, really: where does it all go? You've got the same 168 hours in a week that everyone else has. Why does it seem like there's never enough time to do everything you need to do?

Figuring out how you currently use your time is the first step toward making intelligent decisions about your time management. Be honest with yourself and think through everything you do in a day and a week. You probably don't realize how much time many of your routine activities actually take.

Make a list of what you do for all of the hours in a week. Ask yourself how much time you spend:

- Sleeping (don't forget naps)
- Preparing meals, eating, cleaning up
- Getting ready to go out or go to school
- Commuting
- Attending class
- Studying and doing homework
- Working
- Participating in extracurricular activities
- Exercising and playing sports
- Socializing
- Doing other leisure activities, like watching TV or messing around on your computer

The idea isn't to cut down on all unnecessary activities and focus every spare moment on your school work; it's to understand where your time goes so you can make choices about how to use it better. This means making time not only for things that are important, like school work, but also for the activities you really enjoy, like hanging out with friends.

Many universities suggest that you spend two hours studying for every hour you spend in class. That means if you have 15 hours of lectures and 6 hours of labs every week, you should count on spending another 42 hours reading, reviewing and doing homework. That's 63 hours that are spoken for; knock out another 56 hours for sleep, and you're left with only 49 hours for everything else, including eating and personal hygiene. If you're going to have any time for doing those things that keep you happy and sane, you're going to have to take control of how you use your time.

Making a Schedule

Have you ever spent a week feeling like you have all the time in the world, and then the following week you suddenly realize that you've got two midterms and a paper due? There is a piece of technology that can help you avoid this kind of crisis. The ancient Babylonians, Egyptians, Chinese, and Mayans each invented this thing called a calendar, which you can use to create a schedule of upcoming events, so you can anticipate deadlines and get work done in advance.

Semester schedule

Avoid being surprised by assignments and exams by making a master schedule that records all the deadlines for all your classes, all in the same place. This will allow you to see how the workload in one class will affect the time you can dedicate to another, so you can plan for busy times by getting to work on assignments early.

On a calendar (preferably a computer-based calendar, so it's easy to make changes and keep things legible), list all your semester's deadlines and other obligations, starting with your class schedule and all the assignment due dates and exams. Then add all your planned extracurricular activities, social events, and weekend trips home. Be sure to keep the schedule updated as new assignments are given and due dates are changed.

Your semester schedule is yours and you can change it as you see fit. Don't think of it as a little dictator controlling your time, but as a friend who is giving you fair warning about what's coming up in your life.

Weekly plan

Use your semester schedule to make a more specific plan at the beginning of each week. List all your deadlines and homework assignments for the week, and look forward in your semester schedule to see if you should be preparing for deadlines coming up in the next few weeks. Then figure out how much time you need to spend reading and reviewing for your classes, and make a list of all the extracurricular and social activities you have planned.

Time Management Tips

- Plan! Plan! Plan! You can't effectively manage your time if you don't know what you need to accomplish.

- Keep track of deadlines.

- Start work on big projects and on studying for exams early, to avoid a time crunch the day before a test or due date.

- Write weekly and daily to-do lists, and monitor your progress.

- Set specific study goals for each week and each study session.

- Plan to dedicate your most productive hours of the day to your most important tasks, and save relaxation or socializing for when your brain is tired.

- Think of school as a job; there is work you have to get done, and the main goal of your life right now is to do it.

- Don't let social activities distract you from your school work and other responsibilities. Reward yourself for having completed tasks with social outings, instead of putting off doing tasks in order to hang out.

- Be smart about employment. Some people can't afford not to work, but letting your marks and your sanity fall to pieces for minimum wage is probably not a wise investment of your time.

Now assign each of these activities to a day of the week, keeping in mind how long it will take to do each of them. Be sure to leave yourself enough time to sleep, eat properly, and exercise, as well as some time to relax.

The key to making your schedule work is to make it balanced and realistic, so don't assign yourself 16 hours of reading all on the same day, because you'll never be able to pull it off. If Superman was a student, even he'd need a couple of minutes to eat and go to the bathroom.

Daily plan

Every morning, take a look at your weekly plan and figure out what you have to accomplish that day. Figure out which tasks have to be done at specific times, then plan the rest of your day around them, giving priority to the most important tasks.

The time of day you choose to accomplish each of your tasks does matter. It's often a good idea to get after those tasks you're dreading the most right away, to get them out of the way so they're not hanging over your head all day. You should also plan to do your school work at a time of day when your brain works best, and do sports and other leisure activities when your brain is tired.

As you go down your list, cross off tasks as you complete them, then reward yourself at the end of the day for completing the list. The reward you give yourself can be that thing that you really wanted to do all day while you were doing school work, whether it's watching TV or hanging out with friends.

If you don't finish your list, ask yourself why. Was it because you procrastinated, because you ran into difficulties, or because your list was unreasonably long? With practice, you'll get better at estimating how long tasks take and at making more realistic to-do lists.

Procrastination

Do you find yourself putting off your most difficult tasks until it's late and you're too tired to do them? Do you spend the first hour of every scheduled study session returning emails and reading Internet news? Do you constantly find yourself scrambling to finish essays the night before the deadline?

If you answered yes to any of these questions, you may have a problem with—Hey! Come back here!

You're going to read this right now, if you know what's good for you. Ever heard of the Tooth Fairy? Well, there's a Procrastination Fairy, too. His name is Jacques, he's got arms as thick as telephone poles and he has an enormous procrastination mallet he uses on naughty students like you.

Procrastination is a problem everyone struggles with. It can hurt your marks and rob you of time for doing the things you really want to do. It can also make you anxious and unhappy because you have to live with the thought of all of those incomplete tasks nagging at you.

The good news is that all it takes to battle procrastination is self-awareness and a little bit of determination. A healthy fear of Jacques doesn't hurt, either.

The basic mistake that leads to procrastination is that you're doing things backwards. *First* do the things you have to do and *then* do the time-wasting stuff. You'll probably find that if you do things in the right order, you'll waste your time doing things that are way more fun than what you did while you were procrastinating. Instead of sitting at your computer playing Tetris while you're putting off that paper you're supposed to write, write the paper

Top Time Waster of All Time: The Internet

"I've certainly gotten better over the years at not spending endless amounts of time on Facebook, YouTube, Sporcle, HF Boards, etc., but I'll still occasionally catch myself in the middle of research, for example, stopping what I'm doing and going back to one of them almost unconsciously."

— Nick Frost, English, University of Alberta

"The Internet is my hugest source of procrastination. I'd say that browsing Facebook, YouTube and StumbleUpon take up 95% of my wasted time. It's kind of addicting, one funny or interesting video or article always links to another, and then another, and I don't always realize how long I've been on the Internet until an hour later."

— Michelle Reid, environmental science, McMaster University

first and then you'll be able to do whatever you want—and we bet that with your paper off your mind, you'll spend your time on something a lot better than Tetris.

If, after assessing how you use your time, you still can't figure out how to squeeze in all that studying you should be doing, make a list of your top five time wasters. Do you spend a lot of time chatting with your roommate? Have an addiction to reading celebrity news? Spend all your time hanging out at the campus pub with the boys?

Don't just swear off your time wasters, because you'll miss them, and you probably won't stick to your pledge. Instead, set boundaries for yourself by scheduling specific times when you're allowed to do things you like. For example, one of the authors of this book allows herself to look at Facebook only twice a day, once before she starts working and once at the end of the day. Her co-author is absolutely not allowed to have even a single beer until after he's done working for the day.

Familiarizing someone else with your schedule can be useful for avoiding procrastination. Ask a friend, roommate, or study partner to hold you accountable to your schedule. Check in with each other every day to discuss what you were supposed to accomplish and whether you did it.

Often, procrastination is the product of being surrounded by distractions. Friends barging into your dorm room for a chat, or the sight of your video-game system sitting there alone, with nobody to play with it—these are nearly irresistible inducements to procrastinate.

It's helpful to find a place to go and study where you can separate your school life from the rest of your life. If you go to the library every day between 10 A.M. and 2 P.M., you'll begin to associate that time and place with work, and it will be easier to focus. And by separating the locations where you study and where you live, you'll avoid finding yourself accidentally doing laundry when you're supposed to be reading.

If you find yourself procrastinating when faced with an imposingly large project, try breaking it down to smaller chunks, so you can take on a few small tasks every day and make perceptible progress.

4.2 Life Outside the Classroom ✓

Many of the best experiences at college and university have nothing to do with studying or going to class or writing papers. Your campus may be one of the most exciting places you've ever been. There are thousands of people your age with lifestyles similar to yours who are engaging in fun and interesting activities every day, from hanging out at the campus pub to pushing for social change to learning how to dance the tango.

There are a million reasons to get involved in activities outside of class; the most obvious is that it is a lot more fun than sitting in your dorm room alone. It's also much easier to meet your fellow students while doing something fun than while you're sitting in a lecture theatre, listening to an old guy talk about math.

Your extracurricular activities can also be about much more than having fun and socializing. The myriad clubs and activities available at every campus are great opportunities to explore your interests and potential future career. Are you curious about what being a high school counsellor might be like? Volunteer with the University of British Columbia's Speakeasy service as a peer counsellor. Thinking about giving photography a go? Join the amateur photography club at the University of Toronto.

There is also a ton of stuff you can do that isn't formally organized. You may discover your life passion is bowling by going to your friends' weekly bowling night. Or you might develop a new interest in reading philosophy after chatting with a fourth-year philosophy major you randomly met at a pub. If you're open-minded you will surely discover a whole new world of possibilities on your campus.

In this section:

- Explore your interest in pretty much anything, from comic books to Bangladeshi culture, by joining **Clubs**.

- Stay in shape, have fun, and meet fit hotties by participating in **Athletics**.

- Learn to properly run a meeting and how your university functions by becoming part of your **Student Government**.

- Change the world by getting involved in **Activism**.

- Improve your writing and meet interesting people by checking out **Campus Media**.

- Go to great concerts and listen to fascinating lectures at **Events**.

- Just take it all in by enjoying **General Campus Life**.

Clubs

Whatever you're passionate about, odds are good that out of the thousands of students on your campus, you'll find at least one person who is interested in that subject as well, no matter how obscure it is. And if there are more than a few of you, then someone has probably already organized a club.

As well as being fun and offering the chance to meet people, clubs provide you with a feeling of community, something you might find lacking at large campuses. Clubs connect you to a large group of people who have at least one thing in common with you.

If you're at a big school, there is likely an established club for almost everything you can think of and a hundred other things you never even imagined. You can play table tennis at the University of Saskatchewan, learn to crochet at the University of British Columbia, practise your breakdancing moves at the University of Toronto, and do . . . um, *something* . . . with the members of the Fetish and Kink Enthusiasts Club at McGill University.

Types of clubs

Most schools have a large number of faith-based clubs, where you can meet fellow Christians, Hindus, Muslims, Baha'i or atheists. They often welcome people of other faiths to come and learn about their beliefs.

Some clubs are concerned with a specific ethnicity, identity, or language. There are Ethiopian, Syrian, Bangladeshi, Brazilian, Celtic, Chinese, Ukrainian, German, Filipino, and almost-every-other-national-ethnic-or-linguistic-group clubs at campuses across Canada. These clubs are generally very inclusive and are concerned with promoting a culture and/or a language, rather than excluding outsiders. They often organize interesting events and provide opportunities to speak foreign languages.

Clubs related to a specific field of study are also very common. English clubs provide a venue where students can discuss literature, and engineering clubs are known for pulling pranks (members of UBC's Engineering Undergraduate Society famously hung a VW Beetle from the bottom of the Golden Gate Bridge). These clubs can connect you to students who are further along in their degree and can be invaluable sources of information on everything from academics to career opportunities.

Some clubs are designed to help students network with people in their future industry, develop leadership skills, and get work experience. Business schools organize entrepreneurship and finance clubs (which are open to students from any faculty), and clubs like AIESEC organize international internships. (See **Section 4.5: Going Abroad** for more on AIESEC.) Leadership clubs and groups like Model Parliament and Model United Nations give students the opportunity to practise diplomacy, negotiation, and communication skills.

Finally, there are dozens and dozens of clubs related to specific hobbies. There are choirs and bands, film clubs where you watch and discuss movies, clubs for comedians, clubs for clowns, and clubs for practitioners of the papery art of origami. There are billiards clubs and backgammon clubs and chess clubs. There are culinary clubs and coffee-lover clubs, debate clubs and self-defence clubs.

If the club you want doesn't exist, you can always start your own. Schools and students' unions are usually very encouraging and can provide a lot of help with organizing a new club. New clubs are often provided with space, and you can even get a small budget and other resources to help you organize events.

These examples barely scratch the surface of what's available on Canadian campuses. Take the time to check out the club listings on your school's or your student union's website and peruse your options.

improve your resumé by having fun

Getting involved is also a great way to spruce up your resumé—and it doesn't matter what activity it is. Maurice Fernandes, a senior recruitment manager at Ceridian Canada, says participation in any extracurricular activity demonstrates that a job applicant has time management skills and is a well-rounded person. Using a science major who is an amateur musician as an example, he says, "It shows she can juggle the demands of her academic career with her love of the piano. Also, she doesn't have a fear of performing in front of people."

Athletics

Athletics are fun, they help you stay fit, and they can be a great way to clear the cobwebs out of your mind after a day of lectures. They are also an excellent way to meet people, particularly if you want to meet fit, athletic people of whatever gender you find sexy.

If you are a serious athlete, you can try out for a varsity team for a chance to represent your school in provincial, national, and international competitions. Big schools have top coaches who train athletes in dozens of sports. For instance, the University of Toronto has over 900 varsity athletes on 44 teams playing 26 different sports. Varsity sports range from those you're familiar with from high school, like soccer, football, and basketball, to some you may never have heard of, like fencing, dragon-boat racing, water polo, and cricket.

Less competitive athletes can join intramural sports leagues, where teams play against other students from the same school. At some schools, intramural teams represent a faculty, a department, or a college, so you can have wrestling matches that pit the English department against the engineers, or football games between business students and social scientists. Intramural leagues often have several divisions, each of which offers a different level of competitiveness, so you can choose the division that is right for your game.

For students who want to stay active but whose schedules don't permit them to commit to doing something every week, campus athletic centres also offer drop-in sports, where you can just show up and join, for example, a pickup soccer or basketball game. You can also drop in for non-competitive sports such as casual swims, weight training, or running groups, or for fitness classes like aquafit, pilates, or yoga.

Between student clubs, your school's athletic centre, and the student discounts you can get elsewhere, you'll never have cheaper access to sports equipment, so it's a great opportunity to try out all kinds of different physical activities. Student clubs can hook you up with people to try new sports with, and athletic centres often offer classes to teach you how to do sports that would be hard to just pick up on your own. For example, the University of Calgary Outdoor Centre offers courses in kayaking, snowshoeing, rock climbing, and even hang gliding.

Student Government

When you register for school, you automatically become a member of your institution's students' union. Membership fees will be added to your tuition bill, whether you like it or not. What you get from those fees, however, is mostly up to you.

Students' unions provide tons of services. For example, the Alma Mater Society at the University of British Columbia (the largest students' union in the country) offers free tutoring, it advocates for students who have conflicts with the university, it runs a food bank, provides a health and dental plan, helps students rent housing off-campus, runs a sexual assault centre, provides transit passes, co-ordinates volunteer opportunities, offers counselling services, and operates an art gallery, a radio station, a movie theatre, and a lodge at Whistler, where students can stay on hiking or skiing trips.

In addition to providing services, students' unions are mandated to advocate on the students' behalf. Every students' union interprets this role differently; some students' unions do their advocacy entirely within the institution, representing students' interests in dealing with the school's administration by asking for lower fees and pushing for more services. Other students' unions take a broader role and lobby municipal, provincial, and federal governments for tuition freezes, grants, and tax breaks for students. Some students' unions go beyond advocating for students by organizing campaigns on non-student issues, from fundraising for cancer research to marching against the war in Afghanistan.

Your students' union is a democratic organization, operated by a board or an executive committee made up of students elected by the students of your school each year. If you want a say in how your students' union is run, you can start by voting for candidates in the elections, or better yet, you can run for office.

If you're interested in student politics, get involved and learn how your students' union works. Students' unions are always looking for volunteers to help run programs and to sit on student committees. Some students begin their involvement with student government because they don't like the way something is being done at their school. Is there something at your school that drives you crazy? Do you think all the concerts that are currently being organized are lame and you want to organize your own events? Or did you notice that the second floor of the library is impossible to get to in a wheel-chair? Are you angry that tuition is going up yet again this year? Go and talk to one of your elected student representatives about your issue and ask how you can get involved. If there isn't already a committee set up to address the issue, the union will help a motivated student like you get one started.

Getting involved may lead you to run in a campus election. As an elected official, you can vote on motions about the operations of the union, and you can represent the school at provincial and national student events. Your union represents the student perspective in the administration of the insti-tution, so you could sit on a committee with your school's president and representatives of the faculty and staff and work out the details of how the school will be run, for example writing new policy or approving the budget.

It hardly needs to be said that being elected to the students' union execu-tive can be an amazing learning experience. You'll gain insight into the oper-ation of large organizations and how money is managed at institutions with budgets as large as a student's union or a university. You'll be given a level of responsibility most people don't get until they're well into their careers. As a bonus, these positions usually carry a (modest) salary, so being a student union official is like having a part-time job.

Your involvement with the students' union doesn't have to stop at the local level. Many students' unions are affiliated with a national student organization, such as the Canadian Federation of Students and the Cana-dian Association of Students Associations, and you may have the opportu-nity to work on a national level for one of these groups or to participate in a national campaign.

Meet People and Learn a Ton

"I'm the vice-president internal for our Residence Hall Association, which is the student group responsible for building a community, supporting networking, liaising with campus groups, and advocating students' rights. This position has given me the opportunity to meet hundreds of people, meet my best friends, work with various types of teams, and learn how to host various-sized social events such as floor movie nights, concerts, beverage gardens, and res-wide dances."

— Alison McLeod, business administration, Simon Fraser University

Activism

The anti-war protests of the 1960s have a special place in the public imagination, but post-secondary political activism began long before then and continues to influence public discourse today, whether it's the 2009 protests over the elections in Iran or the G20 activism organized at the University of Toronto in 2010.

Before you decide that activism doesn't suit someone of your political persuasion, we should emphasize that all kinds of activism take place on Canadian campuses, with competing groups often taking up opposing sides of an issue. Institutions of higher education are places of free inquiry, and it shouldn't be supposed that faculty and students are unified in a single political opinion.

If you're passionate about an issue, your school can be a great place to organize a movement and try to make a difference. You're surrounded by other passionate, intelligent young people, and resources are available to students who want to become politically engaged. The three main ways you can get involved at university are through a club, through your students' union, or by showing your support at organized events.

Check your school's club listings to see if there is already a group that is concerned with the issues you care about. You'll find a wide variety of politically oriented clubs focused on issues such as medical research, environmentalism, social justice, animal rights, war, and globalism. Many clubs are affiliated with charitable or political organizations outside your school, such as Engineers Without Borders, the Young Liberals, and community service organizations like food banks and soup kitchens.

Finally, keep an eye out for political events on your campus. There are often demonstrations, lectures, movie screenings, and debates organized

Expand Your Career Prospects

"I'm a social science student, and my faculty doesn't have a whole lot of job opportunities for undergrad students. When you volunteer in something you're interested in, you have a skill set you can put on your resumé that sets you apart from the others in your program. You also have opportunities to make friends and show off your competency to people who might be able to hire you, who otherwise wouldn't notice you. I've made a lot of job and academic contacts through my extracurricular work, and it's turned into job and career prospects that otherwise wouldn't be available to me."

– Sandra Duffey, social work, McMaster University

on campus by various political groups. Even if you disagree with the perspective being put forward, these events are great opportunities to learn about different issues and to explore your own opinions.

Student Media

Student media are a unique kind of club where you can develop new skills, meet interesting people, explore possible career paths, and make your voice heard by others, all while having a great time.

Most universities and colleges have at least one student publication, and many larger schools have two or three student newspapers plus a radio station. Most of these media are completely student-run, giving students the opportunity to write, edit, photograph, and design entire newspapers and to program and DJ a 24-hour radio station. Some university publications are run by the school's faculty, such as literary journals run by creative-writing departments, but all of them showcase student talent and are focused on a readership made up of students.

Contributing to a student paper can be a great way to develop your writing skills. Your paper will let you break out of the standard academic form of writing and explore other styles of expression, and student editors will provide feedback on your writing that your professors may not have time to give you. Plus, you'll gain experience interviewing people, researching stories, and constructing coherent, convincing arguments.

Even if you don't want to be a journalist when you graduate, chances are your job will involve some writing. If you do aspire to a career in writing, a student newspaper is the perfect place to get that first publication credit to put on your resumé.

Extracurricular Activities Can Lead to a Career

"In that first year at York, I got involved with the school paper, which introduced me to Canadian University Press, which made me forget about my plans to transfer to a school with a journalism program. I learned more through the school paper and CUP than I believe I ever could have in four years at journalism school. It was my CUP experience that helped introduce me to the contacts that gave me my first job in my field—before I graduated. While grades and classes are important (they are what you pay for, after all), they are not everything. Explore your interests in extracurriculars."

– Sarah Millar, film studies, York University

There are plenty of non-writing positions available as well. Student papers are always looking for photographers, cartoonists, layout artists, designers, advertising sales people, and business managers. Someone has to pay the bills and manage the cash flow, so if you're looking for experience in running a small business, this could be your big chance. And many student newspapers offer a (modest) salary, so this could be a fun way to earn your beer money.

Even if you're not interested in contributing to student media, pick up your school paper or dial into your school's radio station and find out what's going on at your school and what issues people are talking about.

Events

There is always something buzzing in the exciting intellectual and not-so-intellectual life on campus. Take the time to look at the posters around campus and at the event ads in your school's paper.

On the intellectual side, faculties and clubs often host lectures from famous academics, authors, intellectuals, and politicians—and these events are usually very cheap or totally free. Sometimes these talks are in-depth explorations of an idea that is of intense interest to everyone in one major and of no interest to anyone else, but often they are broadly appealing to anyone with intellectual curiosity, such as discussions of contemporary trends, politics, and current events. And you never know what famous world figure might come to your school: co-author Ben once saw Mikhail Gorbachev speak at the University of Calgary.

The various artsy departments of your school often organize artsy-type events, showcasing the work of your fellow students, the faculty of your school, or others. The art department will have exhibits and the music department will certainly host concerts, sometimes featuring leading musicians from around the world.

Many clubs and societies hold parties. This might be in the form of a welcome-back barbecue in September, or a beer garden organized by the engineering student society. These parties are often open to all students, so even if you're not an engineer, you should go, because beer is delicious and meeting new people is an important part of the complete campus experience.

General Campus Life

Aside from these organized events and co-ordinated experiences, it's possible to have a great time just by being on campus. It's like a small city full of intelligent young people, and there's always something going on, much of it totally unplanned.

Something really great is happening out there right now, but we don't know what it is, so we can't tell you how to find it. We can only tell you that commuting to and from campus to attend classes and spending no other time at school is a mistake.

Someone is definitely having fun at a campus pub somewhere in Canada right now. Oh sure, that pub may be just a cheap, dirty, crowded bar, but there's nowhere better to feel the old school spirit than in a cheap, dirty bar crowded with your fellow undergraduates.

If it's not too cold out (or maybe even if it is), someone is playing Frisbee out on the green. Somewhere, some engineers are pulling a prank by defiling the business building with a banner saying objectionable things about the business faculty. Somewhere, some art students are engaging in performance art, some drama students are publicly and loudly acting like weirdos, and some English major is tacking up posters containing jokes so obscure that only other English majors get them.

But we don't know where. So go and look.

4.3   Your Changing Social Life

Going to college or university will bring changes to more than just your school life. You can expect that your social life and your relationship with your parents will be transformed, particularly if you move away from your hometown.

When you leave your parents' home for the first time, you might also be leaving the group of friends you've had since childhood, and maybe a boyfriend or girlfriend as well. These relationships don't have to end, but they will have to change to some extent, because you won't be able to maintain the same face-to-face contact you're used to.

Everyone's personal relationships are unique, and we can't tell you exactly what's going to happen, but we'll give you a heads-up about some issues other students ran into while undergoing the same transition.

In this section:

- Cope with your changing relationships with your parents, friends, and that special someone when you're **Leaving the Nest**.

- Protect your off-line self from your online self by learning about **Your Online Social Life**.

Leaving the Nest

Your friends

One of the toughest parts of going away to school can be leaving the comfort of your social circle for a city and a school where you may not know anybody. Going off on your own is part of growing up, however, and many people find it to be a liberating opportunity to redefine themselves as individuals.

Moving Away Can Let You Rethink Your Life

"A big difference for me was the new establishment of myself. Coming in to school without any connections to specific people, teams, or clubs gave me the opportunity to reconstruct my 'McGill Life' exactly how I wanted it to be."

– Kady Paterson, education, McGill University

Friends are an amazing source of support, but their long memory of you can also define who you are socially and prevent you from changing. When you're surrounded by people who have known you your whole life, it can be hard to become someone other than that kid who sprayed milk out of her nose in sixth grade, or that nerdy eighth-grader who was obsessed with Pokémon, or whoever else they've defined you as being. Going off to school on your own will let you start over again in a new social context and allow you to become a new, updated version of yourself.

This doesn't mean that you have to cut all ties with your old social world. With luck, you'll be able to get the best of both worlds and maintain those old friendships while making new friends and growing socially at school.

Make it a priority to stay in touch with the people who are important to you. Make video chat dates with your old friends to replicate those face-to-face conversations you used to have. Don't neglect staying in touch with people you're not used to calling on the phone. You're not going to maintain those contacts just by running into them anymore, so your relationship will have to move over to a new medium. Siblings are often an example of this kind of relationship—you're not going to talk to your sister over breakfast cereal while you're away at school, so think about giving her a phone call.

But don't put all of your time and energy into talking to people back home. You can't expect to be happy at school when your heart is somewhere else. Keep your friendships going, but live your life where you are and take advantage of your campus's social life.

Your parents

Your leaving home might be really hard on your parents, particularly if you're the first or the last kid to leave. Your parents might start acting like weirdos. Your mom might start crying for no reason, or your dad might call

sometimes you're not ready to move on

When Susan (not her real name) moved from her small hometown to residence at the University of British Columbia in first year, she left behind her boyfriend and a tight-knit group of friends who had known each other since elementary school. She didn't know very many people at her new school and found herself lost among the thousands of students on her campus. Instead of making friends with other students in her residence, she spent her evenings hiding in her room talking on the phone to her boyfriend and mom. She was so homesick that after her first semester she transferred to a school closer to home.

But a year later she had grown up a little and felt independent enough to again attempt the transition back to Vancouver. This time she was determined to make it work, and instead of living in the past, she fully embraced her new city and kept in touch with her old friends while making new ones.

"Not everybody is ready to change their whole life for university even though that's what people expect of you when you graduate from high school. I just needed that extra time, and I don't see the need to rush things."

you eight times a day to ask you what you're doing—or he might act like he isn't going to miss you at all because he doesn't want you to worry about him.

You've probably got enough to worry about right now, and parental weirdness might lead to arguments as you define your new relationship and the new bounds of parental control. You might feel like telling them to take a long walk off a short dock (if you're into 1950s slang, that is), but try to be understanding and see things from their point of view. Give your parents the benefit of the doubt and assume that they're reacting out of stress because they love you and they'll miss you.

Then establish some rules. Boundaries are important if you and they are ever going to get used to being apart. For example, promise your mom you'll call her every week, but make her promise that she won't call you three times a day.

You may find yourself engaged in struggles for independence. Your parents may be used to having a say in every decision you make in your life, and they don't see why that should change now (especially if they're helping you pay for school), while you feel like you're an adult now and ready to make your own choices. It can be particularly difficult if your parents have decided that you're going to medical school when you want to study theatre.

Understand that they are used to protecting you and telling you what to do, and that your relationship's transition from childhood to adulthood isn't going to happen overnight. Your parents might seem unreasonable, but don't just disregard their advice. They've known you for your whole life and they've been around on this planet for a lot longer than you have, so there's a good chance they know something you don't.

Try to be honest with your parents, and discuss your issues rationally instead of leaping at every opportunity to rebel. Explain your position to your parents and ask them to clearly state their expectations. When both positions are said in words, one or all of you might realize how unreasonable you're being.

The long-distance relationship

Many students find themselves in a long-distance relationship when they go away for school because their high school love stays home or goes away to another school. Luckily, technology has made it much easier to maintain a long-distance relationship; you can text all the time, talk face-to-face on Skype, and keep in touch with social networking sites.

Even so, long-distance relationships are a lot of work and can be emotionally difficult because you seldom get to see each other. As a couple, you're going to have to learn to communicate better. It's important to establish some ground rules so each of you knows what is expected. Are you planning to be monogamous? If so, where is the line drawn? Are you allowed to hang out alone with people of the opposite sex?

Once your rules are in place, you're going to have to trust your partner. From this distance, it's impossible to watch your partner and make sure he or she is being faithful. Calling all the time to see if you can catch your beloved doing something wrong won't work, and you'll seem more like a cop than a lover. Suspicion and jealousy will make life hell and could tear your relationship apart.

By the same token, you'll have to be honest with your partner when he or she asks what you're doing, and trust that he or she won't be unreasonably jealous. Lying is no foundation for a relationship, and if your partner finds out that you've lied about what you're up to, it will make it even harder for him or her to trust you.

Set some boundaries for contacting one another. If you talk on the phone ten times a day, you're not going to have time to have a real life on your new campus, and you're going to be miserable if you think about nothing but the next time you'll be together.

Find unique ways to do nice things for each other. You can't give back rubs from this distance, but you can send letters in the mail and buy or make little presents that let your partner know you're thinking of him or her.

Your Online Social Life

In many ways, online social networking tools like Facebook, Twitter, and MSN Messenger make it easier for students to stay in contact with old friends and make new ones. You can chat with your high school best friend who's at a different university, find out about events on campus, and keep up to date on what your friends at home are up to—all from the comfort of your room.

However, as useful (and addictive) as Facebook may be, you have to be cautious about what you post online. Concerns about privacy are very real; although you may think that the photos and comments you post are for your friends' eyes only, chances are that people you never even thought of will see them, like a professor or your mom. When it comes to the Internet, it's best to assume everything you post could be read by anyone. And once a photo of you vomiting into a fish bowl is posted, it's very difficult to delete. The Internet is a bit like a tattoo; think long and hard about whether you'll still want that photo, status update, or group associated with you 5, 10, and even 20 years from now.

Photos are particularly dangerous. Ask yourself if you would want a potential employer to see that photo before you post it. Once you put pictures out there, you lose control over how they are used.

Take this example: Carole Park, an arts graduate of the University of Toronto, arrived on campus one morning to find her Facebook profile published in the student newspaper *The Gargoyle* and distributed all over the university. Carole, who was editor of a rival newspaper, had mocked *The Gargoyle*'s design in a recent issue, and this was their revenge. "It was so embarrassing. After it was published I realized I didn't want all of that info out there. I don't know why having it on paper is any different, but it is."

Even joking around online can be misunderstood. The United States Secret Service once investigated an Oklahoma student when agents discovered a comment about assassinating former president George Bush and replacing

be careful about
what you say online

Emily B., who goes to a university in New Brunswick, learned the hard way to be careful about what she posts. She was fired from her job as a bartender because of an exchange of wall posts with a co-worker. The two students joked about another co-worker's boyfriend, who regularly took alcohol from behind the bar. "I didn't think anything of it. But apparently the manager checks it quite a bit and reads a lot of conversations."

him with a monkey. And two students from Louisiana State University lost their sports scholarships when they badmouthed their coach online.

4.4   Diversity on Campus

Your high school was probably attended by students from only a small part of the city or town you're from. Your post-secondary school is going to be full of people from all over the province, the country, and possibly the world.

Depending on your background, you may never before have met people like the ones you're sharing a campus with. You might run into such exotic specimens as out-of-the-closet gays, Dutch exchange students, Sikhs in turbans, and farm kids from the Prairies. You might encounter some of the loudest, most self-assured Christians, atheists, Jews, and Zoroastrians you've ever met. You might find some people's customs and values strange; some of them might not even know the rules of hockey (or if you're not a hockey fan, some of them might never shut up about hockey).

If you keep an open mind, you'll find that the diversity that surrounds you will become part of your education. Understanding the way other people view the world can help you better understand your own worldview. Learning about other cultures and backgrounds is fascinating, and being able to connect and work with different people is a valuable skill in a globalized world, especially in a country as ethnically and culturally diverse as ours.

And if you're part of a minority group, now is your time to shine. While you may have felt out of place in high school, in your college or university you'll meet others who share or understand your experiences, you'll be free to openly be yourself, and you'll have access to organizations and services designed especially with you in mind. But even at a place as enlightened as a university, you might occasionally meet closed-minded people who don't treat you as you ought to be treated. Luckily, your school has resources and services to ensure a tolerant and fair environment.

While this section focuses on services for only a few groups of students, you should be aware that clubs, financial assistance, and service centres are available at most schools for female students, mature students, students with children, and many other groups.

In this section:

- Find out how universities support **Students with Disabilities**.

- Learn about **Ethnic Diversity** on campus.

- A brief word regarding **Sexual Orientation**.

- What to do if you experience **Discrimination and Harassment**.

Students with Disabilities

School administrators and the government have long recognized that it is important to accommodate students with disabilities, from providing accessible buildings for students in wheelchairs to offering academic assistance to people with learning disabilities.

Every post-secondary institution has a department that co-ordinates programs to help students overcome disability-related challenges. These range from providing alternative course resources (for instance, Braille or audio-book-format textbooks for blind students) to making special arrangements for students to take exams.

The first step to ensuring that you will have the support you need is to register with this department. Even if your disability is a minor one, it helps to touch base with a counsellor at the beginning of your education so you can readily access services if you need help later. You may need a doctor's letter or other documentation to register; your registration will be kept confidential.

Once you have registered, there are many services available to you. Depending on your disability, you might be able to get special tutoring or arrange to take a class in an alternative format that is better suited to you. For instance, some schools offer captioning of lectures to deaf students. If you are unable to take notes in class because of an injury or disability, you can request a note taker to accompany you to class. In some cases, students with disabilities can get deadlines extended so they can take a few extra weeks to complete assignments and papers. If you are unable to take a full course load, you can apply to retain full-time status with fewer classes.

Technology has made studying much easier for students with some disabilities. Voice-recognition software allows students who are unable to easily use computers to type papers, send emails, and surf the net. Other programs can convert written text into audio and can map out ideas visually. Most schools have the latest technologies, and many have special computer labs designed for people who struggle with using standard computers.

Exam period can be even more daunting for students with disabilities than it is for other students. Perhaps you have difficulty concentrating for a three-hour exam because of an attention-deficit disorder, or a physical disability prevents you from writing quickly enough to tackle an essay question. Your professor and your institution want to provide you with an environment that will give you the best opportunity to demonstrate that you understand the course material, so consult a counsellor about what accommodations can be made. Depending on your situation, the school may allow you to take extra time to complete the exam, bring a computer to help you write, or take the exam alone in a room where you won't be distracted by other students.

Of course, academics are only one part of the post-secondary experience, and students with disabilities may need additional assistance outside the classroom. Many schools have special residences for students with physical disabilities, or offer help finding appropriate on- and off-campus housing. Disability departments can also assist with arranging transportation.

Many schools and provinces offer awards, grants, and bursaries to help students with disabilities pay for school. The federal government provides additional grants and special student-loan provisions for disabled students. (See **Section 5.2: Scholarships, Bursaries, and Government Grants**, and **Section 5.3: Borrowing Money** for more information.)

disabled students
can enjoy everything
university has to offer

Dan Pagan, an arts student at the University of Calgary, has been deaf since birth. While Dan can lip-read and speak a little, he mostly uses sign language and interpreters in class lectures and tutorials. It's difficult to watch interpreters translate what the professor is saying and take notes at the same time, so he has volunteer note takers to help him.

Dan says that, unlike in high school, university students are understanding and accepting of his deafness. Living in residence helped him make lots of friends, and he's involved in many extracurricular activities, including the student newspaper, students' union, and a wide range of clubs. Dan says acknowledging your limits, asking questions constantly, taking risks, and getting involved can help any student, especially those with disabilities, have a rewarding and successful university experience.

Universities and colleges are excellent places to advocate for disability issues. Most schools have a disability-focused committee or club, organized either by the students' union or as part of the institution's structure. For instance, the University of British Columbia has a network of disability liaisons who are appointed by each academic department to inform the university about issues and challenges facing the disabled community. These groups engage in activities like organizing awareness campaigns and carrying out accessibility audits. They may advocate for more disability-friendly policy or organize volunteers to provide peer support and tutoring to disabled students. Check your school's website to get involved.

Ethnic Diversity

University and college campuses are supposed to be havens of tolerance and diversity (we'll get back to that tricky *supposed* part later in this section). On most campuses, you'll find a wide variety of related student clubs and service organizations. The University of Manitoba, for example, has student groups for Aboriginals, Bangladeshis, Germans, Indonesians, Icelanders, Afghanis, Iranians, Filipinos, Ukrainians, and Zambians, among many others.

There is also a variety of religious clubs, including Jewish, Muslim, Sikh, and Baha'i groups, as well as several Christian groups.

These clubs and groups are a great way to meet other people with similar backgrounds or experiences as you. They also add to the richness of the university environment by organizing cultural events where students of all backgrounds can learn about and enjoy different cultures.

Some clubs are also focused on activism or advocacy, and you may be interested in getting involved. Activities range from documentary screenings detailing issues of importance to their ethnicity to protests intended to draw attention to conflicts in their home country.

There are also many programs and services designed to help international students succeed. These range from peer tutoring programs, where students can meet with other students to improve their English, to assistance in arranging housing, finances, or other things that may be difficult for those unaccustomed to how Canadian systems work.

Sexual Orientation

For many gay, lesbian, bisexual, and transgendered students, university symbolizes liberation. No longer do they have to cope with the bigoted prejudices of some people in their small hometown. They are suddenly surrounded by hundreds of students who are openly gay, and because campuses are so tolerant they feel free to be themselves.

Unfortunately, this isn't to say you won't encounter any discrimination—as long as prejudice is found in society, it will be found on campuses. If you're in need of support and community, most universities and colleges have clubs for gay, lesbian, bisexual, and transgendered students, where they can

No One Really Cares Who You Date

"Dating and romance in general are a lot easier for queer university students than in high school. You're mostly away from your parents, so there isn't as much policing, and my experience has been that no one really cares if you have a boyfriend or girlfriend. If your peer group shuns you for being gay or bi, it's so easy to find people who support you for who you are."

– Sandra Duffey, social work, McMaster University

meet other gay students and enjoy a safe space free of discrimination. These clubs also often engage in advocacy and education.

All institutions have policy in place that prohibits harassment or discrimination on the basis of gender or sexual orientation, and most schools have educational campaigns and training programs set up to encourage a fair and equitable learning environment.

Discrimination and Harassment

One of the by-products of studying in a place where freedom of speech and intellectual exploration are cherished and activism is encouraged is that occasionally people are going to say and do things that offend and upset you. Sometimes these incidents must be tolerated. After all, you are expecting people to tolerate your perspectives, so you have to do the same as long as their opinions—however distasteful—are being expressed respectfully.

For instance, Jewish students with family in Israel might have to tolerate the presence of pro-Palestinian protesters on campus, no matter how unsettling they find the protests. An encounter like this doesn't have to be an entirely negative experience; you might be able to learn something about your opponents' perspective if you engage them in a respectful argument.

Your Sexuality Doesn't Need to Define You

"You are going to see a huge spectrum of homosexual personalities when you go to university. If the conversation came up, I would rarely hide my sexuality, but after seeing how accepting everyone was and how the vast majority simply did not care, I went back to allowing my studies or extracurriculars define me instead. Being a member of a varsity sports team, I was encouraged to be open and honest with my team members, who never once acted differently around me. Even the more conservative students I met never once took issue with it."

— Brian (not his real name), business, Queen's University

Of course, there is a limit to what should be tolerated, and the moment that intelligent discourse deteriorates into threats or hate speech, you should not be expected to simply grit your teeth and walk away. If you believe that campaign material or speakers on campus are stepping over the boundary into harassment or hate speech, or if you feel unsafe, you need to act.

Every school has employees whose job it is to prevent discrimination and harassment. Look up the office responsible for dealing with discrimination at your school on the web or schedule an appointment with a counsellor to discuss your concerns. If the incident is more serious and requires immediate attention—for example, if you witness an assault or targeted vandalism—go directly to the police for help.

Not all discrimination and harassment is as overt as a racist speaker at a protest. It's possible to experience systematic discrimination from professors, TAs, school administrators, and other people in positions of authority. If you feel like you are being treated unfairly because of your ethnicity, gender, sexual orientation, or disability, consult your school's discrimination office or a counsellor.

4.5   Going Abroad

This is a great time to go overseas. You're in the process of enlightening yourself, and what better way to learn about the world than to go out and actually see it? There are things you will discover on the road that you can never learn in a classroom.

Travelling abroad will put you in a lot of situations you'd never find yourself in at home, and the experience will teach you a lot about yourself. You'll also return home with new ideas about Canada, because experiencing a foreign land will help you see your home country in a new light.

You're probably broke, and you're going to need to spend some money to go to another continent. But there are ways of doing it on the cheap or getting your trip subsidized. You may think that it'll be a better time to travel after you've graduated, when you've got more money, but for a lot of people there are bigger barriers to travelling after graduation. It can be difficult to arrange for time off work and to get out of things like mortgages, car loans, and marriages.

So it's settled: if you have a burning desire to spend time abroad, now's the time. Well, maybe not *now*—it's going to take you a few months to plan and save money for your trip—but soon.

There are a lot of different ways for a student to blow this popsicle stand we call Canada. You can go overseas and study, volunteer, work, travel, or all of the above. And if you can't muster the cash or the courage to go to another country, there are plenty of places to travel inside this enormous country of ours, and there are government programs that can help you subsidize your trip.

In this section:

- Continue your education in another country by **Studying Abroad**.

- Give a little something back to the world by **Volunteering**.

- Develop work skills and build your resumé with **International Internships**.

- Earn some dough while you're on your trip by **Working Abroad**.

- Learn about organizations that can help you **Travel in Canada**.

- Have the time of your life travelling on the cheap by **Backpacking**.

Studying Abroad

If you don't want to delay your graduation by taking time off for travel, studying at a school in a foreign country might be the best option for you. You can study abroad for a semester or a whole year, or you can find spring or summer courses that might take as little as a month to complete.

While you won't have as much time to get around as you would if you spent the time backpacking, going to school and living in a foreign country will give you a much deeper understanding of a place than just breezing through as a tourist. You'll have the opportunity to learn the language and to make friends with locals and other international students.

Studying abroad can also be an opportunity to improve your education. Overseas universities will offer courses that aren't available at home, and the country you study in can afford educational opportunities you'd never have in Canada—for example, studying Spanish among native speakers in Madrid or studying archaeology surrounded by pyramids in Cairo.

The easiest way to be sure that the courses you take overseas will be credited toward your degree is to go through an exchange program. Exchange programs can save you money, too; through an exchange, you'll pay the same tuition you would pay at your home university rather than expensive foreign-student fees. Most public Canadian universities have exchange agreements with dozens of universities around the world, and if the school you really want to attend isn't on your school's list, a counsellor may be able to work something out specifically for you. Even if a formal exchange program is not an option, it may still be possible to get credit for classes taken at foreign institutions, although it's a little more complicated to arrange and it can be more expensive.

Volunteering

Volunteering in a developing country can be one of the most rewarding experiences you'll have in your life. Working within a community will allow you to forge deep connections with a country, and your experience will look great on a resumé, particularly if it's related to your field of study, such as medicine, engineering, teaching, or social work.

Frustratingly, it can be quite difficult to find an overseas volunteer posting that won't cost you a lot of money. It turns out that it's expensive to give your time away. It can cost a charity thousands of dollars to maintain a volunteer overseas. For it to be worthwhile for them to spend that money, the volunteer they're paying for has to be a motivated and highly trained individual who has committed to a year or more in the posting.

Some organizations offer short-term postings to less-qualified applicants, but they charge a fair pile of money for the opportunity. For example, we found a one-month posting doing orphanage work in Ethiopia that costs $2,900, and a three-month stint teaching English in Ghana for $3,900—and those prices don't include airfare.

Some schools offer volunteer postings through their co-op or international service learning programs. Your institution may also help with fundraising, or even provide grants to help cover the cost.

International Internships

International internships offer on-the-job training and an experience that looks great on a resumé. Internships don't pay much money, but they do

study or volunteer?

When Kali Penny, a Simon Fraser University health sciences student, was trying to spruce up her medical-school application, she was faced with the choice of taking extra courses to boost her GPA or getting some international experience. After careful consideration, she chose to volunteer in her field in India for a semester—and she never regretted the decision. "I would recommend going overseas. You'll do so many things you'd never get to do here and meet people you'd never get to meet."

usually provide accommodation and a living allowance to help cover the cost of living overseas.

The two main organizations offering internships to English-speaking Canadian students are IAESTE (the International Association for the Exchange of Students for Technical Experience), for engineering, science, and other technical students, and AIESEC (Association Internationale des Étudiants en Sciences Économiques et Commerciales), which offers internships focused on management, IT, engineering, social development, and education. Both organizations connect students to companies abroad and facilitate the process of going overseas.

Working Abroad

Getting a job in a foreign country can allow you to live overseas without having to go into debt to do it, but unfortunately, it isn't legal to get a job just anywhere you like. If you're eligible for a foreign passport, then you're one step ahead of everyone else. If not, then you'll be happy to know that it's surprisingly easy for young Canadians to get work visas in many countries.

Canada has reciprocal working-holiday agreements with 21 different countries. The terms of the agreements vary from country to country, but generally they allow Canadians under 31 to apply for one-year work visas, subject to various restrictions.

Getting a visa doesn't guarantee you a job, of course, but it does allow you to work legally. Unless you have work skills that transfer easily to a foreign country (for example, hairdressers do very well), you'll likely be working in the service industry or as unskilled labour.

Working in the service industry overseas won't necessarily be an experience that will greatly improve your resumé, although it won't hurt; some employers like to see that applicants have shown self-reliance and have done something interesting. It will, however, allow you to earn enough money to hang out in, say, Sydney for a year and see a corner of Australia while you're at it.

If you're a bit leery of getting on a plane for a foreign country with nothing more than a work visa and a backpack full of clothes, the Canadian Federation of Students runs a program called the Student Work Abroad Program, or SWAP. SWAP helps students with the visa application process and offers various kinds of support before departure, on arrival, and during your stay overseas.

Another popular option for working abroad is teaching English. Native English-speaking teachers are in demand by schools all over the world. The pay varies greatly, depending on the country. Jobs in less-developed countries and in places that have an easy time attracting teachers because they're tropical paradises (such as Thailand) tend not to pay much. However, students have been known to earn enough money to pay off their student loans by teaching in countries such as South Korea or Japan.

Private schools across Canada offer English-teaching certification, which is required for some overseas teaching positions, and will give you an advantage over non-certified applicants. These schools also help their graduates find jobs and provide access to online job databases.

the benefits
of travel

For Beth Gallagher, a Simon Fraser University biology student, volunteering overseas was about much more than just learning about Africa. She spent three months during the summer teaching English, biology, and physical sciences to Grade 9 students in a refugee camp in Malawi as part of a World University Service of Canada program. She learned how to deal with language barriers, differing work styles and paces, and a lack of resources. "I've never had to improvise so much in my life. I had to figure out how to do science experiments without test tubes."

Travel in Canada

Going to another province isn't exactly going "abroad," but it still counts as leaving home. We live in an enormous country with two official languages, innumerable cultures and subcultures, and incredibly diverse geography. There is a lot of this world to see within our borders, and there are programs that can help you see it while continuing your education and building your resumé without spending a lot of money.

Katimavik is a federally funded volunteer service organization that offers six-month programs to Canadian citizens aged 17 to 21. During your six-month stint, you'll live and volunteer in two different communities across Canada and get work experience while you learn about interpersonal relations, living a healthy lifestyle, environmental stewardship, and our country's official languages.

Katimavik charges a relatively modest participation fee, and they cover the cost of transportation, housing, and food. Your six months of volunteering will teach you new skills, connect you to communities in other parts of your country, and introduce you to fellow citizens your own age from across Canada.

Explore is another federally funded program that can help you see your own country on the cheap while teaching you something. Explore provides bursaries to pay for students to take five-week intensive French- or English-language courses at educational institutions across Canada, many of which provide university credit for having completed the course.

So you get a trip and a free French course—What's the catch? you ask. There isn't a catch. The government just wants anglophones to speak French and francophones to speak English, and they're willing to pay for you to learn.

Backpacking

Backpacking is just like being a tourist, only with less money. Everywhere you go in the world, you'll find budget travellers hefting dusty backpacks and haggling over the price of cheap hotel rooms. You could be one of them.

Backpacking probably isn't going to help you achieve any of your career objectives, but it is a remarkably effective way to have fun, and you can cover a lot of ground with not a lot of money.

be a global citizen—
closer to home

I n our globalized world and our culturally diverse country, being globally aware and able to understand and work with people from different cultural backgrounds is a valuable attribute in any field.

Travel is the most obvious way to gain this perspective. Not only will travel experience show a potential employer that you have knowledge of a different part of the world, but it will show that you are willing to put yourself in potentially uncomfortable situations and are able to problem-solve your way through language and cultural barriers.

You don't necessarily need to pack your suitcase to gain the benefits of being exposed to a different culture, however. Seek out opportunities to participate or volunteer with community or campus groups. This could be as simple as offering to help tutor international students at your school or volunteering at a community program for new immigrants. You'll probably make some new friends as well.

The classic student travel destination of Europe has gotten a lot more expensive in recent years. Back in the 70s they used to write guidebooks on how to do Europe on $5 a day; these days you'd starve to death if you tried to do it on $50. But regions such as Southeast Asia and Central America are still incredibly cheap and stunningly beautiful places to travel.

The best place to get started with planning your backpacking trip is a good guidebook. Popular choices among budget travellers include the Lonely Planet, Rough Guides, Footprint, and Let's Go. If you're anything like us, just looking at the list of titles Lonely Planet offers will be enough to get you excited about travelling. They've got a book on Papua New Guinea and the Solomon Islands! Who knew it was possible to travel independently to Papua New Guinea?

Backpacking and the other options listed in this section are not mutually exclusive. In fact, whatever you're doing overseas, you should consider taking an extra month before or after your program to put on a backpack and take a jaunt around the place. You'll be surprised at what you can find in this world if you look hard enough.

Finance

POST-SECONDARY EDUCATION is expensive, but it's worth it.

The average university student spends more than $20,000 on tuition alone during a typical four-year undergraduate education. When books and living expenses are added to the tally, the average cost of a degree climbs to nearly $65,000. Colleges tend to charge less for tuition and typically offer shorter programs, but going to college is still a considerable financial decision.

The good news is that in the long run, getting an education makes financial sense. According to recent numbers from Statistics Canada, high school graduates with full-time jobs make an average of $36,000 annually, while college graduates average $41,000, and university grads make $61,000. It doesn't take an economics degree to tell that over a lifetime of employment, you get a pretty good return on your educational investment.

Unfortunately, the return-on-investment part doesn't come until later; right now, you've got to figure out how to pay for school. Unless you're lucky enough to have parents who can afford to pay for your entire education, you'll probably have to piece together your financing from a number of sources.

Half a million new Canadian students figure out how to fund their education every year, most of whom have to pay for at least part of their education themselves. In this chapter, we'll explain how to do it, starting with estimating what your education will cost, and then by seeking out funding, first from sources that won't ask you to pay the money back, like scholarships and grants, and from repayable loans from governments and banks. We'll discuss the role that jobs will play in funding your education, and we'll wrap up the chapter with tips on budgeting and keeping your expenses as low as possible.

It might seem overwhelming now, but you'll figure out how to pay for your education—starting by adding up what it is going to cost.

In this chapter:

- Add up what you'll spend and learn about **Costs and Budgeting**.

- Start your search for funding with free money from **Scholarships, Bursaries, and Government Grants**.

- Round out your funding by **Borrowing Money** from the government and banks.

- Earn extra cash by landing part-time and summer **Jobs**.

- Control your expenses with tips on **Sticking to Your Budget**.

5.1 Costs and Budgeting ✓

Before you start looking for ways to fund your education, you should figure out how much money you'll actually need. How much it will cost you will depend on where you go to school and the cost of your program.

For most students, it's important to try to keep costs as low as possible. You're going to try to get as much money as possible from scholarships and grants, but chances are good that you won't get enough of this non-repayable money to fund your whole education. Most students have to borrow the difference, so keeping your expenses down will have a huge impact on the size of the loan you'll have to repay when you graduate.

This means that you'll have to balance your educational and lifestyle goals with your budgetary concerns. For example, living at home for your first year of school instead of moving into residence could save you from having to take out $8,000 in bank loans, which, at an interest rate of 6%, will also save you about $3,000 in interest charges over the course of a four-year degree.

In this section:

- Figure out your core education expenses by adding up your **School and Textbook Costs**.

- Explore the different **Living Expenses** associated with various living arrangements.

- See how students in different situations spend money by examining **Two Sample Student Budgets**.

School and Textbook Costs

Tuition and other school fees are the easiest part of your budget to predict. Below you'll learn about what expenses you can expect and how much the average Canadian students pays. But you should check with your educational institution to find out exactly how much tuition costs and whether you'll be charged extra fees. Textbook costs are a little more variable, as they depend on what books each of your courses is using, but your school can provide you with an estimate you can work with.

Tuition

In 2010–11, the average annual tuition paid by undergraduate students was $5,138. Tuition costs can vary for a number of reasons. Some programs of study, such as engineering or nursing, cost more. Tuition also varies between provinces. Undergrad students in Ontario pay the highest tuition in the country with an average of $6,307 while students who are Quebec residents only pay $2,415 on average.

If you are not a Canadian citizen or permanent resident, you will pay considerably more. Average international student fees in 2009–10 were $16,768.

The per-semester tuition estimates published on your university's website are based on a full-time schedule. However, tuition is almost always charged per class or per credit (exception: the University of Toronto charges undergraduate students a flat rate), so your budget should take into consideration how many classes you are planning to take.

Compulsory fees

Many students make the mistake of thinking that their university expenses end at tuition fees. However, students pay $702 on average in mandatory extra fees each year. This amount typically includes fees for your school's athletic centre, student association, student newspaper, building improvements, and more.

Books and supplies

On average, students spend $872 on books and $120 on supplies per year, but the amount you spend will depend on what program you're enrolled in, as some courses require more expensive books and supplies. For example, science, engineering, and programs like graphic design typically require more expensive textbooks than other classes.

Some courses require that you have special supplies or equipment. Cooking school may require you to buy your own knives and your own chef's uniform. You'll need an instrument for music school.

Whatever your program of study, you'll probably need to have access to a computer. Your school will have computer labs you can use, but it's a lot easier and more convenient to work in the privacy of your home or dorm room, so you'll probably want to get your own. Before you run out and buy an expensive, brand-new computer, ask yourself what you need it for and whether you really need to spend that much money. It doesn't take a whole lot of processing power to run word-processing software or a web browser.

Medical and dental plans

Most universities and colleges offer medical and dental plans for undergraduate students, usually administered by the student association. If you're not otherwise covered, it's great to have these plans because they can save your year's budget from being destroyed by a dental emergency. If you are already covered by your parents' medical plans, some schools allow you to opt out and refund you the cost.

Dissecting Your Tuition Payments

Below is a summary of the tuition and other fees paid by a fourth-year science student taking four classes per semester at the University of British Columbia for one academic year. As happens at all universities and colleges, UBC students are charged considerable costs in addition to tuition, for things such as athletic and transit fees. So be careful to account for these extras when budgeting for the year.

TUITION DETAILS FOR 2009 WINTER

Term 1 Assessments		Term 2 Assessments	
Description	Amount	Description	Amount
BIOL 408 001	$ 442.95	BIOL 408 001	$ 442.95
MATH 405 101	$ 442.95	CONS 440 101	$ 442.95
ISCI 300 001	$ 73.83	ISCI 300 001	$ 73.83
FRST 415 201	$ 442.95	MATH 345 201	$ 442.95
Athletics and Recreation Fee	$ 189.66	Upass	$ 95.00
AMS Fee	$ 35.00	Total	$1,497.68
Athletics and Intramurals	$ 21.00		
Med/Dent Fee	$ 216.31		
Sexual Assault Fund	$ 3.00		
Science Undergrad Society Fee	$ 22.37		
AMS Student Services Fee	$ 9.00		
Student Aid Bursary Fund	$ 1.00		
SUB Renewal Fee	$ 30.00		
Ubyssey Publication Fee	$ 5.00		
Upass	$ 95.00		
Total	$2,042.02		

Due Date	Description	Assessed	Paid	Balance
October 9, 2009	September Instalment	$2,042.02	$2,042.02	$0.00
February 7, 2010	January Instalment	$1,497.68	$1,497.68	$0.00

In this case, our UBC student paid a total of $3,539.70 for two semesters of classes, of which $2,805.36 was tuition and $734.34 was extra fees. These fees included levies for various students' union (called the Alma Mater Society or AMS at UBC) services, the campus newspaper (called the *Ubyssey*), an upgrade to the student union building, the medical and dental insurance plan, and a transit pass (labelled Upass).

As you can see, our student was required to pay in two instalments, one in October and one in February. Payment deadlines vary greatly, and it's important to check with your school, as some universities require full payment for the entire academic year up front. At many schools missing a payment can result in being deregistered from classes.

Save Big on Textbooks

Textbooks can be extremely expensive, but there are a few tricks you can use to cut down on your textbook expenses.

- Go used: Buy used textbooks from the campus bookstore or from other students. Sure, they may come with a stain or someone else's highlighting, but they'll be way cheaper.

- Check the library: If you don't need the textbook throughout the entire course, consider checking it out from the library when you need it. Other people in your class may think of this, so grab a copy early.

- Search online: Google your required textbooks and see if you can find them for cheaper than the campus bookstore price. Be sure to order early, giving yourself time for the books to arrive, and be aware that shipping and handling charges may apply.

- Share: If the course doesn't require constant reading from the textbook, try splitting the cost and sharing the text with a friend who's taking the same course.

- Look for an older edition: Depending on the course, you may be able to get away with using an older edition of the text, which will typically cost way less than the most recent version. Beware of major changes between editions, however, such as missing chapters.

- Borrow: If you have a friend who's already taken the same course and still has the textbook, ask if you can borrow it. Don't forget to return the favour if someone asks you to lend a book in the future.

- Rent: Some schools have a textbook-lending system, where you rent your textbook from the campus bookstore at a reduced price, and when the term is over, you return the book.

- Sell back: Don't forget to sell back your textbook if you know you won't need them again. Most campus bookstores have buy-back days at the end of the term. You won't get back the same amount you paid, but it's certainly better than nothing.

Living Expenses

Living expenses vary according to your living arrangement. You might not have a choice about where you'll live while you're in school, or you may have considerations that are more important to you than your finances, but you should give some thought to what the different living arrangements cost.

Living at home

There are plenty of reasons some people don't want to live at home with their parents, but the financial reasons are all in favour. Depending on your arrangement with your parents, living at home could get you free rent, free laundry, and free meals, plus you'll defer all the costs that come with setting up your own house, like buying furniture.

Living in residence

Again, there are plenty of good reasons for living in residence, but this option is relatively expensive. Costs vary widely, depending on the university, the residence, the room type, and the meal plan you choose. Here are some examples of prices for various styles of rooms at different universities for an eight-month, two-semester school year starting in September 2010:

- Single dorm room with a medium meal plan at the University of Victoria: $7,696.
- Furnished room in six-room apartment-style residence with kitchen and no meal plan at the University of Saskatchewan: $3,075.
- Cheapest double (shared) room plus cheapest meal plan at Dalhousie University: $8,210.

Living off-campus

It's difficult to generalize about off-campus living expenses, because rent and other expenses vary greatly from city to city. However, you should expect to pay a minimum of $400 per month to share a two-bedroom apartment in a not-so-fancy building. Your rent may or may not include utilities, such as electricity or gas, and it probably doesn't include cable TV or Internet. Be sure to ask your landlord about these expenses and add them to your budget if necessary.

Other expenses that need to be budgeted for include the one-time costs of setting up an apartment. You might be able to bring your bed from home, but you probably don't have a kitchen table, a couch, or pots and pans, cutlery, and dishes. Even if you get them second-hand, they all add up. Also, don't forget that you will be required to pay a damage deposit and possibly first and last months' rent when you rent the apartment, depending on which province you live in. (See **Section 2.2: Renting Off-Campus** for more details.)

Groceries

If you have a meal plan with your residence, this cost will be limited to snacks, but if you live off-campus, it will be quite a bit more. Canlearn.ca—the government website about funding your education—estimates you should budget $300 per month or $2,400 for a September to April school year. It depends a lot on your appetite, your eating habits, your discipline, and your cooking skills, but some students may need to budget more than this amount. (For tips on cooking cheap meals, see **Section 6.6: Eating Well and Being Active**.)

Transportation

Some schools offer cheap transit passes that you pay for along with your tuition. In the example in the "Dissecting Your Tuition Payments" box, the student's University of British Columbia tuition includes something called Upass, which is an all-zone transit pass for Metro Vancouver for the low price of $95 per semester (about one-sixth the normal price).

If your school has a deal like this, then you don't need to budget for any additional transportation costs. Otherwise, you should count on paying around $65 per month for transit passes, although this varies from city to city.

> ### Be Realistic About Your Expenses
>
> "Here's the big problem when people are creating budgets: they say, 'Oh, I'm not going to spend money on cigarettes. I'm not going to go out.' By the second week they say, 'I can't live like this,' and they blow their budget."
>
> – Elena Jara, education counsellor, Credit Canada

If you have a car, add up your monthly insurance and lease payments, and estimate the cost of oil changes, parking, and gasoline for how much you think you'll be driving. Include a small reserve fund for incidental expenses and minor repairs. If you're on a tight budget, you might find it a better idea to sell the car or cancel the insurance on it and leave it parked at home.

Clothing, toiletries, and other essentials

It's easy to forget to budget for all of the little odds and ends that keep you clothed, clean, and smelling nice. If you have expensive tastes in clothing, it can add up to a lot.

Canlearn.ca suggests that students who live in residence during the 2010–11 academic year will spend an average of $2,184 per year on these personal items. Students who live off-campus and have to pay for house-cleaning supplies, laundry, and so forth should budget $3,064.

Other monthly expenses

Do you have other monthly expenses, like your cellphone bill? Are you a member of the cheese-of-the-month club? Include these expenses in your budget, or prepare to go without your cellphone or monthly cheese.

your
rainy day fund

Make sure you keep a little extra money set aside for emergencies—no, this isn't for when you're feeling a little bummed out and you feel like buying a new sweater. This money is for when your computer breaks or when you get stuck having to take a taxi home when the bus is no longer running.

Pocket money

Don't assume that when you start university, you're going to turn into a paragon of financial responsibility and never spend money on going out. If you fail to budget for spending money, you'll end up robbing your grocery budget so you can afford to go for a beer. Instead, budget for a reasonable amount of discretionary spending in the neighbourhood of $100 per month.

Two Sample Student Budgets

Below are budgets for two fictitious students. Charles and Katy each have budgets of around $20,000 for their eight-month school year, but because of differences in their schools, their programs, and their lifestyles, they spend their money in very different ways. (Read Section 5.5: Sticking to Your Budget to find out how Charles and Katy piece together their education funding.)

Charles Brown is an 18-year-old who plans to pursue a four-year bachelor of arts degree at the University of Western Ontario starting in September 2010. He will live in residence with a roommate and participate in the campus meal plan.

Katy Green is a 21-year-old third-year nursing student at the University of Alberta. She lives in an off-campus apartment with roommates, cooks her own meals, and loves the Edmonton transit pass included in her tuition.

EDUCATION COSTS		EDUCATION COSTS	
Tuition	$ 4,937.00	Tuition	$ 6,902.00
Compulsory extra fees	$ 937.00	Compulsory extra fees	$ 814.00
Medical and dental	$ 174.00	Medical and dental	$ 438.00
Books	$ 871.00	Books	$ 871.00
Supplies	$ 120.00	Supplies	$ 120.00
TOTAL EDUCATION COSTS	$ 7,039.00	TOTAL EDUCATION COSTS	$ 9,145.00

LIVING COSTS		LIVING COSTS	
Room charge (includes laundry)	$ 5,130.00	Rent	$ 3,600.00
7-day meal plan	$ 3,640.00	Groceries	$ 3,200.00
Phone	$ 320.00	Phone	$ 320.00
Clothing, necessities, extras	$ 2,184.00	Clothing, necessities, extras	$ 3,064.00
Spending money	$ 800.00	Spending money	$ 800.00
Public transport	$ 828.00	Public transport (Upass)	$ 183.00
TOTAL LIVING COSTS	$ 12,902.00	TOTAL LIVING COSTS	$ 11,167.00
TOTAL ANNUAL EXPENSES	$ 19,941.00	TOTAL ANNUAL EXPENSES	$ 20,312.00

5.2 Scholarships, Bursaries, and Government Grants ✓

The very best way to fund your education is with money that you don't have to pay back. There are four main sources of this free money: government grants, awards offered to high school graduates, scholarships and bursaries awarded through your university or college, and awards given by private sources.

Generally speaking, scholarships are awarded on the basis of achievement (academic, athletic, or other) and bursaries are awarded on the basis of financial need, to help students who might otherwise not be able to afford to go to school. Bursaries awarded by governments are usually called grants.

The good news is that there are a lot of potential sources of financial support. For starters, any student who receives student loans is automatically eligible for grants from the government. There are also over 60,000 scholarships and bursaries available to students in Canada.

The bad news is that each award has its own eligibility requirements, and most of them need to be applied for separately. There are so many scholarships available from so many different sources that some of them are never even applied for. If you do your research, stay organized, and diligently apply for awards, some of this free money will end up belonging to you.

In this section:

- Learn to take advantage of **Government Grants**.

- Find out how to qualify for **Awards from Your High School**.

- There are as many **Awards from Your University or College** as courses offered.

- Research **Private Sources**, who offer scholarships for all kinds of reasons.

- Once you've tracked them down, it's time to start **Applying for Scholarships and Bursaries**.

Government Grants

Grants from the federal government

Depending on your province or territory, you may be awarded thousands of dollars in non-repayable grants just for applying for a student loan. Residents from Yukon Territory and every province except Quebec may be eligible for the Canada Student Grants Program. (Quebec, the Northwest Territories, and Nunavut have their own student-aid programs and don't participate in the Canada Student Grants Program.) When you apply for a Canada Student Loan, you are automatically applying for these grants.

There are three main categories of grants in this program: grants for people from low- or middle-income families, grants for students with children, and grants for disabled people.

Eligibility for grants from the first category depends entirely on your family income. If you've been out of high school for less than four years, you're generally considered a dependent student (with some exceptions), which means that your family income includes your parents' income. If you're classified as an independent student, then the assessment is based on your income alone, which makes it much easier to qualify.

Income levels for eligibility depend on the cost of living in your province and the number of people in your family. There is a province-by-province chart on canlearn.ca that will help you figure out if you're in the low- or middle-income categories.

Low-income students who are going to school full-time receive $250 per month of study ($2,000 for an eight-month school year); middle-income students get $100 per month of study. Low-income students who are going to school part-time are also eligible to receive $100 per month.

Parents with dependant children are eligible for an additional $200 per month per kid. Students with permanent disabilities are eligible for another $250 per month, plus up to $8,000 for any special equipment or services they might need to go to school.

Grants and awards from provincial and territorial governments

The financial aid offered by the provincial level of government varies widely from province to province. Some provinces offer only a few awards to help specific groups of students, while others give awards to almost everyone from the province. Some provinces focus exclusively on needs-based grants, while others offer significant merit-based scholarship programs. For instance, British Columbia automatically awards a scholarship to every high school graduate who scores 86% or higher on three of their provincial exams and earns at least a B in English.

Some grants are awarded automatically, but many are given only to students who specifically apply for them, so you should research the grants that are available both in your home province and the province you plan to study in.

In general, most provinces focus their funding on grants for students who have greater difficulty accessing post-secondary education. People with disabilities (including learning disabilities), single parents, Aboriginal students, and people from rural or northern communities are eligible for additional grants in some provinces. Ontario in particular has a wide range of grants targeted at specific groups of students, including those who are part of the first generation of their family to attend post-secondary education.

Some provinces also have grants to reduce the debt that students owe, either during or after their education. Every year Manitoba awards bursaries that reduce the balance of some students' Manitoba student loans. Other provinces, including New Brunswick and Prince Edward Island, have similar programs.

Having opted out of the Canada Student Grants Program, Quebec has its own comprehensive grant program, focused on low-income students and students with disabilities who cannot get enough money in student loans to cover the costs of going to school.

Yukon, the Northwest Territories, and Nunavut offer generous grant programs, including extra funding to pay for transportation to and from schools in the south. All three territories focus their funds on students who attended high school in the territory, and Nunavut and the Northwest Territories have grants for Aboriginal students.

Even if you can't think of a reason why they might give you a grant, take a moment to check your province's student-aid website.

Awards from Your High School

At some high schools, all students are automatically considered for scholarships or bursaries when they graduate, but it pays to ask. Your guidance

brainstorming your unique qualifications

The best place to start your scholarship and bursary search is to make a list of your attributes, activities, and achievements that might qualify you for awards. Being an exceptional student helps a lot, obviously, but there are many other areas of achievement that can help you win financial awards. Write down all of your volunteer experiences, hobbies, interests, athletics, music and theatre activities, leadership experiences, and anything else you can think of. Ask yourself what you are proud of having accomplished. Did you win a service award from your high school for helping out? Did you found a high school newspaper? Did you perform at a dance festival? Any of these types of activities may help you win awards.

Many awards are available to students on the basis of what groups they or their family are connected to, or some other special circumstance. So make another list of any other connections you can think of. Ask your parents if they belong to any unions or social clubs and if their employers offer scholarships. Has anyone in your family served in the military? What is your ethnic background? Does your place of worship offer scholarships?

These questions are all based on actual scholarships and bursaries available to Canadian students, and this is just the beginning. Financial awards are offered for the most unexpected reasons, which might explain why some of them are never applied for.

counsellor can be an invaluable resource for tracking down money for your education. Ask what awards are available, whether you need to apply for any of them to be considered, and whether there are any special awards that match your personal circumstances.

Don't just assume that the scholarships go only to the best basketball player or the top physics student in your graduating class. There are many scholarships for students with very specific qualifications, such as being of a certain ethnicity or volunteering with a specific community organization. There are also lots of bursaries that go to students with financial need. Think about what special qualifications you may have, and talk to your guidance counsellor.

Awards from Your University or College

Each university and college has a whole office full of people whose job it is to help you find money to pay for your education. Your school's financial-aid website will have lists of awards or search engines you can use to find awards you are eligible for, often including awards from private or government sources. There may be awards that aren't listed online, though, so it's a good idea to make an appointment with a financial-aid adviser.

> ## Apply for as Many Awards as You Can
>
> "Hit everything. Be persistent, check for new scholarships constantly, and get very good at letter writing. Paint yourself as a hardworking student just trying to 'make it,' and put lots of emphasis on volunteer work and big projects."
>
> – Andrew Bates, English, University of British Columbia Okanagan

Create a list of your attributes, activities and achievements. Use your quirks and qualifications as search terms to find scholarships that are meant for people like you. The weirder the scholarship qualification (left-handed lawn bowlers of half-Latvian, half-Somalian descent), the less likely anyone else will have applied for it, and the more likely it will be awarded to you if you're eligible. If you talk to a financial-aid counsellor, tell him or her about the things on your list, and you might learn about a scholarship that could be claimed only by you.

Searching the awards database at Wilfrid Laurier University, for example, turns up scholarships and bursaries for female, Aboriginal, and first-generation students. There are also awards for music students, athletes, people considering becoming cystic fibrosis researchers, students in wheelchairs, people who have lost a parent in an impaired-driving accident, and people of Afghani heritage. You never know what you're going to get a financial award for, so get out those search terms and look.

There are two types of awards available at universities and colleges: general awards for all students and entry awards. At most universities, entrance awards are available only to students who are enrolling in full-time classes and who have never been to university before. If you are planning to start your first year as a part-time student, you may want to reconsider, because enrolling as a part-time student could make you permanently ineligible for

scholarships can come from unexpected places

Erin, one of the authors of this book, got a pleasant surprise when she graduated high school: she found out that the McDonald's franchise where she worked flipping burgers offered scholarships. She applied, and they awarded her $500—many weeks' worth of burger-flipping money. They didn't advertise the fact, though, so it goes to show, it's worth asking.

many entrance awards. Try applying for the awards as a full-time student and see what you can get before you make the decision to go part-time.

Some schools automatically consider all prospective students for entrance awards on the basis of their application, but not all do. When you apply for a school, ask a financial-aid adviser or someone at the registrar's office whether you should make a separate application for entrance scholarships. The scholarships and bursaries you are offered might be a factor in your decision about which school to attend.

Many entrance scholarships are designed to help students pay for their entire degree, granting new awards each year as long as the student maintains his or her grades above a certain level. For example, a Chancellors' Scholarship from the University of Saskatchewan awards lucky winners $5,000 in funding every year, provided they keep their average above 80%. It's a lot of pressure, but it's what is called tough love; if you live up to your end of the bargain, that's $20,000 over four years in free cash to pay for your education. And besides, keeping your marks up can lead to your being awarded even more scholarships down the road.

Beyond entrance awards, there are general awards available to all undergraduate students, so your quest for scholarships and bursaries shouldn't end after you're admitted. Apply for scholarships every year and keep checking the website, because application deadlines for different awards occur throughout the year. Even if you think your grades aren't quite good enough for an award, you should still apply. At many schools, some scholarships and bursaries are never awarded, for the simple reason that not enough students apply for them.

Searching for Scholarships Online

One of the most effective ways to search for scholarships and bursaries is by making use of online search engines. Here are some useful online resources that you should check out:

- scholarshipscanada.com has over 7,500 awards listed. Search by school, field of study, or source.

- studentawards.com matches you with awards you are eligible for after you create a detailed profile. It will also send you email updates when new scholarships become available.

- schoolfinder.com helps students find a school that suits them and features a scholarship search engine.

- aucc.ca—Association of Universities and Colleges of Canada—manages scholarships and applications for many private sources, primarily corporations.

- oncampus.macleans.ca—Maclean's OnCampus—offers a comprehensive search tool you can use to search for awards by school.

- globecampus.ca/money-finder—Enter information about your average marks and family income, and Globe Campus assesses how much you qualify for in loans and grants and suggests specific scholarships.

Tip: When creating online profiles for these sites, answer the questions with as much detail as you can, so you can find as many awards as possible.

Doesn't it make you sad to think about all that education money sitting there, lonely and unspent, just because nobody cared enough to ask for it? Poor, poor little bursary, all alone in the financial-aid office, waiting for someone to come and love it. Will it be you?

Private Sources

Many private organizations offer scholarships and bursaries, and they give them out for all kinds of different reasons. The best place to start is to make a list of organizations that you and your family are associated with—including places of worship, employers, unions, and community groups—and find out if they offer scholarships.

Most private organizations publicize their awards through high schools, universities, and online scholarship and bursary databases. These are the only places you're likely to find awards you're eligible for from groups you're not associated with, unless you plan to phone every company, union, and benevolent society in the country on the off chance they have an award for you.

Applying for Scholarships and Bursaries

There are so many scholarships and bursaries to apply for that it could take over your life if you let it. If you focus your efforts and keep yourself organized, however, it shouldn't be more than a part-time job. Compile a folder (paper or electronic) that includes:

- Your updated resumé.
- Information about your financial situation, including that of your parents.
- Copies of your high school or university transcript and proof of your enrolment or acceptance to university or college.
- Letters of reference from family friends, teachers, employers, coaches, or other leaders of activities you've participated in.
- A portfolio of examples of your work, if you are planning to study music, art, design, or other creative subjects.
- Copies of all the scholarship applications you've prepared, including essays you had to write as part of the application (you can reuse these).

Keep a detailed and organized list of all the awards you've found that you're eligible for. There are likely more scholarships out there than you have time to apply for, so prioritize the ones you think you have the best chance of winning. Your list of awards should include the deadline dates and when you sent in your application. You should also make a note of whether you've sent a thank-you note for any awards you won.

While there isn't anything you can do to make your marks look any better than they actually are, how you present your extracurricular activities can make or break your application. You don't need to brag, but don't be so modest that you leave out achievements because you assume other people won't think they're important. Do you like to do pottery just for fun? That counts; it helps to paint a picture of yourself as a well-rounded and interesting person, even if the activity is completely irrelevant to your biology studies.

The dreaded essay

Perhaps the most intimidating part of applying for scholarships and bursaries is essay writing. Approach essays as you would any other written assignment at school; start by carefully reading the question to make sure that you are addressing exactly what they want to know, not what you wished they'd asked. Make sure to go back and reread the question several times while you are writing your essay to make sure you haven't veered off course.

Many essay topics are about you rather than about the academic subjects you're used to writing about. Even if you feel like you are not particularly interesting, everyone has a story, and the adjudicators are interested in getting to know you. It's important to be honest. Exaggeration or cheesy claims about how you first knew you wanted to be a forensic scientist when you were two years old come across as insincere.

Write about what you're passionate about. If you're genuinely interested in your topic or the part of your life that you are writing about, chances are your essay will be more interesting.

If you are having difficulty starting your essay, try talking about the topic with your family or friends while you take notes. They might remind you of something about yourself that you didn't think of. You can gauge from their reactions to the conversation what is interesting and what is not so interesting.

Try to find a theme that ties together your life experience rather than writing a chronological account of everything you've ever done. For instance, think about how your experience playing soccer for years as a child led you to be interested in pursuing a degree in physical education. Frame your experiences as a cohesive story about how your past shaped you into who you are today and what you want for your future.

Try to be as specific as possible. Don't just write that you developed an interest in history in your Grade 10 history class. Tell your adjudicators about how you got excited about history when your teacher, Mr. Jones, told you the story of the Second Defenestration of Prague. This will make the personal story you are weaving in your essay more compelling and memorable.

> **T**he Second Defenestration of Prague was a 1618 argument that ended in three men being "defenestrated," or thrown out a window. They fell 30 metres but survived because they landed in a nice soft pile of manure. This fact won't help you write a scholarship application, but we thought it would be good for a laugh.

Back up your claims about your good attributes with concrete examples. Instead of claiming that you work well with others, provide an example of a time you achieved something you're proud of with a group. (For more essay-writing help, read **Section 3.4: Writing Papers and Essays**.)

Rolling in Free Dough

University of British Columbia English literature graduate Amanda Reaume estimates that she received about $60,000 in scholarships for her undergraduate and graduate education. They didn't just fall in her lap, though—she had to work at getting them. Now Amanda is director of Getting In, a scholarship consulting service, and she shared with us her secrets for getting your own scholarship windfall:

- Start early. At the very latest, you should start researching scholarships the summer before you plan to apply for university—a full year before you graduate from high school.

- Stay organized. Create a comprehensive list of potential scholarships you plan to apply for, complete with due dates and requirements.

- Get appropriate reference letters. Give the people writing your reference letters information about scholarship requirements and ask them to write letters tailored to the scholarship you're applying for—but you have to be organized and give them enough time to write a really great letter.

- Be yourself. Scholarship committees are looking for people who are authentic and who participate in clubs or activities because it means something to them, not just so they can win a scholarship.

- Create a coherent story. Students who are strong writers have an advantage when applying for scholarships. Pay careful attention to language and grammar, and relate your accomplishments in a concise manner in your application essay.

- Apply, apply, apply. Some scholarships receive only one or two applications, and others receive none at all. Apply for as many scholarships as you can. That being said, don't waste your time applying for scholarships you're obviously not qualified for.

Reference letters

Many applications will require reference letters from teachers, family friends, employers, and anyone else who knows you well and will make a credible referee; your buddies from your hockey team won't work, but your hockey coach might give a great reference. Make sure you ask for these letters well in advance so your referees have ample time to write a good letter. It is best to start thinking about who might make a good reference early, so you have time to build relationships with them. Your high school English teacher might be reluctant to write a letter for you if you never spoke in class or asked for help. The people who act as references for you will be more likely to write a better letter if they know you well.

Section 7.4: Reference Letters is about getting reference letters from professors, but a lot of the advice is applicable here, too, so check it out.

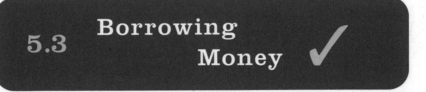

5.3 **Borrowing Money** ✓

Unless you're very lucky, you're probably not going to get enough money from scholarships, bursaries, and grants to pay for your entire education. You might have a tidy pile of money in the bank, or parents or other family members who can afford to foot the bill, but if you're like most students, you'll have to borrow money to pay for your education.

This is probably your first encounter with debt. Now's the time to learn about credit ratings and interest rates and how to manage debt so it doesn't take over your life. You'll want to borrow money again in the future, to finance buying a house or a car, so it's important to keep your record clean.

Fortunately, the government has done a lot of things to make taking out student loans as easy as possible and has some programs in place to help you out if you get into financial trouble after graduation. Still, student loans are real loans, and they'll affect your future in a real way, so it's extremely important that you understand what you're getting yourself into.

In this section:

- Find out **Where to Borrow Money.**
- Learn tips for **Applying for Government Student Loans.**
- **Managing Your Student Loans** will keep you out of financial trouble.
- When government loans aren't enough, you may have to turn to **Private Sources of Credit.**
- Lay a good financial foundation by learning about **Managing Debt.**

Where to Borrow Money

Unless you have generous friends or family members who are willing to lend money at low interest rates, your best bet is to apply for a government student loan. The federal, provincial, and territorial governments lend money to students, and they offer friendly terms.

The main advantage of government loans is that interest is not charged until you graduate. That alone can save you thousands of dollars over the years you'll be at school. Then, when you graduate, you're given a six-month grace period to get your feet on the ground before you have to start making payments. And if you don't find a job after you graduate, or if you don't make enough money to make payments, they have programs that can help.

There's a catch, though: the government probably won't lend you enough money to pay for everything. Nearly 75% of students who take out government loans also borrow from private sources, like banks and credit card companies, and some students aren't eligible for any government loans at all.

Banks offer students lines of credit that are very flexible and that allow you to borrow money in small increments as you need it. However, if you don't yet have a credit history, you might have to get a parent to co-sign the loan with you, which means that if you mess up the payments, Mom or Dad will be on the hook along with you. Another serious disadvantage is that banks are in the business of making money, so they'll charge you interest from the day you take out the loan, and they'll probably require you to make payments while you're still in school.

So, if you need to borrow money, it's best to borrow as much as you can from the federal and provincial or territorial governments and minimize the amount of money you borrow from the bank.

Financial Glossary

Borrowing money can be a confusing process, especially if you don't understand the specialized vocabulary that goes along with it. Read the following glossary to get up to speed on the terms used by your student-loan officers and bankers.

- Principal: The original amount of a loan, on which interest is charged.

- Interest: The price paid for borrowing money. It is expressed as a percentage of the principal charged per year.

- Compound interest: Interest charged on both the principal and on the unpaid interest. For example, if you're paying 10% interest on $100, at the end of the year you owe $110. The next year, the interest will be 10% of $110, or $11, and the total owed will be $121. In reality, interest is usually compounded monthly or even daily.

- Fixed or floating interest rates: Fixed interest rates remain the same for the life of the loan. A floating interest rate changes as the market or prime rate changes.

- Prime, or prime rate: The interest rate charged by banks to customers with the best credit scores. Many loans will have their interest rates expressed as prime plus a number of percentage points. For example, if a loan is at "prime +3" and prime is currently 3.25%, interest will be charged at 6.25%.

- Line of credit: A pre-established amount of money you are able to borrow from a bank whenever you need it.

- Default: Failure to meet the legal obligations of a loan, such as missing payments. Defaulting can result in being charged penalties, being hounded by a collections agency, and being given a bad credit rating.

- Collections agency: A company hired to persuade people who have not paid their bills or loan payments to cough up the money.

- Credit report: Your financial history, including all your good credit history plus the last seven years' worth of bad credit history.

- Credit rating: The rating assigned to you by each of the past lenders listed in your credit report.

- Credit score: A number calculated from your credit report that evaluates you as a risk to lenders. Having a higher credit score can make it easier to get loans and can lower the interest you'll be charged on loans.

Applying for Government Student Loans

Where your loan comes from depends on what province or territory you live in:

- *Alberta, British Columbia, Manitoba, Nova Scotia, and PEI* have stand-alone student loan programs, so you'll get two loans, one from the federal government and one from your provincial government.
- *Newfoundland and Labrador, New Brunswick, Ontario, and Saskatchewan* have integrated student-loan programs, so you'll get one combined loan that is managed through the federal program.
- *Quebec, the Northwest Territories, and Nunavut* don't participate in the Canada Student Loan Program, so you'll get one loan through your province or territory.
- *Yukon* has no student-loan program, so you'll only get a loan from the federal government.

No matter where you're from, you only have to make one application to get all your government loans. As of the 2010–11 academic year, every province and territory except Nunavut allows you to apply online.

Application deadlines vary by province, but you should apply for your student loan as soon as you know which university you're going to, so you

if all else fails, appeal

Joey, a political science student at McMaster University, was always frustrated that his assessed expenses were lower than his actual expenses. For example, Canada Student Loans allowed $55 per month for transit, while a Hamilton transit pass cost $82. When he had to get a part-time job to cover the gap, he notified his student loan program of the change in his financial circumstances, and they recalculated his assessed need and asked him to pay back part of the loan.

So Joey saved up receipts for food, transit, rent, clothing, and prescriptions and appealed the assessment of his need. He won. While he didn't get any extra student loans, he did win the right to work and earn more money without becoming ineligible for maximum student loan funding.

can get the money in time to pay for tuition. However, it is possible to get a loan after the semester has begun if your financial situation changes (for example, if your mom gets laid off and can't afford to help you anymore) or if you space out and forget to apply.

Each province and territory has eligibility requirements for their student loan programs, which can be found on the provincial student-aid website. Generally, you're required to be a Canadian citizen or a landed immigrant, to have lived in your home province for 12 months, to be enrolled at a post-secondary institution that meets the criteria (all publicly funded schools count, but check if you're going to a private college or university), and to be able to demonstrate a legitimate financial need.

It is this last criterion that gives many people problems. Your financial need is calculated by taking your expected educational expenses, including the cost of tuition, books, housing, food, and other expenses, and subtracting your resources, such as personal savings, assets, part-time-work income, grants, awards, and, if you're deemed a "dependent" student, a parental contribution calculated using your parents' income and assets—even if your parents aren't actually giving you any help. You can estimate your assessed need using the online calculator at canlearn.ca.

Your assessed financial need will determine the size of the loan you will get. The Canada Student Loan Program isn't designed to cover the entire cost of your education, just to give you a helping hand. In most cases, you'll be eligible to get a maximum of 60% of your assessed need from the Canada Student Loan Program. Your province will kick in some extra dough, but depending on your province, there's no guarantee you'll reach 100% of your assessed need.

Because they're not even trying to give you all the money they think you need, it's important to keep your assessed need as high as possible, so you can maximize the amount they'll lend you and avoid having to take out bank loans. Here are a few tips:

- If you have any assets, their value will be subtracted from your assessed need because the student loan program will assume that you'll sell the asset to fund your education. Don't declare assets you need for your studies, like your computer.
- You have to report the income you made in the four months before school, but be careful not to overstate your income. Don't include anything you made outside of the four-month period.

don't declare
equipment you need
for your studies

In her first year of music school, Erin, one of the authors of this book, made the mistake of declaring the value of her $4,000 antique saxophone as an asset on her student loan application. That left her qualified to borrow $4,000 less to fund her education because the student loans program assumed that she'd sell her horn to fund her education. The catch was that Erin was enrolled in jazz studies and she needed her saxophone. She was able to appeal the assessment, but it took a few weeks and it was a hassle.

- Keep apartment leases and receipts so you can prove what your actual expenses are. The government will assign an expense amount to you, based on the provincial average, but it is possible to appeal. If you can prove that your expenses are higher than the assessment, you could win the right to borrow more money.
- If you think your assessed need is unfair, appeal.

Managing Your Student Loans

While you're in school

If you have a student loan, you must regularly update the National Student Loan Service Centre (NSLSC) and your provincial lender (if you have a separate provincial lender) about your educational progress and changes in your financial situation. It's up to you to ensure that both agencies know about changes to your study end date, full-time status, financial situation, and address.

It is particularly important that each of your lenders receives a Confirmation of Enrolment notice from your school each academic year. When you apply for a new loan at the beginning of a semester your application will automatically contain a Confirmation of Enrolment, but, if you don't apply for a loan, it's your responsibility to make sure each of your government lenders receives this document. You can download a form online or get one from your university's financial-aid office.

If your lenders don't receive a Confirmation of Enrolment, they'll assume that you graduated or dropped out and they'll start charging you interest. After six months, they'll start demanding payments. You could end up in default and be forced to pay outstanding interest before they reinstate your interest-free status or allow you to apply for new loans—even if you can prove you never stopped going to school.

One last word of warning about not telling your lenders you're still in school: when you sign your student loan papers, you have to provide your bank account information so your lender can make an automatic deposit. What you may not realize is that you're also giving them authorization to take money out of your account. Your government lenders have the ability to withdraw funds from your account if they think you owe them a payment, which can be a serious problem if you're still in school and you just forgot to send a Confirmation of Enrolment.

Conflicts between the National Student Loan Service Centre and student borrowers do sometimes happen. A file of your loan documents, all paper correspondence, and a record of every telephone conversation you have with an NSLSC agent can come in handy if you ever have a disagreement with the NSLSC.

After graduation

During your last semester of studies, you should contact the NSLSC to make arrangements to start paying back your loan. Yes, you'll have six months before you have to start making payments, but it will help you plan your financial future if you know how much you'll be required to pay each month. You can also find out how much your payments will be by using canlearn.ca's Repayment Assistance Estimator. Even though you don't have to make any payments for six months, interest starts piling up as soon as you graduate, so if you have a job right after graduation, you may as well start making payments and save the extra interest.

What if you don't get a job right after graduation? Relax. A lot of the stuff in this section might be scary or confusing, but the dark cloud of your government student debt has a shiny silver lining. If you have trouble finding a job when you graduate, or if you find a job but it doesn't pay very well, there are programs in place to help you.

If you call the NSLSC and tell them you can't afford your payments, they might suggest something called a "revision of terms." That means they'll let you make smaller payments, but over a much longer period of time. Don't do it—you'll just end up paying more interest.

Instead, you should apply for a program called the Repayment Assistance Plan. The plan is designed to help borrowers in financial difficulty avoid defaulting on their loan and getting a black mark on their credit record.

Under the plan, your payments will be reduced to an affordable level, calculated from your income and your family size. Your payment will never exceed 20% of your family income. While you're making these reduced payments, the federal government will also pay the interest, which will allow you to start paying off the principal. If after five years you are still having financial difficulties, the government will start to make payments toward the principal of your loan as well, so your loan will be completely paid off after 15 years.

Keep in mind, though, that enrolment in the plan is not automatic. To apply, contact the National Student Loan Service Centre.

Private Sources of Credit

If your scholarships, grants, and government student loans don't meet your needs, you might have to apply for a student line of credit from a bank.

The advantage of borrowing from banks is that they don't lend on the basis of assessed need like the government does, so it doesn't matter if your parents make too much money. Lines of credit are also very flexible, giving you the ability to take out money only when you need it and to pay it back if you get a summer job or win the lottery. This money-on-demand feature helps you minimize the interest you have to pay by keeping your loan as small as possible.

The disadvantage of borrowing from banks is that they start charging interest from the first day you borrow money. Banks will ask you to make monthly payments to cover your interest, even though for most students this will usually involve taking more money out of their line of credit to make the payment. It's important to make that payment, though, to maintain a good credit rating and to keep the bank happy.

To be fair, banks do offer some pretty generous terms; for example, at the time we researched this book, Royal Bank was offering student lines of credit with the interest rate set at prime +1% until a year after graduation. Although this is a very low interest rate compared to many other types of loans, it's still prime +1% more than the government charges while you're in school.

Having to pay interest while you're in school can be a drain on your financial resources. If you're paying 8% interest and you're borrowing $500 per month plus enough to pay your monthly interest charges, that first interest bill in September of your first year is going to look like a joke: less than $4.00. But by the middle of your fourth year of borrowing $500 a month, your monthly interest bill is going to get up to more than $100, which is a serious chunk of your spending power. In this scenario, the total interest you'll have paid by the time you graduate will be $2,656—and that's before you've even started paying the principal back. For this reason, it's a good idea to try to maximize your funding from sources such as government loans and scholarships in order to keep the amount you borrow from lines of credit to a minimum.

Getting a line of credit

The most important thing you'll need when you get a line of credit is someone to co-sign the loan for you. Unless you've been out of school and making a steady income for a few years, you will probably not have the credit score you'll need to get a student line of credit on your own.

Most students get one of their parents to be their co-signer (some banks call it a "co-borrower" or "guarantor"). By co-signing your loan, a person is guaranteeing that he or she will pay back your loan if you can't do it yourself, and every payment you miss will show up on your co-signer's credit report as well as your own. It's a pretty big responsibility for the co-signer to take on.

You'll also need to provide the bank with proof that you are enrolled in school and a budget showing your expected expenses and your financial resources, including government grants and loans, scholarships, and savings from your summer job. Most students are given a credit limit of around $5,000 per year, but if you can show that your needs are greater (and if your co-signer's credit is sufficient), banks will grant as much as $10,000 per year in credit.

Getting a line of credit from your own bank is really convenient because it will show up on your online banking, and you'll probably be able to access your line-of-credit funds from an ATM, but it's a good idea to shop around for the lowest interest rate. Banks want to establish relationships with young people who are getting an education and might prove to be good customers in the future, so they compete with one another for your business. You can turn that to your advantage; just because a bank is a huge financial institution, don't assume that loan managers don't have authority to negotiate. You might be able to negotiate a lower interest rate, particularly if another bank is offering a better rate.

Credit cards

Some banks offer special deals on credit cards for students. They can even make it sound like it will save you money, by offering you perks like points toward free movie tickets or 1% cash back for the money you charge on your credit card.

Credit cards can be a very convenient way to pay for things and they can help you establish a good credit history, but they're a terrible way to borrow money. Student credit cards charge interest rates of at least 18.5%—more than double what you'll pay on a student line of credit.

In most cases you aren't charged interest if you pay off your entire balance at the end of each month. But if you carry any debt forward, interest is applied to everything on your bill. The interest keeps piling up until you pay off the entire balance, and the interest is calculated daily from the day of each purchase. If you get behind, the 1% cash back your credit card gives you will cover only about 20 days' worth of interest, with the rest coming out of your pocket. And if you carry a large balance for a couple of months in a row, you could pay more in interest than you'll receive in cash back all year.

Never take out a cash advance on a credit card unless the cash is absolutely needed to save a human being's life—and concert tickets don't count! Credit card companies charge interest on cash advances from the moment you withdraw the money, and they often charge an even higher rate of interest than they charge for purchases. There has got to be somewhere else you can get that cash from, and if there isn't, you probably can't afford whatever you're thinking about buying.

You know yourself. If you think you can be disciplined and always pay your bill, you might want a credit card—but be careful. If you think there's a chance you'll miss payments, save yourself the headache and don't even apply for a credit card. You've got enough other debt to worry about.

If you do get in trouble and you're faced with the decision of whether to run up your line of credit or leave a large balance on your credit card, always borrow from the line of credit: the interest rate is much lower. Use your line of credit to pay off your credit card and then cut up your card. Don't give yourself the opportunity to get into financial trouble twice in the same year. (See **Section 5.5: Sticking to Your Budget** to find out how your university can help if you are strapped for cash because of an emergency.)

Managing Debt

When you start school and you get your student loans, that future day you'll have to start paying them back might seem like a long way away. However, if you spend more than you need to and borrow more money to pay for it, your future self is going to hate the present you.

And who wants to be hated by his or her future self? Nobody, that's who.

The thing about debt that can make it a trap isn't the principal, it's the interest. Lenders charge interest on the principal *and* on the unpaid interest. This can cause debt to snowball and gain momentum as it rolls down the hill of your life's finances.

You've been caught in the debt trap if you can barely afford to pay the monthly interest on the money you've borrowed, so you are never able to make a significant payment against the principal. Each month, the principal is almost unchanged, the interest stays high, and you're stuck with the same huge debt.

An example of the debt trap

Rich and Bill both relied on student loans to pay for their education. Rich was financially prudent and got only $20,000 in loans, while Bill got addicted to buying vintage Star Wars figurines online and spent his scholarship money on Han Solo dolls, so he had to take out $30,000 in loans.

Rich and Bill both found jobs after graduation, and they could each afford to put $4,000 per year against their student loans. In the first year, Rich was charged $2,000 in interest, and the other $2,000 of his payment went toward paying off his principal. Because Bill had a bigger loan and had to pay more interest, only $1,000 of his $4,000 went against the principal in his first year.

Year 1	Rich	Bill
Starting Principal	$20,000.00	$30,000.00
Interest Rate	10%	10%
Annual Interest	$ 2,000.00	$ 3,000.00
Annual Payment	$ 4,000.00	$ 4,000.00
Minus: Interest Paid Year 1	($ 2,000.00)	($ 3,000.00)
Equals: Principal Paid	$ 2,000.00	$ 1,000.00
Debt Remaining End of Year 1	$18,000.00	$29,000.00

Year after year, Rich was able to pay off more of his principal, so he was charged less interest, enabling him to pay off even more of his debt the following year.

Most of Bill's payment went to interest, so his principal declined slowly and his interest costs remained high.

If we fast-forward to year 5, we'll see that more than $2,900 of Rich's payment went to his principal, so at the end of the year he had already paid off more than 60% of the debt he started with.

Year 5	Rich	Bill
Starting Principal	$10,718.00	$25,359.00
Interest Rate	10%	10%
Annual Interest	$ 1,071.80	$ 2,535.90
Annual Payment	$ 4,000.00	$ 4,000.00
Minus: Interest Paid Year 5	($ 1,071.80)	($ 2,535.90)
Equals: Principal Paid	$ 2,928.20	$ 1,464.10
Debt Remaining End of Year 5	$ 7,789.80	$23,894.90

Because his interest costs were so high, Bill barely made a dent in his principal, so he has continued paying more than $2,500 a year in interest. At the end of year 5, he still owed almost $24,000—more money than Rich owed at the very beginning, five years before. In fact, while Rich will be finished paying his debt a little over seven years after graduating, at this rate

Bill will take 14 1/2 years to pay off his debt—twice as long as Rich, even though he borrowed only 50% more. By the time Bill finally finishes paying off his loan, he will have paid a total of $28,228 in interest, compared to the $9,128 Rich will have paid.

To put that another way, Bill's $30,000 loan will cost him a total of $58,228 to repay. Rich's $20,000 loan will cost $29,128.

Sure, it's fun to pay interest, but you can probably think of a lot of things you could spend an extra $18,900 on that you'd enjoy even more. Limiting your spending now will help you stay out of the debt trap later.

Your credit history

So, you might be thinking, "Paying off a student loan sounds like a lot of work. Why don't I just not pay them back and see what happens?"

The answer is that someday you might want to get something that will require a credit check, like a credit card, a mortgage on a house, or a car loan. Or you might want to rent an apartment. Or get a cellphone. You get the picture.

In Canada, whenever someone lends you money, issues you a credit card, or extends credit to you in any way, they report a credit rating to two credit reporting agencies, called Equifax Canada and TransUnion Canada. If you always make your payments on time, they report a good rating. If you ever mess up, your rating gets worse.

All your credit ratings get put together on a credit report, which is what anyone who does a credit check on you looks at. If you have a long history of paying your bills on time, you'll look like a good credit risk, and people will be more inclined to give you a loan and maybe even give you a better interest rate. If you don't pay your bills or repay your loans on time, you'll look like a bad credit risk, and they may not want to do business with you at all.

The good news is that taking out student loans and paying them back on time is a great way to establish a good credit history. Most utility bills don't generate positive credit experience (they report only when you mess up), but most cellphone plans do, so get a cellphone in your name and always pay the bill. Another way to build a good credit history is by taking out a credit card with a manageable credit limit, always making the minimum payments, and at least occasionally paying off the full balance.

A credit card can be a big risk, though. If you don't think you have the discipline to resist overusing it, then don't get one.

avoiding the
debt trap

Laurie Campbell, executive director of the non-profit Credit Canada, has helped hundreds of students and recent graduates who were in over their heads in debt. Here are Laurie's tips for keeping yourself out of trouble:

- Limit the number of credit cards you have to either one or none. If you don't have a stable income, you shouldn't be relying on credit for your financial well-being.

- When you get your student loan at the beginning of the semester, divide it into the number of months the money has to last. Resist the temptation to blow it in the first couple of weeks.

- When you leave school, contact your student loan department immediately to find out what your payments are going to be and when you have to start repaying.

If you do find yourself having trouble making payments on your debts, you should:

- Stop using your credit card immediately.

- Try to pay off your highest-interest debts first, while making minimum payments on the others.

- Contact a not-for-profit credit counselling service for help.

5.4   Jobs ✓

Income from working is probably going to be a significant part of how you fund your education, regardless of whether you're swimming in scholarships and help from your parents or you're paying for your own education through loans and the sweat of your brow. If tuition is paid for, you'll still probably want to earn some spending money, and even if you don't need the extra cash, there are a lot of other benefits of working, such as learning about industries you may one day work in.

Working is such an important part of your education that there's a whole other section on the subject later in this book; **Section 7.2: Co-ops and Summer Jobs** includes advice about what kind of jobs will help you in your future career and tips to help you land that job. For now, we'll stick to questions of money and the pros and cons of getting a part-time job during the school year.

Questions of money

You probably don't have a lot of earning power at this point in your life. Maybe the best you can get is a job that pays $10 per hour, which looks like chicken feed when measured against the overall cost of your education.

Well, that $10 an hour might make all the difference to your finances. It might not be possible for you to get enough money in scholarships and loans, and that extra money you earn by working might be what it takes to get you through the year.

And if the $3,000 you save up over a summer keeps you from taking out $3,000 more on your line of credit in the next school year, it could also save you $1,000 in interest over the next four years of school—and that $4,000 in reduced debt might be what prevents you from falling into the debt trap after you graduate (see the example in **Section 5.3: Borrowing Money**).

Besides, if you get some experience on your resumé this summer, you might be able to get a better job next year. It's a hell of a ladder to climb, but you've got to start somewhere, so you might as well put your foot on the first rung.

Pros and cons of part-time jobs

You can greatly decrease your debt by taking a part-time job during the school year as well as having a full-time job in the summer. Before you run out and look for work, though, make sure it makes sense for your situation. Taking a part-time job can actually end up costing you more money in the long run.

Evaluate whether you can handle the workload from school along with the time commitments you'll have to make to the job. Find out how flexible your prospective employer can be with the scheduling of your shifts in case you need to work fewer hours during exam period. It's only worthwhile to take a part-time job if it doesn't hurt your grades and if it leaves you with enough spare time to preserve your sanity. (Check out **Section 4.1: Time Management** for more thoughts on the matter.)

what to do
with your summer
savings

When you're saving up money for school during the summer, it makes no sense to put your money into a savings account and make 2% interest while you're paying 7% interest back to the same bank on the money you owe on your line of credit. If you owe the bank money, use your savings to pay down your debt now: you'll save yourself interest and free up space on your line of credit so you can borrow more next year if you need to.

On the other hand, your government student loans are interest-free while you're still in school, and paying them down doesn't guarantee that more money will be available to you in the future, so it makes more sense to keep the money on hand than it does to pay off government loans.

If you're considering taking fewer classes in order to have time for a part-time job, you should do the math first to make sure that it makes financial sense. Taking fewer classes so you can work may add extra semesters to your education, which means extra living expenses and, if you've got a student line of credit from a bank, more interest you'll have to pay before you graduate. So even though you'll make more money, you might end up with larger student loans than you would have if you had not worked and just concentrated on your studies.

Also, the income you earn from a part-time job might decrease the amount of interest-free government student loans you're eligible for. And if you take few enough classes that you lose full-time status, you'll be eligible for less loan and grant money.

But don't let all these negative considerations discourage you. It is entirely possible to find an awesome, career-building, financially beneficial, school-friendly part-time job. You just need to think about how the specific job will work with your specific situation before you commit to it.

5.5 Sticking to Your Budget

So, you've figured out what your first year at school is going to cost and you've managed to find money to pay for it all. Now comes the hard part: you're going to have to stick to your budget.

At the beginning of the semester you might have access to more money than you've ever had in your life; your scholarships, government grants, and student loans just showed up, and you've got a line of credit from a bank that will let you borrow a few thousand dollars anytime you want it. Even after tuition is paid, you're feeling pretty flush.

Now you've got to resist the temptation to go shopping or to buy rounds of beer for your friends. It looks like a lot of money, but it's got to last for months, so it's time to finish your budgeting process and figure out what you can afford to spend on shopping and rounds of beer, and what you have to save up to make sure you don't go hungry at the end of the semester.

In this section:

- Having figured out your expenses and resources, complete your budget by **Putting It Together**.

- Avoid short-term financial crunches by paying attention to your **Cash Flow**.

- Learn how to get along while **Living by Your Budget**.

- Find out how to get out of a bind with **Emergency Bursaries and Student Loans**.

Putting It Together

Earlier in this chapter you figured out how much your education is going to cost and where you are going to get funding, but your financial planning doesn't end there. You also have to manage your budget to ensure your resources last throughout the year.

Continuing our example from **Section 5.1: Costs and Budgeting,** let's look at how our two fictitious students, Charles Brown and Katy Green, are going to pay for their year of school.

Charles Brown has saved some money from a summer job, he got a couple of scholarships, and his parents have agreed to give him $1,250 per semester, plus they co-signed a line of credit for him.

Katy Green has worked as a waitress full-time all summer and will continue to work part-time during the school year. She's classified as an independent student, so she is eligible for a low-income-family Canada student grant.

Total Annual Expenses	$19,941		Total Annual Expenses	$20,312
Savings	$ 1,500		Savings from summer job	$ 3,000
Scholarships	$ 3,500		Part-time job while in	
Canada student loan	$ 6,024		school	$ 8,000
Ontario student loan	$ 4,016		Canada student grant	$ 1,977
Help from parents	$ 2,500		Canada student loan	$ 3,341
Bank line of credit	$ 5,000		Alberta student loan	$ 3,545
Total resources available	$22,540		Total resources available	$19,863
Surplus	$ 2,599		Deficit	($449)

With his parents' help, Charles has put together more financial resources than he needs. That doesn't mean he should spend more money, though; it means that he should try to stick to his original spending budget and not use the full amount of the line of credit available to him and save himself from having to repay it after he graduates.

Katy, on the other hand, has come up short. She can't borrow more money because she doesn't have anyone to co-sign a bank loan for her, and she refuses to fund her education with her credit card because she read this book. Taking more shifts at work won't help because the extra income will lower the size of the student loans she's eligible for. Her only options are to either appeal the student loans program's assessment of her needs, or to find ways to cut back her expenses.

Katy doesn't think she'll win an appeal, so she goes back to her budget to cut $56 per month off of her expenses. She decides she can get by on less money for groceries, and she cuts down on the amount she intends to spend on clothes.

Look out, Value Village: here comes Katy!

Cash Flow

Even if you've written a detailed and balanced budget and you stick to it, you still might get into trouble if you don't consider your cash flow. Many schools require that tuition and residence costs be paid up front, and if your financial plan includes earning employment income during the year, you might not have the cash to cover those significant up-front costs. In fact, some institutions ask for your full year's tuition in August, a full month before student loan funds are issued.

Avoid cash flow problems by making sure you know when all your major expenses are due and when you can expect to receive your income. Create a financial calendar by writing down your payment deadlines, monthly expenses, and the dates on which you expect to get funding. Don't just assume that the cheque for your scholarship or student loan will arrive before classes start. Contact your funding sources to confirm the timing of payments, and ask whether you need to provide any information, such as confirmation of enrolment, before receiving payment.

Ensure that you will have enough money in your account to cover each major payment and if you don't, make arrangements to temporarily borrow from a parent or family member until you receive that November scholarship or late student loan. If your family can't help you, apply for a student line of credit from a bank, which will allow you to borrow what you need when you need it, and then repay it as soon as you receive your funding.

Make sure that you have some wiggle room in your schedule, as unexpected delays in receiving cheques are common.

If your tuition is due and you absolutely can't figure out a way to make it work, enquire at your university's financial services office if it is possible to get an extension. Some universities allow students to delay paying tuition until they receive their student loan, although there is usually a fee for the convenience.

Living by Your Budget

Budgeting doesn't end once you've figured out how much money you need. You have to actually live by the budget during the school year and stick to those numbers. If for some reason you can't make it on the amount you've budgeted, you've got to figure out a way around your problem. If you think that living by your monthly budget is hard in September, wait until December, when you'll have to live on even less money because you overspent earlier in the semester.

Living by a budget month after month takes a lot of discipline at first, but once you get used to it, it becomes second nature. It can even become a fun game, figuring out the cheapest way to do things. If you've got problems with spending discipline, you might want to try out the following tips:

- Take out your weekly allowance of spending money in cash every Monday, to make it easy to visualize how much you have left. When you've spent it all, that's it; you're done spending until next Monday.
- Check your bank account balances frequently to make sure you're on track.
- Keep a spreadsheet detailing everything you spend so you can keep track of your spending habits.
- Before you make any major purchase, sleep on it and think about whether you really need that expensive item.
- If you're going shopping for clothes or groceries, make a list of what you need before you go and stick to it—don't buy anything that's not on the list.
- Don't go grocery shopping when you're hungry. You'll end up buying all kinds of stuff you don't really need.
- When you're going out for a night on the town, leave your credit card at home. Decide how much you want to spend and bring only that amount of cash.

Your budget is yours and it's not set in stone. A lot of the numbers in your budget will be guesses you made before you tried living on your own, and sometimes they will have to change when you're confronted with harsh economic reality.

Money-saving Tips

- Check out the tips for saving money on textbooks in Section 5.1: Costs and Budgeting.

- Consider buying second-hand clothes from thrift stores.

- Look for shops and restaurants that give student discounts.

- Driving a car is expensive. Save money on gas and parking by riding public transit.

- Owning a car is expensive. Save money on maintenance, registration, insurance, and lease payments by selling your ride. Alternatively, you can park your car off of the street and cancel the insurance while you're in school, and insure it again when you go home for the summer.

- And while we're being cheap about transportation, can you get by with a cheap bike instead of a transit pass? (Think about winter before you commit to this one.)

- Roam Craigslist and other classified listings for free or cheap furniture. People give away all kinds of perfectly good furniture around the end of the month, just so they don't have to move the stuff.

- If you have dental or medical insurance through your parents, make sure you opt out of your university's health plan.

- Avoid paying for convenience food if you have free or cheap food waiting for you at home. Brown-bagging lunch can save a pile of money; so can making the walk back to res to get your meal plan lunch instead of paying to chow down at a restaurant.

- Check out Section 6.6: Eating Well and Being Active for tips on economical cooking.

- Cancel the bells and whistles on your cellphone plan. Maybe voice mail was invented for people with more money than you.

- Before you spend money on things like movie tickets, concert tickets, baseball game tickets, and so forth, ask if there's a student discount.

If you're lucky enough to find yourself coming in under budget in some of your expenses, remember, there's no rule that says you have to spend the difference. You can always put that extra money aside in your emergency fund, and if you haven't spent it at the end of the year, it will be that much less money you'll have to borrow next year.

Sometimes you'll find it impossible to keep some expenses down to the number you budgeted. For example, you may have budgeted $65 for transportation, but a local bus pass costs $83, and no matter how much you

Tales of Blown Budgets

Here are some hilarious and pathetic true stories of students who spent too much money early in the semester and had to take extreme measures to stretch their budget. Please don't take these as suggestions of what to do if you blow your budget; regard these as reasons to avoid blowing your budget in the first place.

- Mark from Memorial University got his hair cut by a friend in a university bathroom stall to save $10.

- Lina from Concordia University diluted her milk with water to make it last longer.

- Will from Mount Alison University stretched his grocery budget by having nothing but concentrated orange juice for dinner.

- Sheena from Memorial University economized by stealing toilet paper from a campus bathroom.

- Dale from Thompson Rivers University ate Spam! (Not junk email; the inexpensive gelatinous canned-pork product.)

- Keely from the University of Alberta went dumpster diving for not-quite-spoiled produce thrown out by supermarkets.

- Amanda from Simon Fraser University, who is quite thin to begin with, almost stopped eating entirely at the end of one semester, subsisting some days on a cup of bubble tea (which certainly wouldn't be our choice as the best nutritional bang for a buck). Her malnutrition contributed to a severe bout of late-semester depression, which forced her to quit all her extracurricular activities.

- Jodie from Queen's University stole plates and cutlery from a university café and sold them as "complete sets" on eBay. Then she spent the money on beer and still couldn't afford food, so she resorted to cutting slices of bread in half to make sandwiches (we are in awe of her skill with a knife) and stealing gas from the boat her neighbour left parked on the driveway.

negotiate, the jerks at the transit authority won't accept less than $83. When this happens, you'll have to change your budget, either by finding a way to get more money, like getting a part-time job, or by finding ways to cut expenses in other areas to make up the difference.

If you need to cut expenses, remember that you're not alone. You're surrounded by people who are trying to live as cheaply as possible, and the best source of advice for living cheap is someone who has been doing it for longer than you have. Talk to your fellow broke students about ways to save money and places to go for cheap eats and entertainment.

Emergency Bursaries and Student Loans

Sometimes students run into economic crises that are beyond their control and beyond their ability to get out of just by living cheaply. For example, maybe your house burned down and you don't have any clothes or anywhere to live; or maybe there was an unexpected delay in receiving your student loan, and you need money for groceries for a week or two.

Most post-secondary institutions in Canada have some kind of program to provide emergency funding to students who have, through no fault of their own, fallen on hard economic times and can't afford things that are essential to the continuation of their education. You'll probably have to provide some personal financial information, as well as a description of your financial catastrophe and documentation to prove that your story is true, but emergency funding can save you from starving or having to drop out of school.

Depending on your situation and your institution, you may be awarded an emergency student loan or an emergency bursary. Visit your school's financial-aid office for more information.

CHAPTER

6

Health and Safety

WHEN YOU GO to university or college, you'll have to make a lot of decisions about your health and safety, decisions you may never have had to make before. This is in part because of the new situations you'll encounter at your school and in part because you'll probably be more independent than you've ever been.

It's not that your campus is a particularly dangerous place; it isn't. It's just that it's new to you and there are a lot of issues you may never have thought of before. You're going to have to make some decisions regarding alcohol, sex, and drugs while you're at school; these things were probably around in high school, too, but you'll likely find they are much more common on a university campus.

Your independence also makes you more responsible for your own physical health and mental well-being than ever before. Your brain and body need to be cared for properly, and seeing as how you're the one who is going to be responsible for them for the rest of your life, now is a great time to develop good eating and exercise habits and to learn to deal with stress and depression.

Take some time to think about these issues in advance so you know how to respond to them when they arise instead of having to improvise a wise decision on the spur of the moment.

In this chapter:

- Make informed decisions now that you're old enough to legally drink **Alcohol**.

- Understand the risks associated with **Drugs**.

- Get advice from fellow students about **Sex**.

- Learn about **Sexual Assault** and how to help a friend who has been assaulted.

- Learn to beat **The Campus Blues** and cope with stress and anxiety.

- Get tips on diet and exercise to help you with **Eating Well and Being Active**.

6.1　Alcohol

This section isn't what you think: we're not going to tell you not to drink. The decision to drink booze is yours to make, no matter what you read here. The purpose of this section is to provide you with the facts to make informed decisions about drinking.

Many students get their first real introduction to alcohol at college or university. Oh sure, a lot of people get their hands on alcohol when they're younger, but now that you've turned 18 (in Alberta, Manitoba, and Quebec) or 19 (everywhere else) it's legal to buy booze, so you can get it anytime you want—or at least anytime you can afford it.

Now that the legal restrictions are off, your relationship to alcohol is in your control, and it's time for that relationship to become a mature one. For some students, partying and drinking are a big part of university life. It's possible for alcohol to simply be a fun part of your social life without it negatively affecting your studies, safety, health, or friendships. Alcohol can be anything from a pleasant diversion to a life-destroying addiction, and being aware of how you use it will give you control of how it impacts your life.

In this section:

- You might be surprised when you learn **How Much Canadian Students Really Drink**.

- Understand what you might be getting yourself into by examining **The Consequences of Drinking**.

- Limit your exposure to those consequences by following our **Safe-Drinking Tips**.

How Much Canadian Students Really Drink

In our society, stereotypes paint college and university students as a pack of drunken party animals whose lives are a 24-hour kegger, where everyone wears togas, dances, and acts in crazy, zany ways, such as throwing televisions out windows and crushing beer cans on their foreheads. Then, at the end of four years of this, they all somehow get degrees and become sociologists and optometrists.

While it is true that most students do drink (and a disturbing number engage in dangerous drinking behaviour), the average student doesn't drink as much as you might think he or she does. Researchers have found that students have an inflated perception of how much their fellow students consume. At the University of British Columbia, for example, a recent study found that 67% thought the typical student had five or more drinks the last time they partied, while in reality only 24% of students did. In fact, 64% of UBC students never drink five or more drinks in one sitting, and one in ten students have never tried alcohol at all.

If your social group drinks a lot, it's easy to imagine that most other students drink as much as you and your friends do. This perception can encourage you in your drinking because you think it's normal for students to get hammered all the time. The truth is that most Canadian students don't drink heavily very often, and many never drink heavily. Those student party animals are in the minority at institutions filled with high achievers who are spending tens of thousands of dollars to develop their brains and launch their careers.

If you choose not to drink at all, there's no need to feel like you're a loser destined to spend your Friday nights solo. Not drinking is not as unusual as

Student Drinking by the Numbers

Here are some stats from a 2004 study of Canadian university students by the Centre for Addiction and Mental Health:

- Students who drank alcohol in the last 12 months: 86%.
- Students who drank alcohol in the last 30 days: 77%.
- Number of drinks consumed per week by students who drank in last 30 days: 6.4.
- Students who have never drunk alcohol: 10%.
- Students who drank at least 5 drinks in the same day, 2 or more times in the last month: 34%.
- Students who drank at least 8 drinks in the same day, 2 or more times in the last month: 13%.

you might think it is. A national survey found that about one in seven university students hadn't consumed alcohol in the last year and nearly one in four haven't had a drink in the last 30 days.

The Consequences of Drinking

One of the most common consequences of drinking is having a good time. It can loosen you up, mellow you out, lower your inhibitions, and make you more likely to sing karaoke. It can be fun. That's why most people drink.

But . . .

(Yes, predictably, there's a "but.")

Booze can also be destructive. As with a lot of things in this life, as you drink more, the positive consequences tend to lessen and the destructive consequences tend to get worse and worse.

After one drink, a man with an average constitution (that is, someone who doesn't have an alcohol allergy or other medical condition) will feel relaxed, but he will still legally be able to operate a motor vehicle and he won't get even a hint of a hangover the next day.

After three drinks he'll be very relaxed, but he'd better not have any plans to get any school reading done later that night, and he'd better not get behind the wheel of a car. There's a chance he'll have a bit of a headache or feel a bit fatigued the next morning.

After eight drinks, that same man might be loud and obnoxious, and he might do something he will later regret. He might vomit, and he might not have a choice of what or who he vomits on. The next day he might have forgotten part of the night before and he'll probably feel sick, perhaps so sick that he won't be able to drag his sorry, booze-stinking body to class. Or if he does make it to class, he might temporarily be too stupid to understand what his professor is trying to teach him. Then, after class, when he's supposed to be studying for an upcoming mid-term or researching a paper, that man might feel the overpowering urge to just take a nap instead.

You get the idea.

And there are other, more severe consequences that happen less often. The Centre for Addiction and Mental Health's study on student drinking found that a significant percentage of students suffered such drinking-related consequences as getting into serious arguments or fights, injuring themselves, or ending up in trouble with the police. Some reported being physically assaulted, sexually harassed, or even sexually assaulted by other students who were drunk. A significant number of students took risks that they may not normally have taken while under the influence, such as having unplanned or unsafe sex or driving while drunk. (Read more in **Section 6.3: Sex** and **Section 6.4: Sexual Assault.**)

And then there are the longer-term consequences of drinking too much. Drinking can make you fat. A bottle of beer has about 150 calories in it, so an eight-beer bender is like having a Big Mac, a bag of Doritos, and half a litre of Coke—and that's not including the nachos you ate while you were drinking the beer or the slice of pizza you had before you went to bed.

More important, excessive alcohol consumption can contribute to serious diseases. Alcohol has been linked to heart and liver diseases and an increased risk of stroke. Excessive drinking can also lead to addiction—not just a habit, but a real, physical addiction, and yes, it can happen to young people, too.

But we're not trying to scare you. We just want to inform you of the possible consequences before you make your decision.

Drinking Disasters

The Centre for Addiction and Mental Health's study found that 6.5% of students reported an alcohol-related injury. What this stat doesn't capture is how often students do other stupid things that have consequences apart from injury. Below is a list of drinking disasters we've heard of students suffering; we won't include any names, but all these things actually happened to at least one student:

- Vomited on brand-new laptop.
- Took an ambulance to the hospital to get stomach pumped, and had to explain the expense to Dad.
- Lost only set of keys to car and house.
- Gave friend piggyback ride, fell face first on sidewalk, and lost tooth.
- Posted 100 photos of self in wildly inappropriate party costume to Facebook.
- Accidentally pooped in pants.

Safe-Drinking Tips

So you've made the decision to drink anyway. We knew most of you would. To be honest, we've been known to drink, too, on occasion, so we're all in this together. If we're going to drink, let's drink smarter and avoid as many of the negative consequences as we can.

It's important to learn how alcohol affects you. Don't go from never touching a drop to trying to drink a bar dry all in one step. Go slowly—start with a drink or two some night, and pay attention to how it affects you. Learn your limit so you don't go all crazy or start vomiting everywhere.

Make sure you eat before you drink. If you drink on an empty stomach, the booze will go straight to your head, and you'll get drunk way faster and on way less booze than you normally would. And if you're super-thirsty, don't start with beer—drink some water first. Alcohol dehydrates you, which is a big part of what a hangover is. Having a glass of water every couple of drinks isn't a bad idea, either, because it'll slow down your consumption and keep you hydrated.

alcohol
poisoning

I f you notice a friend can't stand up, looks confused, vomits uncontrollably, starts breathing irregularly, or passes out and can't be woken up, then that person probably has alcohol poisoning and they need your help.

Don't try to guess how much they've had to drink and then convince yourself that they couldn't possibly have alcohol poisoning because you've seen them drink that much before; the effects of alcohol differ depending on the physical state a person is in, so it's possible that what was a safe amount of alcohol for your friend to drink on one day will be enough to knock him off his feet on another day.

Don't leave your friend to sleep it off. Every year students die of alcohol poisoning, often by drowning on their own vomit, so it's important that you don't leave them alone. If you're able, roll your passed-out friend over onto his side so they don't choke to death when they puke.

Now call 9-1-1 and get an ambulance. Sure, it's going to be embarrassing and unpleasant for your friend to have to get his stomach pumped, but it beats getting brain damage from an alcohol-induced seizure or choking to death on his own vomit.

Pour your own drinks at parties. The people mixing your drink might think they're being generous by free-pouring rum into your rum and Coke, when really they're accidentally ambushing you by giving you twice as much booze as you think you're drinking.

Don't leave your drink unattended. Date-rape drugs like Rohypnol are invisible and tasteless, and they're unfortunately common. It's easy for someone to pop one in your drink if you turn your back on it for a second. If you go to the bathroom, cover your drink with a coaster and ask a friend to watch it for you.

Always go out with friends, and use the buddy system. Keep an eye on your pals and make sure you check in with each other every half hour or so. That way, if one of you gets too drunk, has their drink spiked, or is being harassed by an aggressive drunk, you can back each other up and get each other out of trouble. Never leave your friend alone if they're wasted, even if it looks like they're having fun and they seem to want to go off with that cute guy or girl. If your friend passes out, that cute guy might take advantage, or

hangover
tips

Had one too many, eh? Well, there's no reason to suffer unnecessarily. Here are some tips for getting yourself back into fighting shape as soon as possible:

- **Drink water:** Alcohol dehydrates you. Water un-dehydrates you. Drink water before you go to bed, or if it's too late for that, then drink water as soon as you wake up.

- **Get active:** Excessive alcohol consumption depletes your body's endorphin levels, and being active the next day helps produce these mood-elevating hormones.

- **Soothe your stomach:** Alcohol irritates your stomach, so take an antacid if you need one.

- **Eat light:** Although you might feel like having a big, greasy meal, you'll feel better faster if you eat easy-to-digest food.

- **Eat a banana:** Booze depletes electrolytes. Bananas contain lots of potassium, an important electrolyte. You do the math.

- **Medicate your headache:** There's nothing like a good old-fashioned aspirin to stop those hangover dwarves from hammering on the inside of your skull.

just leave your friend wherever she hit the ground, because she's not the cute guy's responsibility.

We shouldn't have to even say this in this day and age, but please don't drink and drive. You've seen the videos and heard all the gory tales. They're true. Alcohol is involved in about 30% of the fatalities on Canadian roads, and more than 30% of the drinking drivers in those crashes are aged 16 to 24—your age, probably. Consuming even a small amount of alcohol can impair your judgment and your reactions, so instead of risking ruining your life or someone else's, take a cab, walk, call a friend, get on the bus or, if you absolutely have to drive, don't drink. Those couple of beers you didn't plan to drink and the inconvenience of having to come back to get your car the next day are going to seem like pretty frivolous reasons for having killed someone.

If you think you might have a drinking problem, seek help. Your school and community offer counselling services. If you find yourself unable to say no to a drink, if you start drinking so much you black out or make bad decisions, or if drinking starts affecting your ability to do other things (like attend class), then find someone to talk to. Drinking too much as a student can turn into a lifelong problem.

Slow down. You don't have to get a whole lifetime's worth of booze into you this semester. There'll be plenty of time, but only if you don't overdo it now.

6.2   Drugs ✓

If you haven't encountered drugs before now, you should prepare yourself to run into them at your university or college. Drugs are probably going to be much more common on campus than they were at your high school, and it's worthwhile to inform yourself about them in advance, before you find yourself in a situation where people around you are taking drugs and offering them to you.

By far the most commonly used drug on Canadian campuses is cannabis, which is also known as marijuana or pot. You might also meet students who take other drugs, such as hallucinogens, opiates, and various "party drugs" like ketamine and ecstasy. In addition, abuse of prescription drugs is common; some students use them recreationally or as "study aids" because they believe the drugs improve their concentration.

The information in this section shouldn't be regarded as comprehensive or authoritative. We are not pharmacists, physicians, or substance abuse counsellors. This section is meant only as a brief survey of some of the more common drugs on university campuses.

If you are worried that you or a friend may have a drug problem, contact your school's counselling services and talk to someone.

In this section:

- Read about the most common illegal recreational drug in Canada: **Cannabis.**

- **Study Drugs** are becoming increasingly common on Canadian campuses.

- Find out what **Other Drugs** you may happen across at your university.

Cannabis

Whether you want to or not, you will most likely encounter cannabis at your school, if only by smelling someone smoking it as you pass an out-of-the-way park bench on campus.

Cannabis (a.k.a. marijuana, pot, weed, dope, grass, ganja—and about a dozen other names we've never even heard of before) and cannabis derivatives such as hashish (hash) and hash oil are widely available and widely used on Canadian campuses. A study by the Centre for Addiction and Mental Health found that half of Canadian undergraduate students surveyed had tried cannabis at some time in their life, nearly a third had used it in the past year, and one in six had used it in the last 30 days.

The short-term effects of cannabis vary from user to user. Some people become relaxed and talkative, giggle for no apparent reason, and are prone to becoming heavy users of pizza. Others get anxious, tense, confused, or paranoid. An individual's experience may vary from use to use, depending on their physical and mental state when they take the drug and how much they use, so what might be a pleasant experience on one occasion could turn out to be uncomfortable or even frightening the next.

It has been argued that cannabis is less dangerous than alcohol. The jury is still out on that claim, but it is clear that using cannabis is not risk-free.

Pot makes you stoned. It slows your reflexes, shortens your attention span, alters your perceptions, and impairs your judgment, making it unsafe to drive or do anything else that requires a normal level of care and attention.

Marijuana smoke contains many of the same chemicals as cigarette smoke. It can irritate your lungs, lead to chronic bronchitis, and increase your risk of getting lung cancer.

Mixing cannabis and alcohol can make you much more intoxicated than the same amount of either substance could accomplish on its own. This magnifying effect can be unpredictable and can lead to you getting far more intoxicated than you intended to get.

Regular use of cannabis mixes poorly with higher education because it can impact your ability to think even when you're not stoned. Moderate amounts of pot affect your short-term memory and your analytical ability. Chronic use of large amounts of pot can affect your attention span and memory, and the effects can last for weeks or even months after you stop using it.

And then there's the legality of it. Regardless of whether you believe cannabis should be legalized or not, the fact is that it is presently illegal in Canada. Possession of less than 30 grams of cannabis or 1 gram of hashish carries a maximum sentence of six months in prison and a $1,000 fine for a first offence, although it is a summary conviction and does not normally lead to a criminal record. Possession of larger amounts can lead to a criminal indictment carrying a maximum prison sentence of five years plus a criminal record.

Having a criminal record is no fun. It may be impossible to get certain jobs, and you may find it difficult to travel to the United States with a drug conviction on your record.

Study Drugs

Seeking something stronger than coffee to help them through long study sessions, some students turn to drugs that are normally prescribed to people with ADHD (attention-deficit hyperactivity disorder), such as Adderall or Ritalin, because they believe the drugs help them focus and study better. These drugs are often obtained either by faking ADHD symptoms to get a prescription from a doctor, by illegally ordering the drugs over the Internet, or by fraudulently refilling prescriptions.

Adderall and Ritalin are stimulants closely related to amphetamines and are intended to make users awake and focused. While these drugs might sound like the ideal little study buddy, tests have had mixed and inconclusive results about the impact of the drugs on healthy people's cognitive performance, with some tests indicating that many people actually perform worse. Much of the perceived benefit of these drugs for healthy people might be the placebo effect—because users are convinced that the drug will help them, they imagine that the drug actually did help them, even if it had no effect.

The most common side effects of using prescription dosages of these drugs include nervousness, insomnia, headaches, and nausea. More serious side effects include depression, suicidal thoughts, and personality change.

These drugs can be more problematic when their dosage is not controlled by doctors, but is instead determined by stressed-out students who are convinced they need to take more drugs to pass tomorrow's exam. It is possible to overdose, producing the symptoms you'd pretty much expect from someone who's taken too much of a powerful stimulant: heart palpitations, sweating, confusion, increased blood pressure, convulsions, unconsciousness, and even death.

Drugs of this type can be both physically and psychologically addictive. Students become convinced that they can't perform without the drugs, and drug-induced insomnia and the need to overcome the accompanying exhaustion can create a cycle of dependence. In fact, you'll probably be much better off if you just take care of yourself properly. Drugs are a poor substitute for time management, a proper diet, and a good night's sleep.

Other Drugs

If a drug is used in our society, you can bet that someone is using that drug on college and university campuses. We don't have room to deal with every drug or even every category of drugs here, so the following is general advice.

Some students are going to do drugs. If you're one of those students, we can't stop you, but we can ask you to go about it intelligently, by researching any drug before you take it. You're a student in an institution of higher education, for crying out loud; you know how to research something, how to uncover facts, and how to analyze arguments. Don't undertake a very serious decision without knowing what you're getting yourself into.

There is plenty of information about drugs on the Internet, but be wary of online sources; make sure they are reliable and not some kind of drug fan site. Various organizations concerned with substance abuse provide information, as do provincial and federal government bodies.

Understand that the name of the drug doesn't necessarily describe everything that is in the substance you're considering taking. Street drugs are often adulterated with all kinds of stuff. Your ecstasy tablet might contain other drugs or chemicals, and you have no way of knowing what they are.

Be extremely careful with your dosages. Drugs from different sources can vary wildly in strength, depending on how they're produced and how much they've been cut. And many drugs carry the risk of overdose, which can lead to death or other terrible consequences.

Most drugs are addictive, and developing a physical or psychological dependence can significantly alter your life in the long term. If you're in over your head and you feel like you're losing control, seek help. Your school and your community offer free, anonymous counselling.

6.3 Sex ✓

Most Canadian campuses are full of sex. There are sex-related clubs, lectures about sex, sexy events, sex jokes, sex-advice columns in student papers, lots of sexy people, and free condoms being handed out everywhere. Oh, and there's actual sex—you'll probably never see that unless you're taking part, but you'll hear all about it.

Why all the sex? Well, for one thing, sex can be awesome if you go about it the right way. For another thing, our bodies are full of hormones (particularly when we're in our late teens and early 20s) that cause us to think about sex all the time.

We assume you got all the sex ed. you'll ever need in high school. We're not going to show you pictures of diseased genitals or try to scare you away from ever touching anyone else below the shoulders. (If you didn't learn about safe sex in high school, check out sexualityandu.ca.)

Instead of delving into the plumbing-related issues of sex, this section focuses on what students have told us about their transition from the sexual atmosphere of high school to university or college, and their advice for you.

In this section:

- Take in a preview of **The Sexual Atmosphere on Campus**.

- Get tips from students about **Having Sexual Relationships**.

- A word from the wise: **Not Having Sex** isn't the end of the world.

The Sexual Atmosphere on Campus

Many students are a little surprised at how out-in-the-open the subject of sex is when they first arrive on campus. Sex goes from being a taboo, even scandalous subject at their high school to being one of the most talked-about topics around—and not all the talking is being done by students.

Let's Talk About Sex

"There are very few topics about sexuality that are taboo on campus. Last year I helped run a booth about pornography and fetishes in the student centre. We didn't receive any negative comments, and many people were more than happy to stop by our table on the way to class to talk about porn."

– Sandra Duffey, social work, McMaster University

"I noticed a difference immediately, during frosh week. Many of the cheer themes and many of the jokes made by frosh leaders were explicitly sexual. At my high school, students (and especially student leaders) would have been chastised by the administration for joking about sex at a schoolwide event, but during frosh week it was perfectly acceptable."

– Lori, arts and science, McMaster University

The University of Toronto, for example, has a Sexual Education Centre that organizes events like Sexual Awareness Week and "Porn Reborn," a conference about the evolution and future of pornography. You'll also find condoms being handed out like Halloween candy, except you don't need to be wearing a costume and you can get them any day of the year. In addition, most schools have a club for LGBT (lesbian, gay, bisexual, and transexual/transgender) students, who, when they're not advocating for queer rights, build community by organizing queer-positive parties.

On an individual level, you'll probably find that sex will play a much larger part in the lives of your peers than it did in high school. This is only to be expected; you're all growing up. Many students we spoke to said that in their first year, they were surprised how openly and frankly their peers talked about sex and how much more casual people were about having sex than in high school. One woman from a small town who went to a big-city university reported being surprised by how much more sexually active other students were than the people she knew from home.

You might find some or all of this sex stuff shocking or even offensive. You might wonder why people don't keep their bedroom activities in their bedrooms. Well, the genie is out of the bottle, and unless you've got a time machine that can get you back to the 1950s, you're going to have to learn to live with it. In spite of what it might look like during sexual awareness week, your campus is not a non-stop orgy; most of the activity happening at that busy place actually has nothing to do with sex, and many students opt for monogamy or abstinence from premarital sex. You'll find ways of coping, and you'll make friends who feel the way you do.

On the other hand, you might find this openness about sex exciting, liberating, and wonderful. If so, please be careful, remember what you learned in sex ed., continue to educate yourself, and read the next section.

Having Sexual Relationships

As we've said, the sexual culture at your campus is probably going to be very different from what things were like at your high school, and you might find it confusing and difficult to adjust to at first. For example, you might not be familiar with the concept of the hookup (the casual romantic encounter that may or may not involve actual sex) and that may lead to misunderstandings and hurt feelings.

The best thing you can do is start slow and be careful. Be careful with your feelings, be careful with your body, and understand the health risks you may be taking. Don't have sex for other people. Make sure you're ready and you're doing it for yourself.

The most well-rounded relationship advice we found came from a very wise student at St. Francis Xavier University:

Patricia Graham's relationship pointers

- Think hard before getting involved with someone who may still be involved with his or her ex.
- Think even harder before getting involved with a friend.
- Know yourself well enough to know if you are the type of person who can handle regularly hooking up with someone without becoming emotionally involved.
- Communicate. You shouldn't be afraid to ask tough questions and clarify what you expect from the situation. Both people need to be on the same page. If you are not comfortable with this conversation, you may want to ask yourself if you are truly comfortable with the situation you are in.
- The tough situations you get into and the mistakes you make do make you stronger and allow you to grow.
- Have realistic expectations. Life is not a romantic comedy, and things do not always end up happily, but that is okay.

Not Having Sex

It might seem like everyone else is going crazy having sex, and you don't want to, or for one reason or another, you can't.

Relax. There are plenty of other students at your school who have never had sex or who have had sex in the past and are no longer sexually active. You're not a freak and you're not alone.

We all have our own reasons; some of us are late bloomers, others have ethical or religious reasons, and others have standards they're not willing to compromise. We're all individuals, so there's no reason we should all be doing the same thing at the same time.

Listen To Your Instincts

"My advice would be to follow one's instincts and to err on the side of caution. Never sleep with someone you don't really want to sleep with. It's just not worth it."

– Stephanie Rade, library services, University of Western Ontario

There can be a lot of social pressure to have sex, either from friends or from prospective partners. Caving in to peer pressure is a terrible reason to have sex. Not wanting to disappoint your date and being tired of resisting advances are equally bad reasons.

Good reasons to have sex include wanting to, feeling like you're ready, being in a situation that is right for you, and feeling safe. If a situation doesn't meet those requirements, then don't go through with it.

If you badly want to have sex but you can't find a partner, don't obsess over it. We know that it may feel like you're the only person who has never been laid before, but you've got to calm down. Stop trying so hard and work on your long-term game instead. Develop interests so you'll be interesting

asexuality

It's well known that different people have different sex drives, but did you know that some people have no sex drive at all? They're called "asexual" or "non-sexual," and they have no romantic attraction to people of either sex. Some studies estimate they make up about 1% of the population.

to talk to. Read books. Work on your self-confidence. Go to the gym and get yourself a hot body. Do some charity work. Be happy. Become the person who will be attractive to the kind of person you're attracted to.

6.4 Sexual Assault ✓

Sexual assaults are most common among 18- to 25-year-olds—the age group that makes up the majority of college and university students. When you add alcohol and maybe some drugs into the mix, you're unfortunately going to wind up with a lot of sexual assaults—even at an institution of higher learning.

Educating yourself about sexual assault will help you stay safe and may enable you to help a friend who has been sexually assaulted. It's also important to learn where the line between flirting and sexual harassment lies, to make sure you never inadvertently cross it.

In this section:

- Get the facts straight about sexual assault by learning the difference between **Facts and Myths**.

- Stay safe by **Minimizing the Risk**.

- Learn **What to Do If a Friend Is Sexually Assaulted**.

Facts and Myths

Sexual assault is not a synonym for rape. Sexual assault includes any deliberate sexual contact made without the consent of the other party. That means that sexual assault can consist of anything from rape to an unwanted pat on the ass.

Sexual assaults committed by predatory strangers who ambush their victims on the street at night get the most media attention and loom large in the

You Don't Have to Say Yes

"Remember that no matter how far you are in foreplay or how much fun you're having or what your relationship is with your sexual partner, you always, always, ALWAYS have the right to refuse sex and to refuse unprotected sex."

– Sandra Duffey, social work, McMaster University

public imagination, but they are actually quite rare. In reality, most sexual assaults are committed by someone the victim knows and in a private home. On Canadian campuses, 82% of sexual assaults are committed by dates or acquaintances of the victim.

Sexual assault is a serious problem on Canadian campuses; 28% of female students reported being sexually assaulted in the previous 12 months by someone they knew.

The law is clear: you always have the right to refuse sexual advances, regardless of the situation or your prior relationship with the perpetrator. It doesn't matter if the person spent a lot of money on a nice dinner, it doesn't matter if you've consented to have sex with him or her on previous occasions, and it doesn't even matter if you're married to him or her—you always have the right to say no.

Legally, people can't consent to sex while they're drunk. This can lead to tricky situations: drunk people can ask you to have sex with them, but they're legally unable to consent to sex, so if you do have sex with them, it could later be interpreted as a sexual assault. Intoxication can't be used as a defence in a court of law, so a drunk person can still be legally responsible for committing a sexual assault. This means that two drunk people who hook up are on strange legal ground—neither of them can legally consent to sex, but both are legally capable of committing sexual assault.

This is a problem more often than you might expect. One university counsellor we spoke to related an incident in which two students who were good friends had sex while drunk. Later, both of them independently approached the counsellor for help because they each felt that they'd been coerced into having sex with the other.

The best way to steer clear of these situations is to avoid drunken hookups. If you're going to have sex with someone, make sure he or she is sober when you ask—particularly when you're having sex with that person for the first time. This will help you avoid the issue of sexual assault and help both of you avoid regrettable decisions and irresponsible behaviour, like having unsafe sex.

Most Assaults Are Committed by Someone the Victim Knows

"Stranger-to-stranger violence is nowhere near as common as sexual assaults committed by dates and acquaintances."

– Walter DeKeseredy, criminology professor, University of Ontario Institute of Technology

Finally, sexual assault is never deserved. Nobody is "asking for it" unless they literally (and soberly) ask for it. A person's clothing, reputation, body language, or level of intoxication can never justify any unwanted sexual contact, because none of those things can ever signal a person's consent to that contact.

And please, don't repeat the idiotic sentiments that attempt to justify sexual assault, like "She had it coming, dressed the way she was." The rest of us are trying to institutionalize the social change that will finally give every woman and every man sovereignty over her or his own body, and we'd appreciate it if you did not set back the cause 50 years with that kind of nonsense. The combination of your hormones and your interpretation of other people's clothing can never be justification for violating their right to the security of their person.

Minimizing the Risk

It is never a person's fault if he or she is sexually assaulted; the guilt lies 100% with the perpetrator of the assault and not with the victim. However, there are things you can do to avoid putting yourself in a vulnerable position.

When you're on a date or just hanging out with someone you're romantically interested in—or if you're hanging out with someone who you're not romantically interested in and you've just realized that he or she is interested in you—it's important to communicate clearly about your boundaries. You can't expect anybody to read your mind and it's very easy for people to misunderstand your body language. Express your feelings about sex clearly. It might be embarrassing, but it beats the potential embarrassment, awkwardness, or feeling of violation that comes along with someone making a move on you that you didn't want.

At the same time, this sexual assault thing goes both ways, and both of you have the same rights, so it's important to listen to what your date says

beware
date rape drugs

Unfortunately, date rape drugs—typically pharmaceuticals like Rohypnol— are common on university campuses and at off-campus bars and clubs. A date rape drug is used by slipping it into someone's drink when he or she isn't looking. The victim will get suddenly and severely intoxicated, leaving him or her in a position where they may be taken advantage of sexually. Here are some tips for guarding against date rape drugs:

- Never accept a drink from a stranger.
- Place a coaster over your glass when you aren't drinking from it.
- Keep an eye on your drink and your friends' drinks.
- Ask a friend to hold on to your glass when you go to the washroom.
- Check in with your friends; if they become suddenly very drunk or are having trouble standing or speaking, get them to a safe place and call 9-1-1 or your school's security service.

about what he or she wants. Don't assume that you know what your date wants just because of his gender's reputation for having an insatiable and indiscriminate sexual appetite.

Before you go out, tell someone where you are going and when to expect you home. At bars and parties, use the buddy system. Make a pact with your friends to take care of each other. Check in on each other throughout the night, and never let a friend leave the party alone with someone he or she doesn't know.

If you're ever in a situation where you feel uncomfortable with what's going on, or if you just don't feel right about the vibe someone is putting out, you should trust your instincts and get out of there. Sometimes your instincts are smarter than you are, and it's better to be safe than sorry.

Using alcohol and drugs can increase your vulnerability to sexual assault. Be extremely careful about using too much, especially in an unfamiliar place and around people you don't know well. And if you don't think you have used too much, but you feel really messed up, then you may be the victim of a date rape drug; tell your friends immediately, and go somewhere safe.

What to Do if a Friend Is Sexually Assaulted

If a friend is sexually assaulted, immediately get him or her to a safe place. The victim will be able to think more clearly and make better decisions if they aren't scared.

Listen carefully to what they say, and try to keep calm. Explain that it wasn't their fault, and be sure not to get mad at them for doing something stupid, even if they really were taking a foolish risk; that's not what your friend needs to hear right now. Don't try to force them to tell you what happened; your friend is probably feeling vulnerable and traumatized, and doesn't need to be traumatized further by being made to tell the story over and over again.

Tell your friend that you can assist with getting help—but only if he or she wants it. It's up to the victim to decide whether to accept medical attention or call the police, and it's very important that the victim feels in control of the situation at this point.

If the victim is willing, get medical attention. For a female victim, if there is a women's health centre in your community, go there. Otherwise, go to the emergency room at the hospital. Ask your friend how he or she would prefer to get to the hospital; they might feel scared to be alone in a taxi and might prefer to take public transit. Offer to accompany your friend, and ask if there is anyone else they'd rather have to provide support.

Prompt medical attention can help minimize the risk of an unwanted pregnancy or contracting a sexually transmitted disease. The hospital will also be able to provide counsellors to help your friend; hospital staff will collect and store physical evidence in case the victim chooses to press charges.

If the victim wants to involve the police, the earlier they are contacted, the better the chances that the cops will be able to catch the perpetrator. Calling the police from the hospital or a women's clinic might be the best option, because there will be counsellors on hand to help if the victim needs support in speaking to the police.

Sexual assault can leave long-lasting emotional and psychological scars. Victims often report feeling anger, fear, and confusion more than a year after the experience. Students who are sexually assaulted sometimes have trouble concentrating on school work, and some drop out as a result, so it's important that your friend gets help. Dealing with sexual assault is difficult, but fortunately, your friend doesn't have to do it alone. Your school and your community provide counselling and other services to help sexual assault victims recover. And you can help a lot just by being there and standing by your friend.

Y ou always dreamed of going to university, and after working hard in high school you got into your first choice of school. You're young, smart, and taking the first steps toward a good career. There are tons of people to meet and new things to try on campus—if only you felt like taking advantage of them. Life is going exactly as planned, so why do you feel so lousy?

The reality is that depression is very common among students, especially during those first years of school. Depression is often set off by major life changes, and first-year students have their share of big adjustments to get used to. Even the most ambitious and energetic students can be affected by depression and other mental health issues, and the onset of these conditions often comes as a surprise to their friends and family.

Serious illnesses like depression are not the only mental health issues affecting students, of course. Many students suffer from the stress of meeting difficult academic demands or anxiety from homesickness, which can negatively affect their studies, relationships, and general happiness. Luckily, universities and colleges offer a wide spectrum of services that assist students with improving their mental health.

In this section:

- Learn strategies for coping with **Stress and Anxiety**.

- Help yourself and others by understanding **Depression**.

- Improve your mental wellness by taking advantage of **Counselling Services**.

Stress and Anxiety

Everybody gets a little stressed now and again. Stress and anxiety seem to be an almost universal human affliction, but that doesn't mean that you have to just give up and endure it. If you get to know yourself, you can learn strategies to cope.

The academic challenges of university coupled with the new responsibilities of adulthood make many students feel more stressed and anxious than they did during high school. While stress and anxiety are relatively minor problems for some people, they negatively affect many people's sleep patterns, physical wellness, relationships, and studies.

If you're feeling overwhelmed by the demands of your new life, you may take some solace in knowing that you're not alone. A 2008 survey of student mental health at the University of British Columbia found that students reported that stress affects their academic performance more than any other issue, including colds, flus, sore throat, and deaths in the family.

Sometimes students don't seek help to deal with their anxiety because they figure that being stressed out is just part of life. And while it's true that anxiety affects almost everyone at one time or another, when it starts impacting your life or the people around you, it's time to get help. Anxiety can be much more than just feeling a little nervous; it can render you immobilized and leave you feeling like you can't start tackling any of your tasks. It can make you lash out at people you care about. It can prevent you from sleeping well. Seeking help doesn't necessarily mean that you need anti-anxiety drugs; most people learn to control their anxiety and stress without the need for medication.

Other signs that your stress is getting out of hand include losing your appetite or being hungry all the time, getting unreasonably angry or overwhelmed when unexpected things happen, obsessing about all the tasks you have to do, struggling to concentrate or make decisions, and using alcohol or other drugs to self-medicate.

The first step to dealing with your stress is to identify what is stressing you out. Is there a big mid-term coming up that you haven't studied for? Are you worried about your parents being sad that you are no longer living at home? Once you know the source of your stress, think of things you can do to address it, such as scheduling some study time or calling home.

Sometimes stress and anxiety aren't directly related to any one thing. If you are feeling overwhelmed but don't know why, don't bottle up your feelings.

Coping with Homesickness

- Stay busy. Moping in your dorm room and spending every waking hour chatting with people from home isn't going to make you feel any better. Homesickness will dissipate when your new life is rich and full, so get out there and do new things, like intramural sports and social activities.

- Deal with issues at home that worry you. If you're concerned about what's happening at home (your sister is struggling in school or your parents don't seem to be getting along), deal with these issues as directly as you can. Set your mind at ease by calling your sister and asking how you can help.

- Bring some of home with you to school. Put up photos of your friends and family in your room, or do something that reminds you of home. Getting over homesickness doesn't mean totally leaving your old life behind; bringing a piece of your old life into your new life will likely make you feel happier.

- Plan fun things to do. If you spend the whole semester counting down the days until you go home for Christmas, you're going to be miserable. Instead, plan a fun activity with the new people you've met so you have something to look forward to at school.

Express them by talking to a friend or writing them down. Sometimes just expressing your frustration can help you manage your feelings.

Think critically about the expectations you have for yourself. No one is perfect, and if your expectations are unrealistic, you will never feel like you've accomplished what you set out to do. Be easy on yourself, and focus on the positive, such as what you accomplished that day, or your strengths.

When you're feeling overwhelmed by all the tasks you have to do, it often helps to make a plan of action. Rather than staying in a cycle of inaction because you don't know where to start, break down what you need to do into manageable tasks and write a schedule detailing when you are going to do them.

And above all, take care of yourself. Exercising, sleeping well, and eating decently will do wonders for your mental health.

Depression

While almost every student is going to feel stressed or bummed out at some point during their education, there is a point when these feelings cease to be

Your Mental Health Affects Your Studies

"Six of the top seven reasons students gave for academic difficulties were mental health related. Stress, sleep problems, depression and anxiety, concern for troubled family and friends, relationship difficulties and non-academic use of the Internet."

– Dr. Patricia Mirwaldt, director of student health services, University of British Columbia

normal. If your anxiety or sadness begins affecting your life or studies, you may be depressed.

Depression is a problem many students suffer from. A 2008 study at the University of British Columbia found that 13% of male undergraduate students and 11% of female undergrads seriously considered suicide at least once in the year before. Information from some schools indicates that students are more likely to use antidepressants than any other prescription medication, including birth control pills and acne medications.

Depression is a widely misunderstood disorder. Being sad that your cat died is sadness, not depression. Being unable to get out of bed in the morning because of a crushing feeling of hopelessness is depression. Wanting to drop out of school because of a pervading sense of the futility of trying to do anything is depression, if it lasts for more than a day. Depressed people often feel worthless, helpless, hopeless, self-hating, or inappropriately guilty. They may suffer from insomnia and loss of appetite and be irritable, agitated, or lethargic.

Depressed people often connect their feelings of despair to events that are occurring in their lives or to their ideas about the world as a whole, but the true causes of their depression are usually much more complex than what they have fixated on. A person's depression might be rooted deep in their past or embedded in their brain chemistry, so don't get frustrated if you can't simply talk a friend out of being depressed.

Ultimately, it's up to the person who is depressed to seek help, but there are many things you can do to try to help a friend who is suffering from depression. Start by asking how he or she is *really* doing. People are sometimes more willing to open up if they know that someone cares enough to notice they've been out of sorts. Set aside some time to talk in private. Making this a priority will make your friend feel cared for.

Acknowledge your depressed friend's feelings in a sensitive way, even if you disagree with what they're saying. Don't disregard your friend's feelings

Signs That a Friend Might Be Depressed

- She changes her eating and sleeping patterns.
- He expresses hopelessness, fear of failure, uncertainty about the future, anger, or loneliness.
- She starts binge drinking or taking drugs.
- He sleeps excessively or says he can't sleep.
- She stops attending class or starts getting poor marks.
- He rapidly loses or gains weight.
- She stops hanging out with friends.

as unreasonable or irrational. Make sure you really understand what they're telling you, and let them know that you get it by repeating back what they said. This will make them feel less alone. Express concern, but don't be judgmental. Be positive, and remind your friend that things will get better. Then help them access the school's counselling services.

People can learn to cope with depression, but it takes a lot of work and a lot of self-knowledge. If you're struggling with depression, start with working on identifying the difference between being in a depressed state and a more normal state, and distinguishing the difference between your depressed feelings about yourself and the world and your normal feelings. Understand that depression is, at its root, a problem of perception; when you're depressed, the whole world looks awful, but you have to try to realize it's your perceptions that have changed, not the world.

Pulling yourself out of a depression is hard work, but it's a process that builds on itself. If you can force yourself to accomplish one positive thing (and this might be as simple as getting out of bed, taking a shower, and going for a walk in the park), it might make you feel a little better, which will make it easier to take that next positive step.

Counselling Services

Universities and colleges are concerned not only with students' academic performance and intellectual progress, but also their general happiness.

Mental Health Issues Are on the Rise on Campuses

"Mental health is a huge issue on our campus and most others right now: a greater incidence of significant mental health issues, things like bipolar disorder and schizophrenia; students who are a threat to themselves or others; and a general decline in student mental health."

– Dr. Phil Wood, dean of students, McMaster University

They take the mental health of their students very seriously, and every school makes counselling available to students.

If you're dealing with depression or other mental health issues, now is the time to work on learning to cope with your problems. You've got easy access to free, friendly counsellors who are experienced at working with young people in your position. Counsellors can help you develop strategies for coping with depression, stress, and anxiety that will help you later in life. You've come to this place to learn, so this is a great time to learn how to live with yourself.

Counsellors are in the business of helping not only students with serious mental health issues, but also those who just want to improve their academic performance, acquire skills for time management, or learn to deal with stress. For instance, at Wilfrid Laurier University, students can attend workshops to learn about assertiveness skills, dealing with roommate tensions, developing self-confidence, surviving a breakup, goal-setting, procrastination, perfectionism, and so forth. Even if you feel 100% calm all the time (do you have a pulse?), you can benefit from the resources and workshops available through your university's counselling department.

6.6   Eating Well and Being Active

Y ou often hear people talking about the "freshman 15"—the 15 pounds that all students allegedly gain in their first year of college— as though it's a normal, even inevitable phenomenon. There's nothing you can do about it, so you might as well just get fat, right?

In fact, the freshman 15 is partly a myth. On average, Canadian university students gain less than 15 pounds over their entire university or college career. Part of this weight gain is perfectly normal and healthy: people in their late teens and early 20s (particularly males) tend to broaden out and become more muscular than they were when they were teenagers.

But like most myths, this one contains a grain of truth: many people don't take very good care of their bodies during their first years of post-secondary education. Unhealthy cafeteria food is sometimes to blame, as are new habits, such as snacking during late-night study sessions and eating as a response to stress. Some students lose the habit of being physically active when they're no longer going to gym class three times a week or participating in the team sports they played in high school. And turning 18 or 19 (depending on the province) adds a new high-calorie item to many students' diets: alcohol.

Eating well and being active are important in order to maintain a healthy weight and to perform well intellectually, avoid getting sick, sleep well, and be happy. As we've said elsewhere in this book, this period of your life isn't just a time for book learning, it's also a time for growing as a person, and that includes developing habits for a healthy lifestyle.

In this section:

- Learn to develop **Healthy Eating Habits**.
- Keep your budget in mind and learn about **Cooking Healthy on the Cheap**.
- Find out why **Adding Alcohol to Your Diet** can be unhealthy.
- Watch out for signs of **Eating Disorders**.
- Stay fit with **Exercise**.

Healthy Eating Habits

You might be moving away from home and having to do without your parents' healthy, well-balanced meals for the first time in your life. Or maybe you still live at home, but with your busy academic schedule you eat a lot more meals on campus. Whatever your situation, you probably have more responsibility for feeding yourself than ever before. Now is the time to learn to make healthy food choices and establish good eating habits that will stay with you for the rest of your life.

Beating the cafeteria

It can be difficult to find healthy foods you like to eat when you're restricted to the selection offered by your school's cafeteria or your residence's meal hall. Even if your cafeteria offers healthy choices (and many of them do, nowadays), you'll have to fight the temptation to order those delicious-looking but fat-filled hamburgers and french fries.

It pays to exercise some willpower, however. Eating better will make you feel better, and when you get used to eating healthier foods, you'll find those greasy foods less and less tempting. Here are some tips for choosing nutritious foods:

- Look for whole grains instead of white bread or sugary cereals.
- Opt for lean meats and other sources of protein, like beans, instead of fried or fatty meats.
- Choose water or real fruit juice instead of pop.
- Fill up on vegetables from the salad bar instead of overeating starches or protein.
- Be conscious of how much salad dressing and other toppings, such as sunflower seeds, you're using at the salad bar; they can turn your innocent-looking salad into a high-calorie, high-fat meal.
- Avoid sugar-filled desserts, pastries, and sugary muffins and reach for the fresh fruit instead.

Snacking

Given the freedom to eat whatever they want, many first-year students start snacking much more than they used to. Snacking on healthy foods, like fruit and fresh vegetables, is a good way to keep your energy up and avoid overeating during meals, but continually packing away junk food is very unhealthy.

You've got to plan for healthy snacking, because it's not as though vending machines sell packages of celery sticks. You might be stuck eating a bag of chips or a chocolate bar if you get hungry at school and you don't have a healthier snack with you.

Keep healthy snacks in your dorm room (or at home, if you're living with your parents) so they're on hand if you get the munchies while you're studying and so you can bring them with you to class in case of emergency hunger.

Tips for Healthy Eating

- Don't skip meals. Eating regular meals will help you keep your energy up throughout the day, and you'll be less likely to pass out in your physics lecture from hunger or to eat too much junk food.

- Eat breakfast. Starting your day with a satisfying and healthy meal is important to healthy eating all day long. Many dietitians recommend eating a large breakfast with protein (an egg, nuts in your granola) and having a lighter dinner.

- Pay attention to what you're eating. Make sure your meals cover the main food groups and that you're not eating too many highly processed or fried foods.

- Drink lots of water. Sometimes when you think you're hungry, you're actually just thirsty. Carry a water bottle to stay hydrated.

- Keep healthy snacks on hand. If you can easily grab some fruit or carrot sticks with humus while you're studying, you'll have an easier time avoiding junk food.

Fruit and vegetables are good choices for a quick hit of energy; a little bit of protein, like a handful of nuts, can fill you up for the longer haul.

University and college students generally hang out with their friends more at night than they did in high school, and this can lead to a habit of snacking late at night. Eating late at night is usually a bad idea because your body doesn't have time before you go to bed to properly digest and burn the calories you eat, so it ends up storing them as fat. Plus, if you've already had three meals today, you probably don't need more calories. If you're really starving, try to eat something healthy and low in fat, instead of pizza.

Eating for brainpower

Eating well is key not only to having a healthy body, but also to a healthy brain; the garbage-in, garbage-out rule applies to what comes out of your mind. You can't expect to power a genius's brain on potato chips and beef jerky, or on no food at all.

Don't make the mistake of thinking that you can neglect your body and focus entirely on the life of the mind; your brain needs fuel and nutrition, too, and the condition your body is in impacts how your brain functions. Eating properly will help your body provide your brain with a steady stream of fuel, instead of the manic sugar rushes and the doldrums of hypoglycemia caused by a junk-food-rich diet. Proper eating will also help you sleep well, which has a huge impact on your ability to think and to remember what you've learned.

Cooking Healthy Food on the Cheap

When you're on a budget, filling up on 25-cent hot wings on Wings Wednesday at the campus pub can be tempting, but those wings aren't exactly a well-rounded meal. With just a little bit of work and forethought, you can cook something healthy for even less money.

There are two skills you'll need to learn. First, you need to learn how to shop for groceries, and that means looking at the prices and buying groups of ingredients that can be assembled into meals. It sucks to come home from a shopping trip laden with groceries and find that although you have tons of food, you don't have the complete ingredients for anything. Shopping with particular meals in mind will help you avoid having ingredients spoil.

Second, you'll need to learn to cook, which is much easier than you might think. If you're broke and hungry enough, you'll be surprised at how willing you'll be to overlook your own culinary shortcomings when it comes time to dig in. Start with a few simple dishes and gradually increase your repertoire over time. Before long you'll learn to connect the dots, and soon you'll be inventing your own dishes.

Pasta sauce is a great place to begin. Start with a simple tomato-based sauce in first year, and tweak your recipe by adding other ingredients to later versions. By fourth year, you'll be eating gourmet Italian food from your own kitchen.

Your first grocery shopping trip can be a little painful because you'll be buying all those basic herbs, spices, and other ingredients it takes to establish a kitchen, and those things are expensive if you have to buy them all at once. You might wonder whether cooking is cheaper than eating out; we guarantee you that it is. Once you have that base of staple ingredients, herbs, and spices in your kitchen, they'll last you for many meals, and they'll run out one at a time, so you won't have to buy them all at once again.

Going vegetarian or just eating less meat can save a lot of money, regardless of your ethical convictions. Things like beans, lentils, and eggs tend to be much cheaper sources of protein than meat. If you do buy meat, check out what's on sale as soon as you arrive at the grocery store and plan the rest of your meal around whatever is cheap.

Erin's Delicious and Cheap Dahl

Dahl is a delicious Indian curry that is also possibly the cheapest and easiest food in the world to cook yourself. The spices in this dish can serve as the base spices in any curry, so invest in them once and you can make any leftover veggies in your fridge into curry in no time.

You'll need:

1 tbsp of butter (or substitute cooking oil if you don't have butter)
1 onion (yellow or white works)
3 cloves of garlic
1 cup dry lentils (usually made with green lentils, but yellow or red will work too)
4 cups of water
1 tsp cumin
1 tsp coriander
1 tbsp turmeric
1 tsp chili flakes (add extra if you like a spice kick)
Salt to taste

Melt the butter on medium heat in a saucepan. Peel and dice the onions and garlic and cook them in the butter until the onions are soft (about 5 minutes). Rinse the dry lentils in a colander, then add to the onions and garlic. Add 3 cups of water and the spices. Turn the heat up to high and bring the mixture to a boil. Once boiling, turn the heat down and simmer for 30 minutes or until the lentils break down. Add water if the dahl starts to get too dry. Some people like dahl as a thick curry eaten over rice, others like it as a soup, so add water until the mixture is the consistency you prefer.

Dahl will keep for a week in the fridge, so make a big batch and eat it for lunch at school all week.

Variations:

If you want to try something a little different with this basic dahl recipe, add one or all of the following:
1 tsp ground cloves
Fresh chopped cilantro
Fresh or ground ginger
1/2 tsp cinnamon
2 chopped tomatoes

Students Dish on What to Expect From Campus Food

"The quality and selection is mostly uninspiring. The selections are sufficient, but by the end of the year, you get pretty tired of the same stuff over and over. We don't have any really cheap places on campus to eat. If you're looking for lunch, you should expect to pay around $10."

– Ashleigh Mattern, English, University of Saskatchewan

"At U. of T. almost every library has a cafeteria with fast-food chains like Subway, Pizza Pizza, Tim Hortons, Second Cup, and Starbucks. There is also Hart House, a student lounge where students can get a nutritious lunch including grilled chicken, shawarma, salads, spaghetti, and fish."

– Anastasia Prokubovskaya, life sciences, University of Toronto

"The cafeterias are terribly overpriced for what you get both in quantity and quality. The donair place is probably the best deal: $5–7 for a really filling donair."

– Daniel Finnis, engineering, Simon Fraser University

Buying food in bulk is often very economical, but check out the price per weight and make sure you're actually getting a good deal. Lentils and beans are way cheaper if you buy them dry, and they're easy to rehydrate.

Last and most important, eat breakfast at home. Breakfast is so cheap to make at home and it's so easy to have the things on hand that you have no excuse not to do it. Breakfast cereal is okay, but like most processed foods, it can be high in sodium and sugar, and it's way more expensive than it needs to be. Oatmeal (quick oats, not instant oatmeal), on the other hand, is filling, low in fat, sugar-free, and it's one of the cheapest foodstuffs on the planet—plus, you don't need to worry about it going bad, and the only other ingredient is tap water. Throw in some nuts for protein, some fruit (fresh or dried) for vitamins, and a little brown sugar so it doesn't taste like mushed-up cardboard, and you've got yourself a winner.

Adding Alcohol to Your Diet

Alcohol is bad for your diet because it's empty calories; you take on energy without getting any nutritional benefit, so it's best to avoid overconsuming alcohol. There are a lot of reasons to avoid bingeing (drinking a lot in one night), but for your diet it's especially important to avoid getting in the habit of having a couple of casual beers every day. Even if you never get drunk, regular drinking can add up to a lot of calories.

If you're concerned about gaining weight but you still want to enjoy a drink once in a while, avoid drinks with a lot of sugar in them. Stay away from drinks mixed with pop, or cocktails like mojitos that contain a lot of sugar, and have something mixed with soda water instead. Beer packs a caloric wallop, too, so don't fill up on too many brewskis, either.

Eating Disorders

For some people, finding decent food in the cafeteria is the least of their eating worries. The realities of campus life—academic stress, social pressure, demanding schedule—combined with taking on the responsibility for feeding themselves for the first time make post-secondary students particularly vulnerable to developing an eating disorder, such as anorexia (not eating), bulimia (vomiting after eating), or binge eating.

Eating disorders are incredibly dangerous; depriving your body of nutrition can lead to organ failure, strokes, heart attacks, and death. Many people who recover from an eating disorder struggle their entire lives with the irreversible damage done to their bodies and the psychological scars of the disease.

If you suspect that someone you know is struggling with an eating disorder, get immediate medical help. Here are some signs to watch out for:

- Obsessing over food, diets, calorie intake, and weight loss
- Exercising compulsively and obsessively
- Demonstrating unusual eating habits like skipping meals, eating very small portions, or shifting food around on the plate to make it look like it's been eaten
- Using diet pills, laxatives, or other unhealthy methods of avoiding eating
- Hiding food to avoid eating or to eat later
- Rapidly losing weight
- Vomiting after bingeing on food
- Avoiding eating with others
- Becoming depressed, experiencing dramatic mood swings, or suffering from insomnia
- Losing hair and suffering from headaches and dizziness

there's more to sports than hockey and football

So, you want to stay active and you'd like to do something more social than standing on the Stairmaster, but you're not into hyper-competitive team sports like rugby or soccer. You'll be glad to know that there is a ton of other stuff you can do. Here are some weird options to get you started:

- Frisbee golf: Do you like taking long walks in the park but can't afford golf clubs or green fees?

- Geocaching: A worldwide scavenger hunt using GPS devices.

- Bicycle polo: It's a bit like hockey, except instead of skates, you've got bikes. Or it's like polo, but with less horse poop.

- Hula hooping: People are doing this for fitness now. Who knew?

Exercise

No matter how good your diet is, you'll never be really healthy unless you get regular exercise. Only exercise can tone your muscles and strengthen your heart and lungs. It will also give you more energy, help you concentrate, and make it easier to sleep.

There are plenty of ways to stay active on campus, most of which we went over in **Section 4.2: Life Outside the Classroom**, but if you don't feel like turning pages, here's a quick list of ideas:

- Go to the campus gym.
- Make exercise part of your daily routine by walking or cycling to class.
- Make it part of your social life by running or playing sports with friends.
- Join a campus intramural sports team.
- Try out a new activity through your campus athletic centre or a club.

7

The Future
Is Coming

WE'RE NOT TALKING about ray guns and flying cars; we're talking about *your* future.

The years of school you have in front of you might seem like an eternity, but they have a way of quietly creeping by until one day you realize you're about to graduate and you need to find a job. Many students get so focused on earning their degree or diploma they lose sight of what that degree or diploma is supposed to be preparing them for and what else they should be doing to get ready for the next stage of life.

Thinking about what lies in your future can be exciting, and it can motivate you to do a few things now to help you prepare. Some students think that because school is supposed to prepare them for a career, graduating should be enough. However, the real world functions on different terms than your educational institution, so it's important to engage in activities that will develop skills to complement your academic knowledge.

It can be difficult to know what to prepare for when the future is so unclear. Should you enrol in flying-car-driving lessons? We don't know. But no matter what lies in the years ahead, you'll benefit from broadening yourself as a human being so you'll be more adaptable and better ready to cope with an unpredictable future. You can't learn the technical skills it takes to build ray guns, but you can learn the people skills and organizational skills you'll need to manage a ray gun factory—should the need ever arise.

In this chapter:

- Think about what you want and the steps you'll take to reach **Your Long-Term Goals**.

- Get a leg-up by getting work experience with **Co-ops and Summer Jobs**.

- Explore what **Graduate and Professional School** is all about.

- Lay the groundwork so you can score **Reference Letters**.

- There are as many ways to go about **Launching Your Career** as there are careers.

7.1   Your Long-Term Goals ✓

G oals are vital for motivation. Going to school while doing everything else it takes to be a good, functional human being is hard work, and we all need to have some goal in sight, some greater motivation for doing all the little tasks we do on a day-to-day basis.

Whether you've undergone a formal process of goal-setting or not, you do have goals. We all have them, dozens of them, whether we're conscious of them or not. One of our goals might be to graduate and get a degree. Another might be to get 50,000 points in whatever stupid video game we're playing right now. A third might be to spend more time with a friend we haven't seen much of lately.

Thinking about and writing down your goals will help you achieve them. When they're put down on paper, you can see how they relate to each other and what short-term steps need to be taken so you can achieve your long-term objectives. Recording your goals will help you to measure your progress and stay focused and motivated.

As we said at the beginning of this book, you don't have to know what you're going to do with the rest of your life. Post-secondary education is a process of exploration. You're going to learn so much, it would be foolish to have your mind made up for certain right now. But that doesn't mean you can't make plans and set goals. It just means that you might have to be flexible if something happens along the way that changes your mind.

In this section:

- Think about your **Short-, Medium-, and Long-Term Goals** and how they relate to each other.

- Learn to set **S.M.A.R.T. Goals**.

- Ponder how to progress toward your **Career Goals**.

Short-, Medium-, and Long-Term Goals

If you start writing down a list of everything you can think of that you want to accomplish, you'll probably notice that some of your goals are a lot bigger than others and that accomplishing them will take a lot more effort. One goal might be to lose five pounds. Another might be to become a criminal lawyer.

It'll be a lot easier to relate these goals to each other if you separate them according to the time they'll take to accomplish—that is, into short-, medium-, and long-term goals. You can also group them by subject. For example, your criminal law ambition can be put in the "career" category, while losing five pounds can be put under "health" or "sports"—depending on why you want to lose the weight.

Creating this hierarchy will help you see how your goals are connected to each other and how they build onto one another. You can use this structure to create subordinate, shorter-term goals that act as stepping stones on the path to accomplishing a long-term goal. For example, if one of your long-term goals is to get an honours degree in chemistry, a medium-term goal might be to get a grade of A-minus or better in the chemistry class you're taking this semester, and a matching short-term goal might be to review and rewrite your chemistry notes for 30 minutes after every class.

S.M.A.R.T. Goals

An acronym a lot of motivational-type people often use when discussing goal-setting is S.M.A.R.T. We don't generally trust cute acronyms that spell

know thyself

Goal-setting starts with self-reflection. To be able to set yourself on a career path, it's important that you see your strengths, weaknesses, and aspirations with clarity. "Self-awareness is really the bedrock of satisfaction in life. If you know yourself and are true to yourself, you'll bring your best self to the world."

– Keturah Leonforde, career counsellor, Wilfrid Laurier University

something, but we've given this one some thought, and it looks pretty good. The general idea is to set realistic goals in such a way that you can tell whether you've achieved them. Check it out:

- *Specific:* Your goal should be specific and well-defined. For example, it's hard to know exactly what "be a better person" means, but "beat Mark at ping-pong" is easy to understand.
- *Measurable:* It's easier to track your progress, maintain your motivation, and know whether you've accomplished your goal if it's measurable in some way. In this sense, goals like "improve GPA to 3.20" or "run 15 kilometres" are good goals.
- *Achievable:* Set realistic goals that are possible to achieve. It's just pointless and demoralizing to set a goal that you can't possibly achieve. "Win this year's Vancouver Marathon" isn't an achievable goal if you've only just started jogging this spring, and it's just going to depress you when you're halfway through the race and you realize you're in about 8,000th place. Instead, try making "finish the Vancouver Marathon" your goal, with "finish in under five hours" as a secondary, aspirational goal.
- *Relevant:* Your goals should be useful to you, and they should be in line with your other goals, particularly your long-term goals. If one of your long-term goals is "stay healthy and fit," then the short-term goal "win hot-dog-eating contest" might not align well with your other priorities.
- *Time-framed:* Your goals should have some specific time period attached to them. Feeling like there's a ticking clock will help motivate you to get things done. Plus, having a deadline will let you

know when you haven't made it, instead of waiting until you're 80 years old to realize that you're probably never going to win that marathon.

And that spells S.M.A.R.T.—probably just a coincidence.

While it is a good idea to have specific, concrete goals with deadlines attached, they should also be flexible. Real life is messy, circumstances change, and sometimes goals need to be changed as well.

For example, if a goal isn't achievable within the time frame you originally set, instead of giving up, counting yourself a failure, and hanging your head in shame, it'll probably do you more good to revise the goal. So you flunked a class and you won't meet your goal of graduating in four years— you shouldn't have done it, but there's nothing you can do about it now, so revise your goal to graduating in four years plus a semester.

Or maybe you'll be halfway to accomplishing a long-term goal and realize that you don't want to achieve that goal anymore; you don't want to be a criminal lawyer. This is no time to be dogmatic. Revise your goal, or get rid of it altogether.

Career Goals

Whether you're enrolled in a vocational program with a clear path to employment or your post-secondary education thus far has mostly consisted of a casual exploration of 18th-century literature, one day you're going to have to graduate and get a job. While we are certainly not proponents of the view that the only purpose of education is to lead to a career, it is definitely one of the purposes of education, and it doesn't hurt to think about your future career.

Having a career goal, or several possible career goals, is a good way to provide a context for your educational goals, so you can emerge from college or university as a graduate with one or more sets of employable skills. If the career you're considering involves going to professional or graduate school (such as being a scientist, lawyer, or doctor), the process of applying for the next level of schooling provides a convenient framework of qualifications you can use as short- and medium-term goals.

For instance, a strong medical school applicant will have very good marks, an excellent performance on the MCAT standardized test, a record of community involvement, volunteer and work experience, a demonstrated interest in medicine, and reference letters from several prominent professors. These aren't exactly achievements you can throw together in your last semester of school; a prospective medical student is going to have to plan for this long in advance, and a first-year student hoping to get into med school might identify the following short-term goals:

- Use the university's writing centre to improve your writing, to get higher marks on essays, and to perform better on the essay section of the MCAT.
- Become more involved in the community by joining a sports team, volunteering for a local charity, or getting involved in student government.
- Seek out an opportunity to explore the medical profession by working at a clinic or finding a relevant volunteer position.

Not all careers have such clear paths to success, so your goal-setting might take more research and self-reflection. If you know what kind of job you want, seek out people who are currently involved in that field and ask them how they did it. Make an appointment with a career counsellor at school and see what they have to say. Talk to students who are pursuing a similar career and who are closer to graduating than you and get their perspective. Enquire about whether your school can arrange a mentorship with a professional in your field of interest.

Think about the first job on your future career path and imagine what potential employers will want to see on your resumé. What kind of skills and experience will they want you to have? And remember, employers aren't just looking for high marks and academic accolades; they want to see evidence that a candidate is an interesting, engaged, well-rounded person. Seek opportunities to build that ideal resumé, and develop the skills you'll need in your future career, such as leadership or communication skills.

This is also a good time to think about the other things you want to accomplish in your life. Are you hoping to travel before you start your career? Do you aspire to learn a second language or become a better musician? Personal goals like this are at least as important as your career goals. Don't forget to include them in your plans.

7.2 Co-ops and Summer Jobs

Students who graduate in a less-than-stellar job market sometimes run into the following Catch-22: they can't get a job because they have no experience, but they can't get experience without first getting a job. However, you can avoid this dilemma and ease your entry to the job market by getting on-the-job experience in your future industry before you graduate.

Your summer or part-time job can do more for you than provide the year's beer money. If you find the right job, you can explore your future career options and learn something about the field you're considering. You may also get a leg-up on competing applicants for jobs when you graduate by having relevant skills and experience on your resume.

Enrolling in co-operative education (or "co-op") programs can help you do just that. These programs help connect students to prospective employers in their field of interest so students can get jobs in their future field for one or more work terms before they graduate.

In this section:

- Learn what your school's **Co-op Programs** can do for you.

- Find out what kinds of jobs complement your education by learning **What to Look for in a Job.**

- Read about ways to find great opportunities when you're **Looking for Jobs.**

- A tailored resumé and good interview skills will help you with **Scoring the Gig.**

Co-op Programs

Many schools offer co-op programs, which allow students to take one or more terms off school to get a job related to their field of study while earning

co-op can lead to a job

Engineering grad Danny Haines said if he had not completed a co-op program, he would still be handing out resumés. Danny graduated from the University of Alberta in May 2010 and began searching for a job in a difficult economy. After applying to numerous companies, Danny got in touch with the three companies he had completed co-op terms with. His boss from the first co-op he completed, in 2007, said he wished Danny had called sooner and instantly hired him. Beyond landing him a job, Danny said participating in a co-op program allowed him to see how the basic principles he learned in class were applied in real-world scenarios. Today, Danny loves his job as assistant project manager and views co-op terms as win-win situations for the employer and the student. "Employers get to see if the student would be a good fit for the company. Straight out of school I got to work with a company I was familiar with, I already knew the people who worked there, and I had an idea of the type of work I would do."

credits that apply toward their degree or diploma. Most co-op programs only accept students who are in the latter half of their degree or diploma program, but it's a good idea to start thinking about it early in your studies, while you're planning your program.

Your school will give you various kinds of help in finding a co-op job, such as workshops in resumé writing and interviewing, and access to a database of positions open only to co-op students. Prospective employers will sort through the various applications they receive, conduct interviews with applicants, and select which students they hire. Unfortunately, your co-op program can't force a company to hire you, so you'll have to earn the job yourself on the basis of your resumé and interview.

Once you've found a job, you can take a term off school to work, generally for a period of four to eight months. Your pay will depend on the skills you bring to the job and the difficulty of the work. The money is nice, but the best thing you'll get out of your work term is hands-on, practical experience at a job related to your field of study. Past co-op students we spoke to reported that getting some practical experience really helped them academically when they returned to school by giving them a concrete application to which they could relate the theories they were being taught.

The icing on the co-op cake is that many schools will give you course credits for it. You won't get as many credits as you would in a normal semes-

co-op is like the real world— with training wheels

An advantage to co-op programs is that there is a team of people at your university to help you navigate anything that comes up on the job, from negotiating your salary to resolving conflicts with your boss. "As you encounter issues in the workplace, you have a go-to person at your school. There is an academic support team behind you."

– Keturah Leonforde, career counsellor, Wilfrid Laurier University

ter of school, however, so taking a co-op program will generally mean that you'll take a little longer to complete your degree or diploma. On the other hand, while it might take you five years to get a four-year degree, you could come out with 16 months of work experience with two different employers in your future industry, together with all the industry contacts you made in that period, while your classmates will be starting from scratch.

Not all schools and not all faculties offer co-op programs. Check your school's website for more info.

What To Look for in a Job

A summer or part-time job when you're in school can be about so much more than earning a little extra cash. The right job can provide you with new skills, valuable experience, connections, and experiences to list on your resumé that go beyond grades and courses passed. Even working part-time at a coffee shop will demonstrate to future employers that you can work with other people in a fast-paced environment and that you have the time management skills to also excel academically.

Often, your choice between jobs will be a compromise between the objectives you want to achieve. A job as a waitress might offer flexibility and, when you add up all the tips, it could easily pay better than most other jobs, but it probably doesn't have much to do with the career you want to have when you graduate—unless you're studying hospitality management, that

Show Off Your Time Management with Extracurricular Activities

"Rather than asking, 'How are your time management skills?' and hoping the student doesn't lie to me, I tend to look at where they graduated in their class and what else they did during that time. Were you part of the student union? Were you a varsity athlete? Did you have a part-time job?"

– Maurice Fernandes, senior recruitment manager, Ceridian Canada

"Grades and diplomas are the price of admission these days. What employers are really concerned about beyond that is: What have you done outside of the classroom?"

– Keturah Leonforde, career consultant, Wilfrid Laurier University

is. Other jobs, such as being a lab assistant for a professor in your program, may pay less but are much more relevant to your future career.

Jobs can be an excellent opportunity to test-drive your future career. Identify companies or organizations in your field and approach them about employment opportunities. Even a menial job like working as a janitor or in the mail room of an organization in your field can give you a behind-the-scenes look at what your prospective industry is like. You'll also be establishing an employment record with the organization, and you might even have an opportunity to build contacts.

When you're looking for a part-time job, make sure that the job won't interfere with your studies; there's no point in having a great resumé as a chemist if you flunk out of chemistry. Look for jobs that are flexible and will allow you to take time off when you have to write papers or exams. Often, it's easier to find this flexibility in bigger companies, where there are more employees available to cover the shifts you want to take off. Jobs on campus are designed with the needs of students in mind and often have schedules specifically tailored to work for students. The added bonus is that they're nearby, which saves time you might spend commuting to another job.

Not everyone is going to find a perfect, convenient, resumé-building job, however. You should keep an open mind about jobs that don't seem ideal on the surface. Many employers are interested in candidates with a breadth of experience, and their ideal candidate might be someone who can bring experience from other industries. And who knows, maybe trying out a

think outside the box

There are so many more opportunities out there other than the usual barista and waiter positions. Ricardo Bortolon, a graduate science student at the University of British Columbia, once found a job as a nude model for an art school. He also worked as a labourer at a biohazardous-materials facility. "We would process biohazardous material from sites around B.C. such as hospitals, research centres, and morgues. Sometimes the bins would fall over and open and blood or used diapers or a leg would spill out."

job that isn't remotely related to your area of study will teach you something. It might even make you change your mind about what you want to do in life. At the very least, it'll give you interesting stories to tell when you're a successful practitioner of whatever it is you're studying to practise.

Looking for Jobs

The obvious place to start your job search is online classified services like Craigslist. While these services can be a useful tool, ads posted online often attract hundreds of applications—so many that applicants often don't hear back.

The best way to get a job is through what human resources specialists call "the hidden job market." This market consists of jobs that aren't openly or widely advertised and are usually filled through recommendations.

This may be discouraging news if you feel like you don't know anybody with connections to potential employers, but the reality is that we all know people like that. Networking isn't some kind of dirty, backroom game played only by insiders; it's actually just using the oldest form of mass communication in the world: word of mouth. Often, all that's involved in getting a job is telling a friend that you're looking for a job. That friend might happen to know that his boss is thinking about hiring someone new, so he recommends you. Then the boss takes a look at your resumé and asks you a few questions and decides he'd rather not go through the hassle of posting a job listing when he's got a perfectly good applicant in front of him, and boom, you've got a job.

networking
works

Will Vanderbilt, an environmental science student at McGill University, was disappointed when he didn't get an internship with one of his profs. But minutes after getting the rejection email, he received a job offer from his professor's husband for an even better job, which he didn't even know existed. "Since then, I've been to Nunavut twice, and might get to travel to the Western Arctic later this summer!"

Anyone who's ever looked for a job knows that finding employment rarely happens that quickly. However, there is a lot you can do to improve your chances of finding a position. First, get an idea of what kind of job you want, so you don't send people off on a wild-goose chase finding jobs you don't want. Second, you've got to put the word out; post it on Facebook and tell your friends, family, classmates, professors, mail carrier, greengrocer, bartender, and the guy standing next to you at the urinals (you get the idea: everyone) that you're on the job hunt.

Then you'll want to do some more targeted networking. Make a list of people you know who are connected in any way to your field of interest. If you define the word "connected" broadly enough, you might be surprised how many people you actually know. Go through your list and drop each of the people a quick email asking them to keep an eye out for possibilities.

The next step is expanding your network to your best advantage. You'll have a better chance of knowing where opportunities lie if you thoroughly understand the industry you want to get into. Research by reading trade magazines and talking to people who work in the industry. If the industry has a professional association that you can afford to join, then join it, and read the newsletters, surf the job boards, and make as many contacts as you

fun
fact

Ben, one of the authors of this book, once found a job by telling a bartender he was looking for work. The bartender put him in touch with a customer in the bar who was looking for a new employee, and Ben was hired on the spot.

Online Job Search Resources

- Jobbank.gc.ca: This government site offers tips for job hunting and a large job database.

- Online search engines: Look at sites like Workopolis.com, Monster.ca, and Wowjobs.ca.

- CanadianCareers.com: Explore careers, learn to market yourself, and start finding work.

- BusinessWire.com: Research a specific company.

- NewsWire.ca: Another good research tool to start learning about specific companies.

- CareerKey.com: Provides links to professional associations in many industries.

- CharityVillage.com: Lists news and events as well as job and volunteer opportunities for Canada's non-profit sector.

- Connexions.org: Features a database of non-profit organizations.

- Sources.com: Primarily a source for journalists looking for spokespeople, this website is good for searching for companies and contacts by subject.

- Industry Canada (ic.gc.ca): Features a database of Canadian companies by sector.

- Vault.com: Offers insider information on over 10,000 companies, job hunt tips, and a listing of available positions.

can by attending conferences. Many professional organizations have discounted rates for students.

While you're waiting for all of this to pan out, go back to Craigslist and check out your university's job boards. People get jobs that way, too, and companies who make postings at student employment centres are often specifically looking for students. It doesn't hurt to apply.

Scoring the Gig

Now that you've found the job posting of your dreams, all you have to do is reach out and take it—right? Don't send your dream job just any resumé; tailor your resumé and your cover letter to highlight the skills and attributes you have that suit the position. Have your friends and family read over your resumé and cover letter to catch any mistakes you might have made and to make suggestions about how to improve it. Most university career centres offer free resumé editing services.

In your resumé, be explicit about what skills you gained from each of the experiences you list. Don't assume that your various job titles will be enough to convey the kind of work you did and what you might have learned; instead, briefly detail your responsibilities and your accomplishments at each position. For instance, if you volunteered for a fundraising event, include how much money you raised. In the section describing your education, include any major awards you won, major projects you completed, your honour roll status, and your average, if it was good.

You don't have to brag, but don't short-change yourself by being too modest. The work, education, and volunteering experiences you've had at this point in your life may not seem like much to you, but you gained valuable skills from each of them, and any one of them might be enough to put you above another candidate. If you're having a hard time remembering what you learned from your experiences, ask your family and friends to help; they might have a better perspective on your past than you do.

If possible, make direct contact with your potential employer before you submit your application. Being able to put a face (or at least a voice) to the resumé will help the person who is making the hiring decision see you as a human being and tell you apart from the other applicants. Either go to the business in person or make a phone call, and introduce yourself and ask them how they would like to receive your application.

If you land an interview, take some time to prepare for it beforehand. Learn as much as you can about the company and what they look for in employees. Dress for the interview the same way you'd dress for the job—unless the job has a uniform. Nothing freaks out a McDonald's manager like someone showing up for an interview in a McDonald's uniform. Practise answering standard interview questions, which you can easily find on the Internet.

Be sure to get a good night's sleep before your interview, and absolutely the most important thing to remember is to RELAX! NOW! RELAX FASTER!

Sorry.

Breathe deep.

Think happy thoughts . . .

. . . and . . .

relax.

7.3 Graduate and Professional School ✓

Continuing your studies after getting your bachelor's degree isn't just for future professors; it's also for future doctors, lawyers, and many others who want to use it to advance their career or satisfy their intellectual curiosity. However, the decision to go to grad school shouldn't be taken lightly. Grad school takes a significant commitment of time and finances, and succeeding as a graduate student requires more self-direction and motivation than as an undergrad. Some students find themselves in grad school because they didn't know what to do next or were afraid to enter the job market; these aren't particularly great reasons for dedicating the next few years of your life to study. So take some time to reflect on your abilities, aspirations, and shortcomings before taking the plunge.

If you are considering continuing your education and getting a master's or doctoral degree, you should begin preparing during your undergraduate years. The application process is often quite competitive, and there's a lot you can do years in advance to improve your chances of being accepted.

In this section:

- Answer the question **What Is Grad School All About?**

- Find out what you'll need to apply in **Elements of the Application.**

What Is Grad School All About?

Many people think of graduate school as a pathway to becoming a lifelong academic, like a professor or a researcher. A life in academia is an option, of course, but graduate studies serve different purposes in different fields, some of which are intensely academic, while others are very practical and skills-based.

In many fields, graduate or professional school provides students the practical information needed to apply the more general knowledge they

start thinking
about grad school
now

There are a lot of things you can do as an undergraduate student to increase your chances of getting into grad school. So even if you want to keep the door open, start thinking about what you can do to make yourself a better applicant and address your weaknesses.

"I had been planning to go to grad school since my second year, so I made sure I took courses with tenured or tenure-track professors so I would have lots of choices for references. I also enrolled in an undergraduate thesis course to emphasize focus in my field. I spoke to upper-year students and professors I trusted at the end of my second year, and I am glad I began my prep early."

– Stephanie Rade, library services, University of Western Ontario

"Since I am interested in the medical field, in my first year I applied to different hospitals to get some hands-on experience as a volunteer. I also personally emailed several professors who gave me the opportunity to work in their labs. Working in these different environments I tried to get as much advice as possible from the people who had already gone through the career path that I was just starting.

"The University of Toronto also provides numerous guidance centres that provide information about possible careers and grad school opportunities, and each college has registrars with whom you can make appointments to discuss what your next steps will be after finishing your undergraduate studies. I also leaped at every opportunity to get involved in research, interact with doctors, and be a part of the medical community."

– Anastasia Prokubovskaya, life sciences, University of Toronto

learned at the undergraduate level. For instance, law school can equip philosophy grads with the practical knowledge they need to apply their skills in logic and rhetoric to a career; an MBA program can give engineering graduates the business chops they need to become successful entrepreneurs; a journalism master's program can turn an environmental science graduate into an environment reporter.

The grad school experience varies widely from program to program; you can't just assume that if you loved your undergrad years, you'll love grad school. If you're considering going on to grad school, take a close look at specific programs and find out exactly what is involved in getting a master's degree.

Most non-professional graduate programs involve much less coursework than an undergraduate is accustomed to. Most of the student's energy is instead dedicated to researching a thesis under the supervision of a faculty member, which can be a huge change for students who are used to having more structure to their education.

Professional programs, on the other hand, may have no thesis requirement but will have more courses and may include a work-experience requirement. For example, law students article at a law firm before they are certified to practise law; medical students spend a ton of time working alongside doctors as part of their residencies.

Talk to professors and current graduate students about any graduate program you're considering, and find out what the program entails before you set out on the arduous application process.

Graduate school as a job

Being a graduate student is a bit like going to school, but it's also a bit like having a job, in that you'll probably have responsibilities to people other than yourself. Many graduate students are offered positions as teaching assistants—TAs—as a part of their funding package, for example, and that means marking papers and tests, running tutorials, and even lecturing. Other grad students will find themselves doing their grad research as a part of a larger project involving other graduate students all working under a supervising professor.

The bright side of all of this work and responsibility is that graduate students are often offered funding in return for their toil. Now that being a student is becoming more of a career, you'll likely piece together the funding for your education from a mosaic of research and TA positions and fellowships in addition to the scholarships, bursaries, and loans you used in your undergrad. Your funding will be contingent on your performance as a TA or researcher, however, so your school is partly your educator and partly your employer.

Elements of the Application

Each graduate program has its own unique admission requirements; some put most of the emphasis on marks, while others place more emphasis on work and other extracurricular experience. Take a close look at the application processes of all the programs you're interested in well in advance of your graduation date so you have time to work on your weaknesses or so you can focus on the programs that value your strengths. Typically, you'll have to compile the following items for your graduate or professional school application:

Grades and transcripts

Your GPA will be an important consideration for any program, and your application will have to be accompanied by an official copy of your transcript from your university. Some grad programs require your university to send your transcripts to them directly (presumably so you can't doctor the documents—a B-minus is so easy to change into a B-plus) while other schools will ask you to send it with the rest of your application.

Find out exactly which grades the school looks at. Some will only look at your GPA in the final two years of study, while others will only look at your average in courses that are prerequisites for the program. For example, a med school might not care that you flunked Econ 101 in first year because they're only going to look at your average in the required science courses.

If your marks aren't your strongest point, don't fret. Many programs put more emphasis on other considerations, such as your work experience, extracurricular activities, or community involvement. Check for programs that have lower minimum GPA requirements, but remember that meeting the minimum doesn't guarantee you a spot at the school; many other applicants may have better grades, and the spots go to the most qualified candidates.

Standardized tests

Many graduate programs require applicants to write a standardized test, such as the LSAT for law school, the MCAT for medical school, or the more general GRE for other graduate programs. These tests focus on general knowledge of the field and the ability to write and think logically. They are intended to give the school an objective basis for comparing students who attended different schools with different grading standards and took courses of varying difficulty in their undergrad years.

If you test well, this may be your opportunity to make up for some not-so-awesome marks you got in your undergraduate years. For some students, however, standardized tests can be a nightmare. The amount of weight given to test scores varies from program to program and from school to school, which is something that should be kept in mind when applying.

These tests can be a real voyage into your academic past (How do you multiply fractions?) and perhaps into academic *terra incognita* (What is the meaning of salubrious? Multifarious? Loquacious?), so you might have to devote a considerable amount of time to studying. Many students choose to devote a summer to getting ready to write their standardized test.

Personal statement or essay

Many grad programs will require you to write a personal statement or a short essay as part of the application. You'll often be asked for something autobiographical that says something about your background, your motivations for attending grad school, and what you've done with your life that will make you a successful graduate student. Other programs will ask you to answer a question concerning your field.

In general, the purpose of the essay is to allow the school to learn why you want to be admitted and what you hope to do with the education they're offering, as well as whether you can write clearly and make well-reasoned, compelling arguments. (For more on writing essays, read **Section 3.4: Writing Papers and Essays.**)

Application forms and resumés

Grad schools are interested in what you've done with your life besides school, such as your work, research, volunteer, and travel experience. You may be asked to provide this information in resumé format, which will allow you to control how you present your experiences, or you may be asked to follow their standardized application form.

This can be one of the trickiest parts of an application because, rather than simply presenting what someone else thinks of you, like your grades, you have to discuss yourself and decide how to frame the experiences you've had in the past 20-odd years of life. In competitive programs, all the applicants will have lots of extracurricular experiences. For your application to stand out, you need to highlight why your experience is relevant to the program and why it makes you special, rather than simply list what you've done and hope that the person who reads the line "volunteer camp counsellor 2008 to 2010" understands what you learned from the experience.

Letters of recommendation

Most programs ask for two to four letters of recommendation. We think that this is such an important topic that we wrote a whole section about it. Carry on reading the next section.

perseverance
might be the key

Jim Janson earned a degree in economics from Dalhousie University in the 1980s, but it wasn't until 20 years later that he realized he wanted to continue his education. After more than two decades working in a Halifax-based carnival, he decided to become a lawyer. He wrote the LSAT and received a strong score, but admissions officials weren't convinced that he could handle the academic workload after so long out of university, so he was rejected.

He began taking courses in law and criminology. When he was rejected a second time, he was frustrated—but he stuck to it. Finally, on his third try, he was wait-listed and eventually accepted. "I was very serious about doing it once I decided. I said to myself, 'Well, I'll have to do whatever they tell me I have to do, and I'll get in.' And it worked."

7.4 Reference Letters

If you are planning to study law, medicine, or anything else at the graduate level, you'll definitely need reference letters from professors. Students going on to other opportunities can benefit from them too; a good reference letter can make all the difference to a job application by describing your personality and abilities in a way that will set you above other candidates. Getting a good reference requires preparation, and the way you ask profs for a reference will impact the letter they write for you, so it's important to go about it correctly.

In this section:

- Find out the answer to the burning question **What Is a Reference Letter?**

- Set yourself up to score great reference letters by **Laying the Groundwork.**

- The only way to get that letter is by **Approaching Your Prof.**

What Is a Reference Letter?

A reference letter, or letter of recommendation, is an essential part of your graduate school or professional school application. Most of these schools require that you include two to four reference letters with your application. Some programs will provide a specific form that professors have to fill out to give you a reference, while others will accept letters written in whatever format the professor chooses.

A good reference letter gives the reader insight into your character and personality, as well as your academic abilities, and is written by someone the reader feels they can trust. This means that the best letters will be written by professors who actually know you and your work well and who are respected members of their academic communities. What this effectively communicates to the reader is that someone who is already a member of the academic community believes you have the potential to be a successful graduate student.

There is some disagreement about how much reference letters influence the way professors view a grad school application. Some professors say that even a brilliant letter can't make up for a mediocre GPA or an unimpressive standardized test score. However, a strong letter can make the difference between a successful and an unsuccessful application—especially if the selection committee is on the fence about a candidate.

All reference letters are positive—if they weren't, the professors wouldn't write them at all. The difference between a so-so and a kick-ass reference letter is all in the detail. A letter that says, "Erin Millar got an A in my class and her participation was above average," isn't going to stand out or change anybody's mind about Erin's application. On the other hand, a letter that raves about how Erin demonstrated passion for a subject, showed creativity in

Ask for Letters from People with Cred

"If you are applying to a graduate program with a strong research orientation, the most credible referee will be someone who is also an active researcher in the same field. The more renowned the person is, the more credibility will be given to the endorsement."

– Dr. Dave Mumby, associate professor of psychology, Concordia University, and author of a book about getting into graduate school

the way she approached assignments, and may have accidentally cured cancer in her biology lab just might make the difference between rejection and acceptance.

Laying the Groundwork

The key to getting a good reference letter is approaching the right professor. The biggest challenge for most students is developing relationships with three or four professors so they know them well enough to ask for a letter. You can't expect to cultivate relationships with four professors in the last semester of your degree, so if you're even remotely considering going to grad school, you should start getting to know your profs from the very beginning of your degree. If you never bother to talk to your professors, you might find that even though you have very good marks, none of your professors remember your name.

Here are some ideas for getting to know your professors and creating opportunities to demonstrate what an amazing student you are:

- Participate in class.
- Use your professors' office hours by going in to ask questions or to discuss assignments.
- Look for opportunities to volunteer to work in labs or on research conducted by your professors.
- Consider taking a "directed studies" course, in which you pursue your own topic of study for a semester under the direction of a supervising professor.
- Write an honours thesis and get to know your thesis adviser.
- In third and fourth year, take courses with small class sizes, which give you more opportunity to interact with your professors.

Getting More Than a Generic Letter

"If you want a less generic letter, the key is to develop relationships with your profs—not becoming best friends but demonstrating genuine interest in the course material. During undergrad, I met with many of my profs on a regular basis. When discussing essay topics, I always had a few ideas that I had done some preliminary research on, or at least thought about, and had an idea of where the argument would go. I also met with profs regularly just to discuss the course, the readings, that sort of thing. By doing this I developed a good professor-student relationship with a number of my professors. They knew me and could speak to my character and my genuine interest in the subject material."

– Carson Jerema, political science, University of Waterloo

Of course, there's no point in pursuing these opportunities unless you can show your professors that you're a good student. Make sure that you perform well in these situations by meeting deadlines, working well with others, and producing good research and writing.

To get references from the right professors, you'll have to pay attention and make sure that you take classes with those profs. Many classes and tutorials are taught by graduate students, doctoral candidates, and untenured faculty doing postdoctoral work. These people might be easier to develop relationships with, but you'll also need references from at least a couple of big-league, widely published, respected, tenured professors.

As you get into your third and fourth years of your undergraduate, pay more attention to which profs are teaching the classes you register for. Figure out what your professors' specialties are and the kind of research they are working on so you can get an idea of who these people are. Find out which professors are experts in the subjects within your major that you're most interested in, and try to take classes from them.

Approaching Your Prof

The way you ask professors for a reference can affect how good a letter they write for you. First you have to give them enough time to write a decent letter. Springing the request on them two days before your application deadline

Don't Be Shy

"Don't be sheepish or apologetic. Writing reference letters for students is not a favour that professors grant to their students, it is one of their professional obligations. Crazy as it seems, professors want to get their best students into grad schools, and writing strong letters on their behalf is part of the job."

— Andrew Potter, author, philosopher, and former professor, Trent University

isn't going to result in the letter you want.

Be polite when you ask your professors for a reference, but there's no need to be shy about asking. Writing reference letters is actually part of your professors' job, and they're used to being approached by students.

Make your request in person or over the phone. Email is a little too casual a medium. An actual conversation will give your profs the opportunity to ask questions about what you're applying for and your future career plans, so they can tailor the letter accordingly.

Remind your profs who you are, what classes you've taken with them, and why they should write you a letter. For instance, remind them of the awesome paper you wrote and the excellent mark you earned in the course.

Once your profs agree to write the letter, provide them with additional information about yourself to make writing the letter easier. This can include copies of your transcript and resumé so the profs are familiar with you and your accomplishments. Tell the profs what kind of letter you need and how it must be delivered. Reference letters sometimes need to be sent directly to the school you are applying for or delivered in a sealed envelope. If this is the case, provide your profs with stamped, addressed envelopes.

After you've made your reference letter requests, pay attention to your application deadlines. If a deadline is approaching and you still haven't received a reference letter or confirmation from the school you're applying to that they've received your prof's letter directly, call your prof at least a few days in advance of the deadline with a polite reminder.

When you do get the letter, be sure to write the prof a thank-you note.

7.5 Launching Your Career

I f you're reading this, the last section of the book, you're either thinking about graduation and the beginning of your career or you've been
enthralled by our captivating prose and you can't wait to see how this
suspense-filled advice book ends. If you're in the latter category, let us spoil it
for you: the butler did it.

For readers in the former category, we close this book with inspiring tales
of unusual ways graduates parlayed the experiences of their post-secondary
years into careers. There are a million careers you can embark on, and there
are a million ways to get started, and we're going to tell you about four of
them.

Many students spend their time at school focusing on learning "hard
skills"—concrete capabilities such as the ability to analyze financial statements
or write compelling press releases or collect samples for laboratory analysis.
However, employers are also very concerned with job applicants' "soft
skills," such as their ability to work in a team, bring a new perspective to a
problem, or organize a project effectively.

This section gives examples of ways students can use some of their less
concrete talents and their out-of-classroom experiences to hit the ground
running when they graduate.

In this section:

- Learn how **Getting Involved Outside the Classroom** can score you
  your first job.

- Think about how to apply your **School Projects in Real Life.**

- Find out how some graduates start careers unrelated to their degrees
  by **Following a Tangent.**

- Take advantage of **Relationships with Your Classmates.**

Getting Involved Outside the Classroom

What you do outside the classroom can be as important as your academic activities when it comes to getting a job interview. All the applicants for the job you want may have a degree, and they may all even have the same degree as you, so what sets you apart from the others? After tossing out the resumés of applicants who just aren't qualified for the job, the next thing most employers look for is experience that demonstrates the applicant is motivated, organized, and creative, among many other attributes.

Campuses offer hundreds of opportunities to get involved. (Check out **Section 4.2: Life Outside the Classroom.**) Participate in whatever strikes your fancy, and think about what incidental skills you're gaining from that activity. You can also be strategic about selecting your activities by looking for ways to explore your future field, build contacts, and get relevant experience. Regardless of what your activities are, however, don't assume they don't belong on your resumé because they are unrelated to your field or they seem boring. Employers like well-rounded applicants and aren't necessarily interested only in accountants who were members of the accounting club and did volunteer bookkeeping on the weekends.

Keturah's story

When she applied for her first job after graduating with an M.B.A., Keturah Leonforde almost deleted her volunteer work as a choir director from her resumé because it seemed unrelated to any of the jobs she wanted. But after she netted a gig at a top accounting firm, she was surprised to find out that she owed the position, at least in part, to what she thought irrelevant. "It was your volunteer experience that set you apart," her new boss told her. "On paper, your experience was quite comparable with everyone else, but that volunteer experience was far above and beyond."

Keturah is now a career consultant for graduate programs at Wilfrid Laurier University.

School Projects in Real Life

The classic school-project-turned-success story, narrated by business professors the world over, is FedEx, which was conceived in a Yale University economics paper. As the legend goes, FedEx founder Fred Smith received a failing grade for the project but, hoping to prove his prof wrong, went on to launch what is now one of the largest delivery companies in the world. There's as much fiction as fact in that story—Smith has said that he earned a "gentlemanly C" on the project—but it neatly captures a dream shared by many students: the brilliant concept cooked up in school that leads to success.

The fact is that plenty of real-world, practical ideas that go on to spawn successful careers get their start in the ivory towers of academia. The research you do for an honours thesis could land you a research position at a professor's lab. Your novel approach to an old problem in a school project might be what attracts a potential employer's attention. Or maybe in the course of your studies you'll happen across the need for a service that will be the basis of a future small business.

Parker's story

After an uninspiring co-op term improving door hinges for a 1998 Saturn car, University of Waterloo engineering student Parker Mitchell wanted to find a more fulfilling topic for his final project. He found it in some notes belonging to his professor's late colleague, an engineer who was originally from India. Parker learned that over one billion Indians live without access to clean water, so he set his sights on designing a household device that could provide enough clean water for a family of four and cost less than $15.

Although Mitchell's low-cost water filter never solved India's water problems, the realization that engineering could provide practical solutions to the problems of the developing world changed his perspective on the profession. He and his classmate George Roter later founded Engineers Without Borders, an organization that has brought better agricultural technology to an estimated 10,000 farmers around the world.

Following a Tangent

Sometimes the career that grows out of your education isn't what you would have expected when you started out. It happened to one of the authors of this book: Erin got a bachelor's of music with the goal of becoming a musician and music teacher and ended up a writer after getting involved with her college's student newspaper.

The skills and interests you develop that aren't directly related to your major may lead you to your career. Perhaps you enjoy participating in university sports so much that you'll decide to pursue a career as a swimming instructor and coach instead of doing something with your math degree. Or you might find that you can apply your education in a different way than you originally expected; for instance, although you majored in psychology as part of your plan to become a counsellor, you find your skills useful in the human resources department of a technology company.

Melissa's story

When Melissa Kluger received her bachelor's degree from Queen's University, she had no idea what she wanted to do. So when she got accepted to law school at the University of Toronto, she jumped at the chance to become a lawyer. At U of T she was surprised to discover that no publication for law students existed. At Queen's she had developed writing and editing skills by starting a creative writing magazine, so she decided to start a student law publication.

She always regarded her interest in publishing as a hobby until she started working as a media lawyer and realized how much she missed the creative process. She saw an opportunity in the lack of publications catering to the community of young legal professionals, so she left private practice in 2005 and launched yet another publication, *Precedent Magazine*, which is now in its fifth year.

Relationships with Your Classmates

The thing that launches your career might be right in front of you—or sitting next to you. The friendships you build with your peers in university might evolve into important professional relationships later on. Although right now you might think of your classmates only as study buddies or people to grab a pint with after class, your fellow students might one day be your colleagues, employees, clients, or even your future bosses.

You should also pay attention when you meet someone you work well with. The working relationship you develop with your partner for a term project might translate well into the work world one day, and your classmate might be in the position to hire you or recommend you for a position. The network of people you meet in university will be the basis of your contacts when you start out in the professional world, so don't take your fellow students for granted.

Jared and Ted's story

Jared Smith and Ted Couri happened to sit next to one another during a lecture at the University of Alberta. The two business students started chatting about their career plans, and they found they had a lot in common. Both were set to take over their fathers' businesses.

Together they got involved in AIESEC, a student-run organization that facilitates international co-ops, and eventually became president and vice-president of their local chapter. They worked so well as a team that they attracted more funding and job opportunities than any other chapter in Canada that year.

So after graduating they decided to start a marketing business together, which they started with nothing but a laptop in one of their parents' basements. Over 10 years later the company, Incite Solutions, has more than 30 employees and was named one of Canada's fastest-growing companies by *Profit* magazine in 2008.

Conclusion Want More? ✓

Do you still need more information after reading this book?

That's understandable. Going to university or college is a complicated process, and everyone could use more information and advice than we could ever fit into this little book made out of mashed-up trees (or a finite number of well-ordered electrons, if you're reading this in an e-book).

Fortunately, there's a backup resource for this book that's as big as the world! Wide. Web. Here's the URL: www.campuscompanion.ca—memorize it, write it on your arm, tattoo it on your forehead, and tell your friends. This website is full of links to other sources of information about each of the subjects we covered here, and it includes forums where you can discuss these topics with other students and ask us questions. We certainly don't have the answers to every question, but we've got connections to experts, such as professors and university administrators, and we know a lot of students and recent graduates who might be able to help. We're always interested in learning about the problems students face so we can keep improving and updating this book in later editions.

Remember that you can always research anything you want to know more about on your own. As we've said several times in this book, you're enrolled in a post-secondary institution, so you should get used to tracking down information, evaluating the credibility of sources, and analyzing your research to reach a conclusion. There's no reason you can't approach the problems you're having in your life with the same academic rigour you apply to your school work.

Your life is your own, and these are your decisions to make. We only ask that you take ownership of these decisions and take the time to make considered, informed, conscious choices about how you approach your education and where it takes you.

And damn it, have fun. Don't squander this opportunity to have the time of your life.

Acknowledgements

Although the advice in this book is written in our words, it is based on the insight of so many people who were generous with their time. First and foremost we want to acknowledge our research assistant, Annalise Klingbeil. We benefited enormously from her invaluable perspective.

Thanks also to the dozens of professors, academic advisers, health care professionals, and others who shared with us their knowledge, and to the hundreds of students who offered their stories and wisdom. We can't name you all, but a few of you went far beyond our expectations with your consistently thorough and thoughtful contributions, especially Julia Bolzon, Sandra Duffey, Alex Fox, Patricia Graham, Bronwyn Guiton, Stephanie Rade, Danielle Webb, and Catherine Wells.

We are indebted to our friends and family, especially those who shared their university experiences with us over the years; many thanks to Caitlin Millar and Kali Penney.

This book surely wouldn't have come to fruition without the enthusiasm of everyone at Thomas Allen Publishers. We would especially like to thank editors Janice Zawerbny and Wendy Thomas for their editorial guidance and patience with our writerly neurosis.

Our ongoing exchanges with colleagues about Canada's post-secondary system have surely improved our understanding of universities. Thanks specifically to Joey Coleman and Carson Jerema. Much of the initial research was done with the support of *Maclean's* magazine and former managing editor of special projects Tony Keller.

Finally, we would not have taken on this project if not for the support and encouragement of our agent, Derek Finkle of the Canadian Writers Group.

Index